Thomas Hardy's Personal Writings

Thomas Hardy's Personal Writings

PREFACES · LITERARY OPINIONS · REMINISCENCES

EDITED BY

Harold Orel

University of Kansas Press · Lawrence · 1966

L. C. Card: 66-17465

PRINTED IN THE U.S.A.

BY THE UNIVERSITY OF KANSAS PRINTING SERVICE

TO

BILL AND JANE

Preface

Some years ago, while conducting research for a monograph on the epic aspects of Thomas Hardy's *The Dynasts,* I became aware of a special problem: the wide scattering of the shorter nonfictional writings of the Wessex poet and novelist. Most of them have not been reprinted. They are occasional pieces of varying length, and the obscure publications in which many of them appeared are no longer current.

The most fascinating thing about all of them may be the fact that Hardy prepared them for the press, and carefully wrote them so that they would appear in type exactly as he wished. They constitute a record of Hardy's opinions, extending over a full half-century, that will surely interest his large public throughout the world.

Details about the histories of the various texts reprinted herein are given in Richard Little Purdy's bibliographical study, *Thomas Hardy* (London, 1954). In the years since its appearance that excellent work, a model of textual investigation and annotation, has become the foundation of much Hardy scholarship, including this collection.

I have not included any of the uncollected fiction or poetry that Hardy published during his lifetime (with one exception: the charming "How I Built Myself a House"), and I have not tried to reproduce the many brief, unimportant items listed in Part III of Professor Purdy's volume, "Uncollected Contributions to Books, Periodicals, and Newspapers." Some of these consist of a few sentences or even a quotation selected for a special occasion; their interest is limited. They are summarized in the Appendix, however, on pp. 241-256.

Enough remains to make a substantial volume for all readers who want to know more about Hardy—more than twice as much material as Ernest Brennecke collected for his comparable book, *Life and Art* (New York, 1925), a work long out of print. The literary prefaces which Hardy wrote or revised for the definitive

Wessex Edition of his own writings, as well as the literary prefaces which he contributed to the works of his friends, are gathered here for the first time, providing a fuller understanding of his concept of the creative artist, and of his views of the relationship between art and life.

The interview in which Hardy made clear his wishes for the preservation of Stonehenge as a national monument was shaped and edited by Hardy, and should be considered his work.

In everything Hardy wrote for publication, he was a professional. His dedication to the craft of writing will seem even more complete after one has reviewed the contents of this volume; his distinct, strong-minded, remarkably consistent personality imposes unity upon disparate subjects. The separate categories (the prefaces, opinions on literary matters, reminiscences and personal views, and meditations on Dorset) are all autobiographical to some extent. This is inevitable. Hardy never forgot that he came from Dorset, and that, even when he wrote about London and other parts of the world, he was above all else a man of Wessex.

ACKNOWLEDGMENTS

Special thanks are given to Lloyd's Bank, Ltd., and Miss Irene Cooper Willis, the Executors of the Will of the late Mrs. F. E. Hardy and the Trustees of the Hardy Estate, for permission to reprint the materials.

Other acknowledgments are due to Macmillan and Co., Ltd., for permission to include the Prefaces to the Wessex Edition of both the Wessex novels and the verse; Cecil Pope, Esq., Wrackleford House, Dorchester, for the preface to *A Book of Remembrance*; E. Stanley Smith, Clerk to the Governors, Hardy's School, Dorchester, for the address delivered at the laying of the commemoration stone of the new Dorchester Grammar School; Commander F. T. Hare (R.N.), Frome Vauchurch House, Maiden Newton, Dorset, for the note on South African farmers and the obituary on Mary Hardy, both printed in the *Dorset*

County Chronicle; F. E. Moule, Esq., 103 Lenthay Road, Sherborne, Dorset, for the preface to *Dorchester Antiquities*; W. T. G. Perrott, Hon. Secretary, Society of Dorset Men, 93, The Avenue, Muswell Hill, London, for the preface to the *Year-Book 1907-1908,* the address in the *Year-book 1908-1909,* and the contribution to the symposium, "Which is the Finest View in Dorset?" in the *Year-book 1915-1916,* of the Society; Mrs. Ruth Noyes, Librarian, The English Folk Dance and Song Society, Cecil Sharp House, 2, Regent's Park Road, London, for the letter on country-dances and "The College Hornpipe" (as formerly danced in Wessex) in the *E. F. D. S. News,* and the follow-up letter on English country-dances in the *Journal of the English Folk Dance Society*; and Mrs. Monica Dance, Secretary, The Society for the Protection of Ancient Buildings, 55, Great Ormond Street, London, for "Memories of Church Restoration."

Appreciation for special permission to reprint or to quote from Hardy materials is also expressed to Harper & Row, Publishers, for the letter which appeared in *The Harper Centennial 1817-1917*; George Newnes Ltd., London, for the letter in *John o' London's Weekly* that prefaced the reprinting of *Tess of the d'Urbervilles* in 1925; the Bodley Head, Ltd., for the letter to John Lane included in F. H. Cheetham's *Louis Napoleon and the Genesis of the Second Empire*; Associated Newspapers, Ltd., Northcliffe House, London, for the notes and letters published in the *Daily Chronicle*, the *Daily News*, the *Daily Mail*, and the *Westminster Gazette*; *The Times* (London) for various notes and letters, plus the article "Maumbury Ring," which appeared in that newspaper; Diligent Press and *Twentieth Century* for "G. M.: A Reminiscence"; the *Guardian*, Cross Street, Manchester, for the two letters on Rheims Cathedral, written during the Great War; the National Magazine Co., Ltd., for "How Shall We Solve the Divorce Problem?", originally printed in *Nash's Magazine*; the *Spectator* for the letter entitled *"Far from the Madding Crowd*: A Correction"; the Homeland Association, Ltd., for the preface to *Dorchester (Dorset), and Its Surroundings,* by F. R. and Sidney

Heath; the Royal Society of Arts for "The Ancient Cottages of England," published in a pamphlet entitled *The Preservation of Ancient Cottages*; W. and R. Chambers, Ltd., Edinburgh, for the sketch "Robert Louis Stevenson," contributed to Rosaline Masson's *I Can Remember Robert Louis Stevenson*; and the *New York Times* for Hardy's contribution to the symposium, "What is the Best Short Poem in English?" (July 5, 1914).

I am also appreciative of the many services rendered by Roger Peers, Esq., Curator and Secretary, Dorset County Museum, Dorchester, whose cheerful helpfulness to me as a researcher in the Hardy Collection extended well beyond the call of duty.

For encouragement and help, I would like to thank Professors Warner G. Rice and Karl Litzenberg of the University of Michigan, Professors Charles D. Murphy of the University of Maryland, Sylvester H. Bingham of the University of New Hampshire, Frederic E. Faverty of Northwestern University, Clyde K. Hyder, Charlton J. Hinman, and Dean William P. Albrecht of the University of Kansas, Professor Samuel Hynes of Swarthmore College, and Dean Walter Wright of the University of Nebraska.

This book was made possible, in generous measure, by the support of a grant from the American Philosophical Society. The typing of the final manuscript was paid for by a grant from the Graduate Research Fund of the University of Kansas.

The frontispiece is reproduced by courtesy of the National Portrait Gallery, London.

A Note on the Text

The Prefaces to Thomas Hardy's own writings are reproduced from the Wessex Edition, which Macmillan and Co., Ltd., published between 1912 and 1931 in twenty-four volumes.

It is true that the revisions and alterations made for the Osgood, McIlvaine and Co. edition of 1895-1896, in sixteen volumes, were more thoroughgoing than those made for the Wessex Edition. For the earlier edition Hardy had carefully eliminated inconsistencies, clarified topographical matters, and changed titles of chapters rather freely. In addition, he wrote the Prefaces for the Osgood, McIlvaine text. But his final views, consisting for the most part of afterthoughts in the form of footnotes and carefully dated postscripts, do not change the Osgood, McIlvaine text so much as expand and enrich it. The Wessex Edition must be accounted the definitive text.[1]

Moreover, for the Wessex Edition Hardy prepared a classification of his novels, a schema. (There are no separate Prefaces for these subdivisions.) "Novels of Character and Environment" were by far the most important category, consisting of nine volumes: *Tess of the d'Urbervilles, Far from the Madding Crowd, Jude the Obscure, The Return of the Native, The Mayor of Casterbridge, The Woodlanders, Under the Greenwood Tree, Life's Little Ironies,* and *Wessex Tales.* "Romances and Fantasies" described five of the volumes: *A Pair of Blue Eyes, The Trumpet-Major, Two on a Tower, The Well-Beloved,* and *A Group of Noble Dames.* There were three "Novels of Ingenuity": *Desperate Remedies, The Hand of Ethelberta,* and *A Laodicean.* The uncertain title "Mixed Novels" described the contents of only one book, *A Changed Man.* The remainder of the volumes were verse.

For Volume I of the Wessex Edition Hardy prepared an extended essay, "General Preface to the Novels and Poems." This, taken together with his important "Apology" for *Late Lyrics and Earlier,* indicates the major mood of the remarks attached to what Hardy now considered the authoritative text: autumnal, serene, and proud. He reviewed the controversies which had greeted his novels, and noted that "A Pure Woman" had been added to the title of *Tess of the d'Urbervilles* as an afterthought; he was far enough removed from the bitter outcries against *Jude the Obscure* to view them with some amusement; and he denied again that he was any simple-minded Pessimist. It was too late for him to revise his novels on the basis of riper wisdom; they would lose their "freshness and spontaneity" if he were to seek

1. "The Wessex Edition is in every sense the definitive edition of Hardy's work and the last authority in questions of text." Purdy, p. 286.

to correct their "immaturity." But in the Wessex Edition he did note that some of his writings had appeared before their time, and that their truths had become commonplaces by 1912.

It is not feasible to organize the writing of the Prefaces in any valid chronological order. The Postscripts—although dated later—obviously belong with the Prefaces to which they were added. For this reason, the Prefaces have been arranged in the order of the publication of the books themselves. Hardy dated each part of his Preface to indicate the year of its composition.

Eight Prefaces to the works of other writers are reprinted on pp. 65-88.

All asterisks in Hardy's text refer to Hardy's own notes. Except for a note by a French editor to a preface by Hardy that was printed after his death (pages 59-60), numbers refer to editorial notes, printed on pp. 259-281. Brackets, wherever they appear, enclose the editor's interpolations. Brief comments which explain the occasion of the individual piece are added to the text whenever necessary.

The titles listed in the Table of Contents are those which originally appeared with the separate pieces. Since Hardy was not responsible for the titles or headlines printed over the items which he wrote for or to newspapers, I have taken the liberty of adding after an uninformative or perhaps even misleading title a more truly descriptive title, within brackets. Minor errors obviously made by printers—they are not numerous—have been corrected. Otherwise the original texts are followed faithfully.

All references to the *Life* are, of course, to the "autobiography" which Thomas Hardy dictated to Florence Emily Hardy, and which was published under her name (*The Early Life of Thomas Hardy, 1840-1891,* and *The Later Years of Thomas Hardy, 1892-1928*) in November, 1928, and April, 1930. Macmillan and Co., Ltd., reprinted both books in one volume, *The Life of Thomas Hardy, 1840-1928* (London, 1962). Page citations are taken from this latter edition.

Contents

I.
Prefaces to Hardy's Writings

Desperate Remedies

[1871; Wessex Edition, XV, 1912]

THE following novel, the first published by the author, was written nineteen years ago, at a time when he was feeling his way to a method. The principles observed in its composition are, no doubt, too exclusively those in which mystery, enlargement, surprise, and moral obliquity are depended on for exciting interest; but some of the scenes, and at least one or two of the characters, have been deemed not unworthy of a little longer preservation; and as they could hardly be reproduced in a fragmentary form the novel is reissued complete—the more readily that it has for some considerable time been reprinted and widely circulated in America.

January 1889.

To the foregoing note I have only to add that, in the present edition of *Desperate Remedies,* some Wessex towns and other places that are common to the scenes of several of this series of stories have been called for the first time by the names under which they appear elsewhere, for the satisfaction of any reader who may care for consistency in such matters.

This is the only material change; for, as it happened that certain characteristics which provoked most discussion in my latest story were present in this my first—published in 1871, when there was no French name for them—it has seemed best to let them stand unaltered.

February 1896.

The reader may discover, when turning over this sensational and strictly conventional narrative, that certain scattered reflections and sentiments therein are the same in substance with some in the *Wessex Poems* and others, published many years later. The explanation of such tautology is that the poems were written before the novel, but as the author could not get them printed, he incontinently used here whatever of their content came into his head as being apt for the purpose—after dissolving it into prose, never anticipating at that time that the poems would see the light.

T. H.

August 1912.

Under the Greenwood Tree

[1872; Wessex Edition, VII, 1912]

THIS STORY of the Mellstock Quire and its old established west-gallery musicians, with some supplementary descriptions of similar officials in *Two on a Tower, A Few Crusted Characters,* and other places, is intended to be a fairly true picture, at first hand, of the personages, ways, and customs which were common among such orchestral bodies in the villages of fifty or sixty years ago.

One is inclined to regret the displacement of these ecclesiastical bandsmen by an isolated organist (often at first a barrel-organist) or harmonium player; and despite certain advantages in point of control and accomplishment which were, no doubt, secured by installing the single artist, the change has tended to stultify the professed aims of the clergy, its direct result being to curtain and extinguish the interest of parishioners in church doings. Under the old plan, from half a dozen to ten full-grown players, in addition to the numerous more or less grown-up singers, were officially occupied with the Sunday routine, and concerned in trying their best to make it an artistic outcome of the combined musical taste of the congregation. With a musical executive limited, as it mostly is limited now, to the parson's wife or daughter and the school-children, or to the school-teacher and the children, an important union of interests has disappeared.

The zest of these bygone instrumentalists must have been keen and staying, to take them, as it did, on foot every Sunday after a toilsome week through all weathers to the church, which often lay at a distance from their homes. They usually received so little in payment for their performances that their efforts were really a labour of love. In the parish I had in my mind when writing the present tale, the gratuities received yearly by the musicians at Christmas were somewhat as follows: From the manor-house ten shillings and a supper; from the vicar ten shillings; from the farmers five shillings each; from each cottage-household one shilling; amounting altogether to not more than ten shillings a head annually—just enough, as an old executant told me, to pay for their fiddle-strings, repairs, rosin, and music-paper (which they mostly ruled themselves). Their music in those days was all in their own manuscript, copied in the evenings after work, and their music-books were home-bound.

It was customary to inscribe a few jigs, reels, hornpipes, and ballads in the same book, by beginning it at the other end, the insertions being continued from front and back till sacred and secular met together in the middle, often with bizarre effect, the words of some of the songs exhibiting that ancient and broad humour which our grandfathers, and possibly grandmothers, took delight in, and is in these days unquotable.

The aforesaid fiddle-strings, rosin, and music-paper were supplied by a pedlar, who travelled exclusively in such wares from parish to parish, coming to each village about every six months.

Tales are told of the consternation once caused among the church fiddlers when, on the occasion of their producing a new Christmas anthem, he did not come to time, owing to being snowed up on the downs, and the straits they were in through having to make shift with whipcord and twine for strings. He was generally a musician himself, and sometimes a composer in a small way, bringing his own new tunes, and tempting each choir to adopt them for a consideration. Some of these compositions which now lie before me, with their repetitions of lines, half-lines, and half-words, their fugues and their intermediate symphonies, are good singing still, though they would hardly be admitted into such hymn-books as are popular in the churches of fashionable society at the present time.

August 1896.

Under the Greenwood Tree was first brought out in the summer of 1872 in two volumes. The name of the story was originally intended to be, more appropriately, *The Mellstock Quire,* and this has been appended as a sub-title since the early editions, it having been thought unadvisable to displace for it the title by which the book first became known.

In rereading the narrative after a long interval there occurs the inevitable reflection that the realities out of which it was spun were material for another kind of study of this little group of church musicians than is found in the chapters here penned so lightly, even so farcically and flippantly at times. But circumstances would have rendered any aim at a deeper, more essential, more transcendent handling unadvisable at the date of writing; and the exhibition of the Mellstock Quire in the following pages must remain the only extant one, except for the few glimpses of that perished band which I have given in verse elsewhere.

T. H.

April 1912.

A Pair of Blue Eyes

[1873; Wessex Edition, X, 1912]

THE FOLLOWING CHAPTERS were written at a time when the craze for indiscriminate church-restoration had just reached the remotest nooks of western England, where the wild and tragic features of the coast had long combined in perfect harmony with the crude Gothic Art of the ecclesiastical buildings scattered along it, throwing into extraordinary discord all architectural attempts at newness there. To restore the grey carcases of a mediaevalism whose spirit had fled seemed a not less incongruous act than to set about renovating the adjoining crags themselves.

Hence it happened that an imaginary history of three human hearts, whose emotions were not without correspondence with these material circumstances, found in the ordinary incidents of such church-renovations a fitting frame for its presentation.

The shore and country about "Castle Boterel" is now getting well known, and will be readily recognized. The spot is, I may add, the furthest westward of all those convenient corners wherein I have ventured to erect my theatre for these imperfect dramas of country life and passions; and it lies near to, or no great way beyond, the vague border of the Wessex kingdom on that side, which, like the westering verge of modern American settlements, was progressive and uncertain.

This, however, is of little importance. The place is pre-eminently (for one person at least) the region of dream and mystery. The ghostly birds, the pall-like sea, the frothy wind, the eternal soliloquy of the waters, the bloom of dark purple cast that seems to exhale from the shoreward precipices, in themselves lend to the scene an atmosphere like the twilight of a night vision.

One enormous sea-bord cliff in particular figures in the narrative; and for some forgotten reason or other this cliff was described in the story as being without a name. Accuracy would require the statement to be that a remarkable cliff which resembles in many points the cliff of the description bears a name that no event has made famous.

March 1895.

P.S.—The first edition of this tale, in three volumes, was issued in the early summer of 1873. In its action it exhibits the romantic stage of an idea which was further developed in a later book. To the ripe-minded critic of the present one an immaturity in its views of life and in its workmanship will of course be apparent. But to correct these by the judgment of later years, even had correction been possible, would have resulted, as with all such attempts, in the disappearance of whatever freshness and spontaneity the pages may have as they stand.

To add a word on the topography of the romance in answer to queries, unimportant as the point may be. The mansion called "Endelstow House" is to a large degree really existent, though it has to be looked for at a spot several miles south of its supposed site. The church, too, of the story was made to be more open to the ocean than is its original.

T. H.

June 1912.

[The concluding paragraph did not appear in the Wessex Edition but was added at a later date.]

Far from the Madding Crowd

[1874; Wessex Edition, II, 1912]

In reprinting this story for a new edition I am reminded that it was in the chapters of *Far from the Madding Crowd,* as they appeared month by month in a popular magazine, that I first ventured to adopt the word "Wessex" from the pages of early English history, and give it a fictitious significance as the existing name of the district once included in that extinct kingdom. The series of novels I projected being mainly of the kind called local, they seemed to require a territorial definition of some sort to lend unity to their scene. Finding that the area of a single county did not afford a canvas large enough for this purpose, and that there were objections to an invented name, I disinterred the old one. The region designated was known but vaguely, and I was often asked even by educated people where it lay. However, the press and the public were kind enough to welcome the fanciful plan, and willingly joined me in the anachronism of imagining a Wessex population living under Queen Victoria;—a modern Wessex of railways, the penny post, mowing and reaping machines, union workhouses, lucifer matches, labourers who could read and write, and National school children. But I believe I am correct in stating that, until the existence of this contemporaneous Wessex in place of the usual counties was announced in the present story, in 1874, it had never been heard of in fiction and current speech, if at all, and that the expression, "a Wessex peasant," or "a Wessex custom," would theretofore have been taken to refer to nothing later in date than the Norman Conquest.

I did not anticipate that this application of the word to modern story would extend outside the chapters of these particular chronicles. But it was soon taken up elsewhere, the first to adopt it being the now defunct *Examiner,* which, in the impression bearing date July 15, 1876, entitled one of its articles "The Wessex Labourer," the article turning out to be no dissertation on farming during the Heptarchy,[1] but on the modern peasant of the southwest counties.

Since then the appellation which I had thought to reserve to the horizons and landscapes of a partly real, partly dream-country, has become more and more popular as a practical provincial definition; and the dream-country has, by degrees, solidified into a utilitarian region which people can go to, take a house in, and write to the papers from. But I ask all good and idealistic readers to forget this, and to refuse steadfastly to believe that there are any inhabitants of a Victorian Wessex outside these volumes in which their lives and conversations are detailed.

Moreover, the village called Weatherbury,[2] wherein the scenes of the present story of the series are for the most part laid, would perhaps be hardly discernible by the explorer, without help, in any existing place nowadays; though at the time, comparatively recent, at which the tale was written, a sufficient reality to meet the descriptions, both of backgrounds and personages, might have been traced easily enough. The church remains, by great good fortune, unrestored and intact* and a few of the old houses; but the ancient malt-house, which was formerly so characteristic of the parish, has been pulled down these twenty years; also most of the thatched and dormered cottages that were once lifeholds. The heroine's fine old Jacobean house would be found in the story to have taken a witch's ride of a mile or more from its actual position; though with that difference its features are described as they still show themselves to the sun and moonlight. The game of prisoner's-base, which not so long ago seemed to enjoy a perennial vitality in front of the worn-out stocks, may, so far as I can say, be entirely unknown to the rising generation of schoolboys there. The practice of divination by Bible and key, the regarding of valentines as things of serious import, the shearing-supper, the long smock-frocks, and the harvest-home, have, too, nearly disappeared in the wake of the old houses; and with them has gone, it is said, much of that love of fuddling to which the village at one time was notoriously prone.[3] The change at the root of this has been the recent supplanting of the class of stationary cottagers, who carried on the local traditions and humours, by a population of more or less migratory labourers, which has led to a break of continuity in local history, more fatal than any other thing to the preservation of legend, folk-lore, close inter-social

* This is no longer the case (1912).

relations, and eccentric individualities. For these the indispensable conditions of existence are attachment to the soil of one particular spot by generation after generation.

T. H.

1895; 1902.

The Hand of Ethelberta

[1876; Wessex Edition, XVI, 1912]

THIS SOMEWHAT FRIVOLOUS narrative was produced as an interlude between stories of a more sober design, and it was given the sub-title of a comedy to indicate—though not quite accurately—the aim of the performance. A high degree of probability was not attempted in the arrangement of the incidents, and there was expected of the reader a certain lightness of mood, which should inform him with a good-natured willingness to accept the production in the spirit in which it was offered. The characters themselves, however, were meant to be consistent and human.

On its first appearance the novel suffered, perhaps deservedly, for what was involved in these intentions—for its quality of unexpectedness in particular—that unforgivable sin in the critic's sight—the immediate precursor of *Ethelberta* having been a purely rural tale. Moreover, in its choice of medium, and line of perspective, it undertook a delicate task: to excite interest in a drama—if such a dignified word may be used in the connection—wherein servants were as important as, or more important than, their masters; wherein the drawing-room was sketched in many cases from the point of view of the servants' hall. Such a reversal of the social foreground has, perhaps, since grown more welcome, and readers even of the finer crusted kind may now be disposed to pardon a writer for presenting the sons and daughters of Mr.

and Mrs. Chickerel as beings who come within the scope of a congenial regard.

December 1895.

P.S.—The surmise ventured upon in the note above—that the subject of this book was growing more welcome with the lapse of time—has been borne out by events. Imaginary circumstances that on its first publication were deemed eccentric and almost impossible are now paralleled on the stage and in novels, and accepted as reasonable and interesting pictures of life; which suggests that the comedy (or, more accurately, satire)—issued in April 1876—appeared thirty-five years too soon. The artificial treatment perceptible in many of the pages was adopted for reasons that seemed good at the date of writing for a story of that class, and has not been changed.

T. H.

August 1912.

[The subtitle to which Hardy refers in the first paragraph was *A Comedy in Chapters.*]

The Return of the Native

[1878; Wessex Edition, IV, 1912]

THE DATE at which the following events are assumed to have occurred may be set down as between 1840 and 1850, when the old watering-place herein called "Budmouth" still retained sufficient afterglow from its Georgian gaiety and prestige to lend it an absorbing attractiveness to the romantic and imaginative soul of a lonely dweller inland.

Under the general name of "Egdon Heath," which has been given to the sombre scene of the story, are united or typified heaths of various real names, to the number of at least a dozen; these being virtually one in character and aspect, though their original unity, or partial unity, is now somewhat disguised by intrusive strips and slices brought under the plough with varying degrees of success, or planted to woodland.

It is pleasant to dream that some spot in the extensive tract whose south-western quarter is here described, may be the heath of that traditionary King of Wessex—Lear.

July 1895.

POSTSCRIPT

To prevent disappointment to searchers for scenery it should be added that though the action of the narrative is supposed to proceed in the central and most secluded part of the heaths united into one whole, as above described, certain topographic features resembling those delineated really lie on the margin of the waste, several miles to the westward of the centre. In some other respects also there has been a bringing together of scattered characteristics.

I may mention here in answer to enquiries that the Christian name of "Eustacia," borne by the heroine of the story, was that of the Lady of the Manor of Ower Moigne, in the reign of Henry the Fourth, which parish includes part of the "Egdon Heath" of the following pages.

The first edition of this novel was published in three volumes in 1878.

T. H.

April 1912.

[The next-to-the-last paragraph was added after the printing of the Wessex Edition.]

The Trumpet-Major

[1880; Wessex Edition, XI, 1912]

THE PRESENT TALE is founded more largely on testimony—oral and written—than any other in this series. The external incidents which direct its course are mostly an unexaggerated reproduction of the recollections of old persons well known to the author in childhood, but now long dead, who were eye-witnesses of those scenes. If wholly transcribed their recollections would have filled a volume thrice the length of *The Trumpet-Major*.

Down to the middle of this century, and later, there were not wanting, in the neighbourhood of the places more or less clearly indicated herein, casual relics of the circumstances amid which the action moves—our preparations for defence against the threatened invasion of England by Buonaparte. An outhouse door riddled with bullet-holes, which had been extemporized by a solitary man as a target for firelock practice when the landing was hourly expected, a heap of bricks and clods on a beacon-hill, which had formed the chimney and walls of the hut occupied by the beacon-keeper, worm-eaten shafts and iron heads of pikes for the use of those who had no better weapons, ridges on the down thrown up during the encampment, fragments of volunteer uniform, and other such lingering remains, brought to my imagination in early childhood the state of affairs at the date of the war more vividly than volumes of history could have done.

Those who have attempted to construct a coherent narrative of past times from the fragmentary information furnished by survivors, are aware of the difficulty of ascertaining the true sequence of events indiscriminately recalled. For this purpose the newspapers of the date were indispensable. Of other documents consulted I may mention, for the satisfaction of those who love a true story, that the "Address to all Ranks and Descriptions of Englishmen" was transcribed from an original copy of a local museum; that the hieroglyphic portrait of Napoleon existed as a print down to the present day in an old woman's cottage near "Overcombe;" that the particulars of the King's doings at his favourite watering-place were augmented by details from records of the time. The drilling scene of the local militia received some additions from an account given in so grave a work as Gifford's *History of the Wars of the French Revolution* (London, 1817). But on reference to the *History* I find I was mistaken in supposing the account to be advanced as authentic, or to refer to rural England. However, it does in a large degree accord with the local traditions of such scenes that I have heard recounted, times without number, and the system of drill was tested by reference to the Army Regulations of 1801, and other military handbooks. Almost the whole narrative of the supposed landing of the French in the Bay is from oral relation as aforesaid. Other proofs of the veracity of this chronicle have escaped my recollection.[4]

The first edition of this romance was in three volumes, published in 1880.

T. H.

October 1895.

A Laodicean

[1881; Wessex Edition, XVII, 1912]

THE CHANGING of the old order in country manors and mansions may be slow or sudden, may have many issues romantic or otherwise, its romantic issues being not necessarily restricted to a change back to the original order; though this admissible instance appears to have been the only romance formerly recognized by novelists as possible in the case. Whether the following production be a picture of other possibilities or not, its incidents may be taken to be fairly well supported by evidence every day forthcoming in most counties.

The writing of the tale was rendered memorable to two persons, at least, by a tedious illness of five months that laid hold of the author soon after the story was begun in a well-known magazine; during which period the narrative had to be strenuously continued by dictation to a predetermined cheerful ending.

As some of these novels of Wessex life address themselves more especially to readers into whose souls the iron has entered, and whose years have less pleasure in them now than heretofore, so *A Laodicean* may perhaps help to while away an idle afternoon of the comfortable ones whose lines have fallen to them in pleasant places; above all, of that large and happy section of the reading public which has not yet reached ripeness of years; those to whom marriage is the pilgrim's Eternal City, and not a milestone on the way.

January 1896.

P.S.—*A Laodicean* was first published in 1881, in three volumes. Looking over the novel at the present much later date, I hazard the conjecture that its sites, mileages, and architectural details can hardly seem satisfactory to the investigating topographist, so appreciable a proportion of these features being but the baseless fabrics of a vision.[5]

However, there may remain a compensation of another sort in the character of Paula, who, on renewed acquaintance, leads me to think her individualized with some clearness, and really lovable, though she is of that reserved disposition which is the most difficult of all dispositions to depict, and tantalized the writer by eluding his grasp for some time.

T. H.

October 1912.

Two on a Tower

[1882; Wessex Edition, XII, 1912]

THIS SLIGHTLY-BUILT ROMANCE was the outcome of a wish to set the emotional history of two infinitesimal lives against the stupendous background of the stellar universe, and to impart to readers the sentiment that of these contrasting magnitudes the smaller might be the greater to them as men.

But on the publication of the book people seemed to be less struck with these high aims of the author than with their own opinion, first, that the novel was an "improper" one in its morals, and, secondly, that it was intended to be a satire on the Established Church of this country. I was made to suffer in consequence from several eminent pens.

That, however, was thirteen years ago, and, in respect of the first opinion, I venture to think that those who care to read the story now will be quite astonished at the scrupulous propriety observed therein on the relations of the sexes; for though there may be frivolous, and even grotesque touches on occasion, there is hardly a single caress in the book outside legal matrimony, or what was intended so to be.

As for the second opinion, it is sufficient to draw attention, as I did at the time, to the fact that the Bishop is every inch a gentleman, and that the parish priest who figures in the narrative is one of its most estimable characters.

However, the pages must speak for themselves. Some few readers, I trust—to take a serious view—will be reminded by this imperfect story, in a manner not unprofitable to the growth of the social sympathies, of the pathos, misery, long-suffering, and divine tenderness which in real life frequently accompany the passion of such a woman as Viviette for a lover several years her junior.

The scene of the action was suggested by two real spots in the part of the country specified, each of which has a column standing upon it.[6] Certain surrounding peculiarities have been imported into the narrative from both sides, and from elsewhere.

The first edition of the novel was published in 1882, in three volumes.

T. H.

July 1895.

The Mayor of Casterbridge

[1886; Wessex Edition, V, 1912]

READERS of the following story who have not yet arrived at middle age are asked to bear in mind that, in the days recalled by the tale, the home Corn Trade, on which so much of the action turns, had an importance that can hardly be realized by those accustomed to the sixpenny loaf of the present date, and to the present indifference of the public to harvest weather.

The incidents narrated arise mainly out of three events, which chanced to range themselves in the order and at or about the intervals of time here given, in the real history of the town called Casterbridge and the neighbouring country. They were the sale of a wife by her husband, the uncertain harvests which immediately preceded the repeal of the Corn Laws, and the visit of a Royal personage to the aforesaid part of England.

The present edition of the volume, like the previous one, contains nearly a chapter which did not at first appear in any English copy, though it was printed in the serial issue of the tale, and in the American edition. The restoration was made at the instance of some good judges across the Atlantic, who strongly represented that the home edition suffered from the omission. Some shorter passages and names, omitted or altered for reasons which no longer exist, in the original printing of both English and American editions, have also been replaced or inserted.

The story is more particularly a study of one man's deeds and character than, perhaps, any other of those included in my Exhibition of Wessex life. Objections have been raised to the Scotch language of Mr. Farfrae, the second character; and one of his fellow-countrymen went so far as to declare that men beyond the Tweed did not and never could say "warrld," "cannet," "advairrtisment," and so on. As this gentleman's pronunciation in correcting me seemed to my Southron ear an exact repetition of what my spelling implied, I was not struck with the truth of his remark, and somehow we did not get any forwarder in the matter. It must be remembered that the Scotchman of the tale is represented not as he would appear to other Scotchmen, but as he would appear to people of outer regions. Moreover, no attempt is made herein to reproduce his entire pronunciation phonetically, any more than that of the Wessex speakers. I should add, however, that this new edition of the book has had the accidental advantage of a critical overlooking by a professor of the tongue in question—one of undoubted authority:—in fact he is a gentleman who adopted it for urgent personal reasons in the first year of his existence.[7]

Furthermore, a charming non-Scottish lady, of strict veracity and admitted penetration, the wife of a well-known Caledonian, came to the writer shortly after the story was first published, and inquired if Farfrae were not drawn from her husband, for he seemed to her to be the living portrait of that (doubtless) happy man. It happened that I had never thought of her husband in constructing Farfrae. I trust therefore that Farfrae may be allowed to pass, if not as a Scotchman to Scotchmen, as a Scotchman to Southerners.

The novel was first published complete, in two volumes, in May 1886.

T. H.

February 1895; *May* 1912.

The Woodlanders

[1887; Wessex Edition, VI, 1912]

IN THE PRESENT NOVEL, as in one or two others of this series which involve the question of matrimonial divergence, the immortal puzzle—given the man and woman, how to find a basis for their sexual relation—is left where it stood; and it is tacitly assumed for the purposes of the story that no doubt of the depravity of the erratic heart who feels some second person to be better suited to his or her tastes than the one with whom he has contracted to live, enters the head of reader or writer for a moment. From the point of view of marriage as a distinct covenant or undertaking, decided on by two people fully cognizant of all its possible issues, and competent to carry them through, this assumption is, of course, logical. Yet no thinking person supposes that, on the broader ground of how to afford the greatest happiness to the units of human society during their brief transit through this sorry world, there is no more to be said on this covenant; and it is certainly not supposed by the writer of these pages. But, as Gibbon blandly remarks on the evidence for and against Christian miracles, "the duty of an historian does not call upon him to interpose his private judgment in this nice and important controversy."[8]

The stretch of country visible from the heights adjoining the nook herein described under the name of Little Hintock, cannot be regarded as inferior to any inland scenery of the sort in the west of England, or perhaps anywhere in the kingdom. It is singular to find that a world-wide repute in some cases, and an absolute famelessness in others, attach to spots of equal beauty and equal accessibility. The neighbourhood of High-Stoy (I give, as elsewhere, the real names to natural features), Bubb-Down Hill, and the glades westward to Montacute; of Bulbarrow, Hambledon Hill, and the slopes eastward to Shaston, Windy Green, and Stour Head, teems with landscapes which, by a mere accident of iteration, might have been numbered among the scenic celebrities of the English shires.

September 1895.

I have been honoured by so many inquiries for the true name and exact locality of the hamlet "Little Hintock," in which the greater part of the action of this story goes on, that I may as well confess here once for all that I do not know myself where that hamlet is more precisely than as explained above and in the pages of the narrative. To oblige readers I once spent several hours on a bicycle with a friend in a serious attempt to discover the real spot; but the search ended in failure; though tourists assure me positively that they have found it without trouble, and that it answers in every particular to the description given in this volume. At all events, as stated elsewhere, the commanding heights called "High-Stoy" and "Bubb-Down Hill" overlook the landscape in which it is supposed to be hid.

In respect of the occupations of the characters, the adoption of iron utensils and implements in agriculture, and the discontinuance of thatched roofs for cottages, have almost extinguished the handicrafts classed formerly as "copsework," and the type of men who engaged in them.

The Woodlanders was first published complete, in three volumes, in the March of 1887.

T. H.

April 1912.

Wessex Tales

[1888; Wessex Edition, IX, 1912]

AN APOLOGY is perhaps needed for the neglect of contrast which is shown by presenting two stories of hangmen and one of a military execution in such a small collection as the following. But as to the former, in the neighbourhood of county-towns hanging matters used to form a large proportion of the local tradition; and though never personally acquainted with any chief operator at such scenes, the writer of these pages had as a boy the privilege of being on speaking terms with a man who applied for the office, and who sank into an incurable melancholy because he failed to get it, some slight mitigation of his grief being to dwell upon striking episodes in the lives of those happier ones who had held it with success and renown. His tale of disappointment used to cause his listener some wonder why his ambition should have taken such an unfortunate form, by limiting itself to a profession of which there could be only one practitioner in England at one time, when it might have aimed at something that would have afforded him more chances—such as the office of a judge, a bishop, or even a member of Parliament—but its nobleness was never questioned. In those days, too, there was still living an old woman, who, for the cure of some eating disease, had been taken in her youth to have her "blood turned" by a convict's corpse, in the manner described in "The Withered Arm."[9]

Since writing this story some years ago I have been reminded by an aged friend who knew "Rhoda Brook" that, in relating her dream, my forgetfulness has weakened the facts out of which the tale grew. In reality it was while lying down on a hot afternoon that the incubus oppressed her and she flung it off, with the results upon the body of the original as described. To my mind the occurrence of such a vision in the daytime is more impressive than if it had happened in a midnight dream. Readers are therefore asked to correct the misrelation, which affords an instance of how our imperfect memories insensibly formalize the fresh originality of living fact—from whose shape they slowly depart, as machine-made castings depart by degrees from the sharp hand-work of the mould.

Among the many devices for concealing smuggled goods in caves and pits of the earth, that of planting an apple-tree in a tray or box which was placed over the mouth of the pit is, I believe, unique, and it is detailed in "The Distracted Preacher" precisely as described by an old carrier of "tubs"—a man who was afterwards in my father's employ for over thirty years. I never gathered from his reminiscences what means were adopted for lifting the tree, which, with its roots, earth, and receptacle, must have been of considerable weight. There is no doubt, however, that the thing was done through many years. My informant often spoke, too, of the horribly suffocating sensation produced by the pair of spirit-tubs slung upon the chest and back, after stumbling with the burden of them for several miles inland over a rough country and in darkness. He said that though years of his youth and young manhood were spent in this irregular business, his profits from the same, taken all together, did not average the wages he might have earned in a steady employment, whilst the fatigues and risks were excessive.

I may add that the action of this story is founded on certain smuggling exploits that occurred between 1825 and 1830, and were brought to a close in the latter year by the trial of the chief actors at the Assizes before Baron Bolland for their desperate armed resistance to the Custom-house officers during the landing of a cargo of spirits. This happened only a little time after the doings recorded in the narrative, in which some incidents that came out at the trial are also embodied.

In the culminating affray the character called Owlett was badly wounded, and several of the Preventive-men would have lost their lives through being overpowered by the far more numerous body of smugglers, but for the forbearance and manly conduct of the latter. This served them in good stead at their trial, in which the younger Erskine prosecuted, their defence being entrusted to Erle. Baron Bolland's summing up was strongly in their favour; they were merely ordered to enter into their own recognizances for good behaviour and discharged. (See also as to facts the note at the end of the tale.)

However, the stories are but dreams, and not records. They were first collected and published under their present title, in two volumes, in 1888.

T. H.

April 1896; *May* 1912.

An experience of the writer in respect of the tale called "A Tradition of Eighteen Hundred and Four" is curious enough to be mentioned here. The incident of Napoleon's visit to the English coast by night, with a view to discovering a convenient spot for landing his army of invasion, was an invention of the author's on which he had some doubts because of its improbability. This was in 1882, when it was first published. Great was his surprise several years later to be told that it was a real tradition. How far this is true he is unaware.

T. H.

June 1919.

[As the date indicates, the paragraph above was added after the publication of the Wessex Edition.]

A Group of Noble Dames

[1891; Wessex Edition, XIV, 1912]

THE PEDIGREES of our county families, arranged in diagrams on the pages of county histories, mostly appear at first sight to be as barren of any touch of nature as a table of logarithms. But given a clue—the faintest tradition of what went on behind the scenes, and this dryness as of dust may be transformed into a palpitating drama. More, the careful comparison of dates alone—that of birth with marriage, of marriage with death, of one marriage, birth, or death with a kindred marriage, birth, or death—will often effect the same transformation, and anybody practised in raising images from such genealogies finds himself unconsciously filling into the framework the motives, passions, and personal qualities which would appear to be the single explanation possible of some extraordinary conjunction in times, events, and personages that occasionally marks these reticent family records.

Out of such pedigrees and supplementary material most of the following stories have arisen and taken shape.

I would make this preface an opportunity of expressing my

sense of the courtesy and kindness of several bright-eyed Noble Dames yet in the flesh, who, since the first publication of these tales in periodicals, six or seven years ago, have given me interesting comments and conjectures on such of the narratives as they have recognized to be connected with their own families, residences, or traditions; in which they have shown a truly philosophic absence of prejudice in their regard of those incidents whose relation has tended more distinctly to dramatize than to eulogize their ancestors. The outlines they have also given of other singular events in their family histories for use in a second *Group of Noble Dames* will, I fear, never reach the printing-press through me; but I shall store them up in memory of my informants' good nature.

The tales were first collected and published in their present form in 1891.

T. H.

June 1896.

Tess of the d'Urbervilles

[1891; Wessex Edition, I, 1912]

Explanatory Note to the First Edition

The main portion of the following story appeared—with slight modifications—in the *Graphic* newspaper; other chapters, more especially addressed to adult readers, in the *Fortnightly Review* and the *National Observer,* as episodic sketches. My thanks are tendered to the editors and proprietors of those periodicals for enabling me now to piece the trunk and limbs of the novel together, and print it complete, as originally written two years ago.

I will just add that the story is sent out in all sincerity of purpose, as an attempt to give artistic form to a true sequence of things; and in respect of the book's opinions and sentiments, I would ask any too genteel reader, who cannot endure to have said what everybody nowadays thinks and feels, to remember a well-worn sentence of St. Jerome's: If an offense come out of the truth, better it is that the offense come than that the truth be concealed.

T. H.

November 1891.

Preface to the Fifth and Later Editions

This novel being one wherein the great campaign of the heroine begins after an event in her experience which has usually been treated as fatal to her part of protagonist, or at least as the virtual ending of her enterprises and hopes, it was quite contrary to avowed conventions that the public should welcome the book and agree with me in holding that there was something more to be said in fiction than had been said about the shaded side of a well-known catastrophe. But the responsive spirit in which *Tess of the d'Urbervilles* has been received by the readers of England and America would seem to prove that the plan of laying down a story on the lines of tacit opinion, instead of making it to square with the merely vocal formulae of society, is not altogether a wrong one, even when exemplified in so unequal and partial an achievement as the present. For this responsiveness I cannot refrain from expressing my thanks; and my regret is that, in a world where one so often hungers in vain for friendship, where even not to be wilfully misunderstood is felt as a kindness, I shall never meet in person these appreciative readers, male and female, and shake them by the hand.

I include amongst them the reviewers—by far the majority—who have so generously welcomed the tale. Their words show that they, like the others, have only too largely repaired my defects of narration by their own imaginative intuition.

Nevertheless, though the novel was intended to be neither

didactic nor aggressive, but in the scenic parts to be representative simply, and in the contemplative to be oftener charged with impressions than with convictions, there have been objectors both to the matter and to the rendering.[10]

The more austere of these maintain a conscientious difference of opinion concerning, among other things, subjects fit for art, and reveal an inability to associate the idea of the sub-title adjective with any but the artificial and derivative meaning which has resulted to it from the ordinances of civilization. They ignore the meaning of the word in Nature, together with all aesthetic claims upon it, not to mention the spiritual interpretation afforded by the finest side of their own Christianity. Others dissent on grounds which are intrinsically no more than an assertion that the novel embodies the views of life prevalent at the end of the nineteenth century, and not those of an earlier and simpler generation—an assertion which I can only hope may be well founded. Let me repeat that a novel is an impression, not an argument; and there the matter must rest; as one is reminded by a passage which occurs in the letters of Schiller to Goethe on judges of this class: "They are those who seek only their own ideas in a representation, and prize that which should be as higher than what is. The cause of the dispute, therefore, lies in the very first principles, and it would be utterly impossible to come to an understanding with them." And again: "As soon as I observe that any one, when judging of poetical representations, considers anything more important than the inner Necessity and Truth, I have done with him."[11]

In the introductory words to the first edition I suggested the possible advent of the genteel person who would not be able to endure something or other in these pages. That person duly appeared among the aforesaid objectors. In one case he felt upset that it was not possible for him to read the book through three times, owing to my not having made that critical effort which "alone can prove the salvation of such an one." In another, he objected to such vulgar articles as the Devil's pitchfork, a lodging-house carving-knife, and a shame-bought parasol, appearing in a respectable story. In another place he was a gentleman who turned Christian for half-an-hour the better to express his grief that a disrespectful phrase about the Immortals[12] should have been used; though the same innate gentility compelled him to excuse the author in words of pity that one cannot be too thankful for: "He does but give us of his best." I can assure this great critic[13] that to exclaim illogically against the gods, singular or plural, is not such an original sin of mine as he seems to imagine. True, it may have some local originality; though if Shakespeare were an authority on history, which perhaps he is not, I could show that the sin was introduced into Wessex as early as the Heptarchy itself. Says Glo'ster in *Lear,* otherwise Ina, king of that country:[14]

> As flies to wanton boys are we to the gods;
> They kill us for their sport.[15]

The remaining two or three manipulators of *Tess* were of the predetermined sort whom most writers and readers would gladly forget; professed literary boxers, who put on their convictions for the occasion; modern "Hammers of Heretics";[16] sworn Discouragers, ever on the watch to prevent the tentative half-success from becoming the whole success later on; who pervert plain meanings, and grow personal under the name of practising the great historical method. However, they may have causes to advance, privileges to guard, traditions to keep going; some of which a mere tale-teller, who writes down how the things of the world strike him, without any ulterior intentions whatever, has overlooked, and may by pure inadvertence have run foul of when in the least aggressive mood. Perhaps some passing perception, the outcome of a dream hour, would, if generally acted on, cause such an assailant considerable inconvenience with respect to position, interests, family, servant, ox, ass, neighbour, or neighbour's wife. He therefore valiantly hides his personality behind a publisher's shutters, and cries "Shame!" So densely is the world thronged with any shifting of positions, even the best warranted advance, galls somebody's kibe.[17] Such shiftings often begin in sentiment, and such sentiment sometimes begins in a novel.

July 1892.

The foregoing remarks were written during the early career of this story, when a spirited public and private criticism of its points was still fresh to the feelings. The pages are allowed to stand for what they are worth, as something once said; but probably they would not have been written now. Even in the first short time which has elapsed since the book was first published, some of the critics who provoked the reply have "gone down into silence,"[18] as if to remind one of the infinite unimportance of both their say and mine.

January 1895.

The present edition of this novel contains a few pages that have never appeared in any previous edition. When the detached episodes were collected as stated in the preface of 1891, these pages were overlooked, though they were in the original manuscript. They occur in Chapter X.

Respecting the sub-title, to which allusion was made above, I may add that it was appended at the last moment, after reading the final proofs, as being the estimate left in a candid mind of the heroine's character—an estimate that nobody would be likely to dispute. It was disputed more than anything else in the book. *Melius fuerat non scribere.*[19] But there it stands.

The novel was first published complete, in three volumes, in November, 1891.

T. H.

March 1912.

Life's Little Ironies [1]

[1894; Osgood, McIlvaine & Co. Edition of the Wessex Novels, XIV, 1895-1896]

A STORY-TELLER's interest in his own stories is usually independent of any merits or demerits they may show as specimens of narrative art; turning on something behind the scenes, something real in their history, which may have no attraction for a reader even if known to him—a condition by no means likely. In the present collection "The Melancholy Hussar of the German Legion" has just such a hold upon myself for the technically inadmissible reasons that the old people who gave me their recollections of its incidents did so in circumstances that linger pathetically in the memory; that she who, at the age of ninety, pointed out the unmarked resting-place of the two soldiers of the tale, was probably the last remaining eyewitness of their death and interment; that the extract from the register of burials is literal, to be read any day in the original by the curious who recognize the village.

Several of the other stories are true in their main facts, if there should be anybody who cares to know it. In respect of the tale of "Andrey Satchel," some persons still living may discern in Parson Toogood one to whom they, or at least their fathers, were not altogether strangers. To present that truly delightful personage as he entirely was, is beyond the power of my uncertain pen. One would like to tell of the second baptisms in old port which he used to perform on the squire's children at the christening dinner; of the bishop's descent one day upon the parsonage to convict Toogood of absenteeism, the latter's breakneck ride across country from a cocking party in consequence, and his breathless entry by his back door just in time to open his front to his visitor, whom he meekly received with a quill behind his ear, and a sermon outspread. He had several imitators in his composite calling of sportsman and divine, but no rival.

T. H.

June 1896.

[This Preface appeared in Volume XIV of the sixteen-volume edition of the Wessex Novels published by Osgood, McIlvaine & Co., London, in 1895–1896, but Hardy chose not to reprint it when preparing for the publication of *Life's Little Ironies* in the Wessex Edition. The reason lay in Hardy's rearrangement of stories. "The Melancholy Hussar of the German Legion" was transferred to *Wessex Tales*; so was "A Tradition of Eighteen Hundred and Four." On the other hand, "An Imaginative Woman" was transferred from *Wessex Tales* in the Osgood, McIlvaine Edition to *Life's Little Ironies* in the Wessex Edition. Rather than tinker with the text of this Preface, Hardy wrote a brief new Preface for the Wessex Edition.]

Life's Little Ironies [2]

[1894; Wessex Edition, VIII, 1912]

Of the following collection the first story, "An Imaginative Woman," which has hitherto stood in *Wessex Tales*, has been brought into this volume as being more nearly its place, turning as it does upon a trick of Nature, so to speak, a physical possibility that may attach to a wife of vivid imaginings, as is well known to medical practitioners and other observers of such manifestations.

The two stories named "A Tradition of Eighteen Hundred and Four" and "The Melancholy Hussar of the German Legion," which were formerly printed in this series, have been transferred to *Wessex Tales*, where they more naturally belong.

The present narratives and sketches, though separately published at various antecedent dates, were first collected and issued in a volume in 1894.

T. H.

May 1912.

Jude the Obscure

[1896; Wessex Edition, III, 1912]

Preface to the First Edition

The history of this novel (whose birth in its present shape has been much retarded by the necessities of periodical publication) is briefly as follows. The scheme was jotted down in 1890, from notes made in 1887 and onwards, some of the circumstances being suggested by the death of a woman in the former year. The scenes were revisited in October, 1892; the narrative was written in outline in 1892 and the spring of 1893, and at full length, as it now appears, from August, 1893, onwards into the next year; the whole, with the exception of a few chapters, being in the hands of the publisher by the end of 1894. It was begun as a serial story in *Harper's Magazine* at the end of November, 1894, and was continued in monthly parts.

But, as in the case of *Tess of the d'Urbervilles*, the magazine version was for various reasons an abridged and modified one, the present edition being the first in which the whole appears as originally written. And in the difficulty of coming to an early decision in the matter of a title, the tale was issued under a provisional name, two such titles having, in fact, been successively adopted. The present and final title, deemed on the whole the best, was one of the earliest thought of.

For a novel addressed by a man to men and women of full age; which attempts to deal unaffectedly with the fret and fever, derision and disaster, that may press in the wake of the strongest passion known to humanity; to tell, without a mincing of words, a deadly war waged between flesh and spirit; and to point the tragedy of unfulfilled aims, I am not aware that there is anything in the handling to which exception can be taken.

Like former productions of this pen, *Jude the Obscure* is simply an endeavour to give shape and coherence to a series of seemings, or personal impressions, the question of their consistency or their discordance, of their permanence or their transitoriness, being regarded as not of the first moment.

August 1895.

POSTSCRIPT

The issue of this book sixteen years ago, with the explanatory Preface given above, was followed by unexpected incidents, and one can now look back for a moment at what happened. Within a day or two of its publication the reviewers pronounced upon it in tones to which the reception of *Tess of the d'Urbervilles* bore no comparison, though there were two or three dissentients from the chorus. This salutation of the story in England was instantly cabled to America, and the music was reinforced on that side of the Atlantic in a shrill crescendo.

In my own eyes the sad feature of the attack was that the greater part of the story—that which presented the shattered ideals of the two chief characters, and had been more especially, and indeed almost exclusively, the part of interest to myself—was practically ignored by the adverse press of the two countries; the while that some twenty or thirty pages of sorry detail deemed necessary to complete the narrative, and show the antitheses in Jude's life, were almost the sole portions read and regarded. And curiously enough, a reprint the next year of a fantastic tale that had been published in a family paper some time before, drew down upon my head a continuation of the same sort of invective from several quarters.

So much for the unhappy beginning of *Jude*'s career as a book. After these verdicts from the press its next misfortune was to be burnt by a bishop—probably in his despair at not being able to burn me.[20]

Then somebody discovered that *Jude* was a moral work—austere in its treatment of a difficult subject—as if the writer had not all the time said that it was in the Preface. Thereupon many uncursed me, and the matter ended, the only effect of it on human conduct that I could discover being its effect on myself—the experience completely curing me of further interest in novel-writing.

One incident among many arising from the storm of words was that an American man of letters, who did not whitewash his own morals, informed me that, having bought a copy of the book on the strength of the shocked criticisms, he read on and on, wondering when the harmfulness was going to begin, and at last flung it across the room with execrations at having been induced by the rascally reviewers to waste a dollar-and-half on what he was pleased to call "a religious and ethical treatise."

I sympathized with him, and assured him honestly that the misrepresentations had been no collusive trick of mine to increase my circulation among the subscribers to the papers in question.

Then there was the case of the lady who having shuddered at the book in an influential article bearing intermediate headlines of horror, and printed in a world-read journal, wrote to me shortly afterwards that it was her desire to make my acquaintance.

To return, however, to the book itself. The marriage laws being used in great part as the tragic machinery of the tale, and its general drift on the domestic side tending to show that, in Diderot's words, the civil law should be only the enunciation of the law of nature (a statement that requires some qualifications, by the way),[21] I have been charged since 1895 with a large responsibility in this country for the present "shop-soiled" condition of the marriage theme (as a learned writer characterized it the other day). I do not know. My opinion at that time, if I remember rightly, was what it is now, that a marriage should be dissolvable as soon as it becomes a cruelty to either of the parties—being then essentially and morally no marriage—and it seemed a good foundation for the fable of a tragedy, told for its own sake as a presentation of particulars containing a good deal that was universal, and not without a hope that certain cathartic, Aristotelian qualities might be found therein.

The difficulties down to twenty or thirty years back of acquiring knowledge in letters without pecuniary means were used in the same way; though I was informed that some readers thought these episodes an attack on venerable institutions, and that when Ruskin College was subsequently founded it should have been called the College of Jude the Obscure.

Artistic effort always pays heavily for finding its tragedies in the forced adaptation of human instincts to rusty and irksome moulds that do not fit them. To do Bludyer and the conflagratory bishop[22] justice, what they meant seems to have been only this: "We Britons hate ideas, and we are going to live up to that privilege of our native country. Your pictures may not show the untrue, or the uncommon, or even be contrary to the canons of art; but it is not the view of life that we who thrive on conventions can permit to be painted."

But what did it matter. As for the matrimonial scenes, in spite of their "touching the spot,"[23] and the screaming of a poor lady in *Blackwood* that there was an unholy anti-marriage league afoot,[24] the famous contract—sacrament I mean—is doing fairly well still, and people marry and give in what may or may not be true marriage as light-heartedly as ever. The author has even been reproached by some earnest correspondents that he has left the question where he found it, and has not pointed the way to a much-needed reform.

After the issue of *Jude the Obscure* as a serial story in Germany, an experienced reviewer of that country informed the writer that Sue Bridehead, the heroine, was the first delineation in fiction of the woman who was coming into notice in her thousands every year—the woman of the feminist movement—the slight, pale "bachelor" girl—the intellectualized, emancipated bundle of nerves that modern conditions were producing, mainly in cities as yet; who do not recognize the necessity for most of her sex to follow marriage as a profession, and boast themselves as superior people because they are licensed to be loved on the premises. The regret of this critic was that the portrait of the newcomer had been left to be drawn by a man, and was not done by one of her own sex, who would never have allowed her to break down at the end.

Whether this assurance is borne out by dates I cannot say. Nor am I able, across the gap of years since the production of the novel, to exercise more criticism upon it of a general kind than extends to a few verbal corrections, whatever, good or bad, it may contain. And no doubt there can be more in a book than the author consciously puts there, which will help either to its profit or to its disadvantage as the case may be.

T. H.

April 1912.

[The earlier titles of *Jude the Obscure,* to which Hardy refers in his second paragraph, were *The Simpletons* and *Hearts Insurgent.*]

The Well-Beloved

[1897; Wessex Edition, XIII, 1912]

THE PENINSULA carved by Time out of a single stone, whereon most of the following scenes are laid, has been for centuries immemorial the home of a curious and well-nigh distinct people, cherishing strange beliefs and singular customs, now for the most part obsolescent. Fancies, like certain soft-wooded plants which cannot bear the silent inland frosts, but thrive by the sea in the roughest of weather, seem to grow up naturally here, in particular amongst those natives who have no active concern in the labours of the "Isle." Hence it is a spot apt to generate a type of personage like the character imperfectly sketched in these pages—a native of natives—whom some may choose to call a fantast (if they honour him with their consideration so far), but whom others may see only as one that gave objective continuity and a name to a delicate dream which in a vaguer form is more or less common to all men, and is by no means new to Platonic philosophers.

To those who know the rocky coign of England here depicted—overlooking the great Channel Highway with all its suggestiveness, and standing out so far into mid-sea that touches of the Gulf Stream soften the air till February—it is matter of surprise that the place has not been more frequently chosen as the retreat of artists and poets in search of inspiration—for at least a month or two in the year, the tempestuous rather than the fine seasons by preference. To be sure, one nook therein is the retreat, at their country's expense, of other geniuses from a distance; but their presence is hardly discoverable. Yet perhaps it is as well that the artistic visitors do not come, or no more would be heard of little freehold houses being bought and sold there for a couple of hundred pounds—built of solid stone, and dating from the sixteenth century and earlier, with mullions, copings, and corbels complete.[25] These transactions, by the way, are carried out and covenanted, or were till lately, in the parish church, in the face of the congregation, such being the ancient custom of the Isle.

As for the story itself, it may be worth while to remark that, differing from all or most others of the series in that the interest aimed at it is of an ideal or subjective nature, and frankly imaginative, verisimilitude in the sequence of events has been subordinated to the said aim.

The first publication of this tale in an independent form was in 1897; but it had appeared in the periodical press in 1892, under the title of *The Pursuit of the Well-Beloved.* A few chapters of that experimental issue were rewritten for the present and final form of the narrative.[26]

T. H.

August 1912.

Wessex Poems

[1898; Wessex Edition, Verse I, 1912]

OF THE MISCELLANEOUS collection of verse that follows, only four pieces have been published, though many were written long ago, and others partly written. In some few cases the verses were turned into prose and printed as such in a novel, it not having been anticipated at that time that they might see the light in their original shape.

Here and there, when an ancient and legitimate word still current in the district, for which there was no close equivalent in received English, suggested itself, it has been made use of, on what seemed good grounds.

The pieces are in a large degree dramatic or personative in conception; and the dates attached to some of the poems do not apply to the rough sketches given in illustration,* which had been recently made, and, as may be surmised, are inserted for personal and local reasons rather than for their intrinsic qualities.

September 1898.

Poems of the Past and Present

[1902; Wessex Edition, Verse I, 1912]

HEREWITH I tender my thanks to the editors and proprietors of the *Times,* the *Morning Post,* the *Daily Chronicle,* the *Westminster Gazette, Literature,* the *Graphic, Cornhill, Sphere,* and other papers, for permission to reprint from their pages such of the following pieces of verse as have already been published.

As was said of *Wessex Poems,* of the subject-matter of this volume much is dramatic or impersonative even where not explicitly so. And that portion which may be regarded as individual comprises a series of feelings and fancies written down in

* The early editions were illustrated by the writer.

widely differing moods and circumstances, and at various dates; it will probably be found, therefore, to possess little cohesion of thought or harmony of colouring. I do not greatly regret this. Unadjusted impressions have their value, and the road to a true philosophy of life seems to lie in humbly recording diverse readings of its phenomena as they are forced upon us by chance and change.

T. H.

August 1901.

The Dynasts, Parts First and Second

[1904, 1906; Wessex Edition, Verse II, 1913]

The Spectacle here presented to the mind's eye in the likeness of a Drama is concerned with the Great Historical Calamity, or Clash of Peoples, artificially brought about some hundred years ago.

The choice of such a subject was mainly due to three accidents of locality. It chanced that the writer was familiar with a part of England that lay within hail of the watering-place in which King George the Third had his favourite summer residence during the war with the first Napoléon, and where he was visited by ministers and others who bore the weight of English affairs on their more or less competent shoulders at that stressful time. Secondly, this district, being also near the coast which had echoed with rumours of invasion in their intensest form while the descent threatened, was formerly animated by memories and traditions of the desperate military preparations for that contingency. Thirdly, the same countryside happened to include the village which was the birthplace of Nelson's flag-captain at Trafalgar.

When, as the first published result of these accidents, *The Trumpet-Major* was printed, more than twenty years ago, I found myself in the tantalizing position of having touched the fringe of a vast international tragedy without being able, through limits of plan, knowledge, and opportunity, to enter further into its events; a restriction that prevailed for many years. But the slight regard paid to English influence and action throughout the struggle by those Continental writers who had dealt imaginatively with Napoléon's career, seemed always to leave room for a new handling of the theme which should re-embody the features of this influence in their true proportion; and accordingly, on a belated day about six years back, the following drama was outlined, to be taken up now and then at wide intervals ever since.

It may, I think, claim at least a tolerable fidelity to the facts of its date as they are given in ordinary records. Whenever any evidence of the words really spoken or written by the characters in their various situations was attainable, as close a paraphrase has been aimed at as was compatible with the form chosen. And in all cases outside oral tradition, accessible scenery, and existing relics, my indebtedness for detail to the abundant pages of the historian, the biographer, and the journalist, English and Foreign, has been, of course, continuous.

It was thought proper to introduce, as supernatural spectators of the terrestrial action, certain impersonated abstractions, or Intelligences, called Spirits. They are intended to be taken by the reader for what they may be worth as contrivances of the fancy merely. Their doctrines are but tentative, and are advanced with little eye to a clear metaphysic, or systematized philosophy warranted to lift "the burthen of the mystery"[27] of this unintelligible world. The chief thing hoped for them is that they and their utterances may have dramatic plausibility enough to procure for them, in the words of Coleridge, "that willing suspension of disbelief for the moment which constitutes poetic faith."[28] The wide acceptance of the Monistic theory of the Universe forbade, in this twentieth century, the importation of Divine personages from any antique Mythology as ready-made sources or channels of Causation, even in verse, and excluded the celestial machinery of, say, *Paradise Lost,* as peremptorily as that of the *Iliad* or the *Eddas.* And the abandonment of the masculine pronoun in allusions to the First or Fundamental Energy seemed a necessary and logical consequence of the long abandonment by thinkers of the anthropomorphic conception of the same.

These phantasmal Intelligences are divided into groups, of which one only, that of the Pities, approximates to "the Universal Sympathy of human nature—the spectator idealized"* of the Greek Chorus; it is impressionable and inconsistent in its views, which sway hither and thither as wrought on by events. Another group approximates to the passionless Insight of the Ages. The remainder are eclectically chosen auxiliaries whose signification may be readily discerned. In point of literary form, the scheme of contrasted Choruses and other conventions of this external feature was shaped with a single view to the modern expression of a modern outlook, and in frank divergence from classical and other dramatic precedent which ruled the ancient voicings of ancient themes.

It may hardly be necessary to inform readers that in devising this chronicle-piece no attempt has been made to create that completely organic structure of action, and closely-webbed development of character and motive, which are demanded in a drama strictly self-contained. A panoramic show like the present is a series of historical "ordinates" (to use a term in geometry): the subject is familiar to all; and foreknowledge is assumed to fill in the junctions required to combine the scenes into an artistic unity. Should the mental spectator be unwilling or unable to do this, a historical presentment on an intermittent plan, in which the *dramatis personae* number some hundreds, exclusive of crowds and armies, becomes in his individual case unsuitable.

In this assumption of a completion of the action by those to whom the drama is addressed, it is interesting, if unnecessary, to

* Schlegel.

name an exemplar as old as Aeschylus, whose plays are, as Dr. Verrall reminds us,* scenes from stories taken as known, and would be unintelligible without supplementary scenes of the imagination.

Readers will readily discern, too, that *The Dynasts* is intended simply for mental performance, and not for the stage. Some critics have averred that to declare a drama** as being not for the stage is to make an announcement whose subject and predicate cancel each other. The question seems to be an unimportant matter of terminology. Compositions cast in this shape were, without doubt, originally written for the stage only, and as a consequence their nomenclature of "Act," "Scene," and the like, was drawn directly from the vehicle of representation. But in the course of time such a shape would reveal itself to be an eminently readable one; moreover, by dispensing with the theatre altogether, a freedom of treatment was attainable in this form that was denied where the material possibilities of stagery had to be rigorously remembered. With the careless mechanicism of human speech, the technicalities of practical mumming were retained in these productions when they had ceased to be concerned with the stage at all.

To say, then, in the present case, that a writing in play-shape is not to be played, is merely another way of stating that such writing has been done in a form for which there chances to be no brief definition save one already in use for works that it superficially but not entirely resembles.

Whether mental performance alone may not eventually be the fate of all drama other than that of contemporary or frivolous life, is a kindred question not without interest. The mind naturally flies to the triumphs of the Hellenic and Elizabethan theatre in exhibiting scenes laid "far in the Unapparent,"[29] and asks why they should not be repeated. But the meditative world is older,

* Introduction to the *Choëphori*.

** It is now called an Epic-Drama (1909).

more invidious, more nervous, more quizzical, than it once was, and being unhappily perplexed by—

> Riddles of Death Thebes never knew,[30]

may be less ready and less able than Hellas and old England were to look through the insistent, and often grotesque, substance at the thing signified.

In respect of such plays of poesy and dream a practicable compromise may conceivably result, taking the shape of a monotonic delivery of speeches, with dreamy conventional gestures, something in the manner traditionally maintained by the old Christmas mummers, the curiously hypnotizing impressiveness of whose automatic style—that of persons who spoke by no will of their own—may be remembered by all who ever experienced it. Gauzes or screens to blur outlines might still further shut off the actual, as has, indeed, already been done in exceptional cases. But with this branch of the subject we are not concerned here.

T. H.

September 1903.

Time's Laughingstocks and Other Verses

[1909; Wessex Edition, Verse III, 1913]

In collecting the following poems to form a volume, I have to thank the editors and proprietors of the periodicals in which certain of them have appeared for permission to reclaim them.

Now that the miscellany is brought together, some lack of concord in pieces written at widely severed dates, and in contrasting moods and circumstances, will be obvious enough. This I cannot help, but the sense of disconnection, particularly in respect of those lyrics penned in the first person, will be immaterial when it is borne in mind that they are to be regarded, in the main, as dramatic monologues by different characters.

As a whole they will, I hope, take the reader forward, even if not far, rather than backward. I should add that some lines in the earlier poems have been rewritten, though they have been left substantially unchanged.

T. H.

September 1909.

General Preface to the Novels and Poems

[Wessex Edition, I, 1912]

IN ACCEPTING a proposal for a definite edition of these productions in prose and verse I have found an opportunity of classifying the novels under heads that show approximately the author's aim, if not his achievement, in each book of the series at the date of its composition. Sometimes the aim was lower than at other times; sometimes, where the intention was primarily high, force of circumstances (among which the chief were the necessities of magazine publication) compelled a modification, great or slight, of the original plan. Of a few, however, of the longer novels, and of many of the shorter tales, it may be assumed that they stand to-day much as they would have stood if no accidents had obstructed the channel between the writer and the public. That many of them, if any, stand as they would stand if written *now* is not to be supposed.

In the classification of these fictitious chronicles—for which the name of "The Wessex Novels" was adopted, and is still retained—the first group is called "Novels of Character and Environment," and contains those which approach most nearly to uninfluenced works; also one or two which, whatever their quality in some few of their episodes, may claim a verisimilitude in general treatment and detail.

The second group is distinguished as "Romances and Fantasies," a sufficiently descriptive definition. The third class—

"Novels of Ingenuity"—show a not infrequent disregard of the probable in the chain of events, and depend for their interest mainly on the incidents themselves. They might also be characterized as "Experiments," and were written for the nonce simply; though despite the artificiality of their fable some of their scenes are not without fidelity to life.

It will not be supposed that these differences are distinctly perceptible in every page of every volume. It was inevitable that blendings and alternations should occur in all. Moreover, as it was not thought desirable in every instance to change the arrangement of the shorter stories to which readers have grown accustomed, certain of these may be found under headings to which an acute judgment might deny appropriateness.

It has sometimes been conceived of novels that evolve their action on a circumscribed scene—as do many (though not all) of these—that they cannot be so inclusive in their exhibition of human nature as novels wherein the scenes cover large extents of country, in which events figure amid towns and cities, even wander over the four quarters of the globe. I am not concerned to argue this point further than to suggest that the conception is an untrue one in respect of the elementary passions. But I would state that the geographical limits of the stage here trodden were not absolutely forced upon the writer by circumstances; he forced them upon himself from judgment. I considered that our magnificent heritage from the Greeks in dramatic literature found sufficient room for a large proportion of its action in an extent of their country not much larger than the half-dozen counties here reunited under the old name of Wessex, that the domestic emotions have throbbed in Wessex nooks with as much intensity as in the palaces of Europe, and that, anyhow, there was quite enough human nature in Wessex for one man's literary purpose. So far was I possessed by this idea that I kept within the frontiers when it would have been easier to overleap them and give more cosmopolitan features to the narrative.

Thus, though the people in most of the novels (and in much of the shorter verse) are dwellers in a province bounded on the north by the Thames, on the south by the English Channel, on the east by a line running from Hayling Island to Windsor Forest, and on the west by the Cornish coast, they were meant to be typically and essentially those of any and every place where

Thought's the slave of life, and life time's fool,[31]

—beings in whose hearts and minds that which is apparently local should be really universal.

But whatever the success of this intention, and the value of these novels as delineations of humanity, they have at least a humble supplementary quality of which I may be justified in reminding the reader, though it is one that was quite unintentional and unforeseen. At the dates represented in the various narrations things were like that in Wessex: the inhabitants lived in certain ways, engaged in certain occupations, kept alive certain customs, just as they are shown doing in these pages. And in particularizing such I have often been reminded of Boswell's remarks on the trouble to which he was put and the pilgrimages he was obliged to make to authenticate some detail, though the labour was one which would bring him no praise. Unlike his achievement, however, on which an error would as he says have brought discredit, if these country customs and vocations, obsolete and obsolescent, had been detailed wrongly, nobody would have discovered such errors to the end of Time. Yet I have instituted inquiries to correct tricks of memory, and striven against temptations to exaggerate, in order to preserve for my own satisfaction a fairly true record of a vanishing life.

It is advisable also to state here, in response to inquiries from readers interested in landscape, prehistoric antiquities, and especially old English architecture, that the description of these backgrounds has been done from the real—that is to say, has something real for its basis, however illusively treated. Many features of the first two kinds have been given under their existing names; for instance, the Vale of Blackmoor or Blakemore, Hambledon Hill, Bulbarrow, Nettlecombe Tout, Dogbury Hill, High-Stoy, Bubb-Down Hill, The Devil's Kitchen, Cross-in-Hand, Long-Ash Lane, Benvill Lane, Giant's Hill, Crimmercrock Lane, and Stonehenge. The rivers Froom, or Frome, and Stour, are, of course, well known as such. And the further idea was that large towns and points tending to mark the outline of Wessex—such as Bath, Plymouth, The Start, Portland Bill, Southampton, etc.—should be named clearly. The scheme was not greatly elaborated, but, whatever its value, the names remain still.

In respect of places described under fictitious or ancient names in the novels—for reasons that seemed good at the time of writing them—and kept up in the poems—discerning people have affirmed in print that they clearly recognize the originals: such as Shaftesbury in "Shaston," Sturminster Newton in "Stourcastle," Dorchester in "Casterbridge," Salisbury Plain in "The Great Plain," Cranborne Chase in "The Chase," Beaminster in "Emminster," Bere Regis in "Kingsbere," Woodbury Hill in "Greenhill," Wool Bridge in "Wellbridge," Harfoot or Harput Lane in "Stagfoot Lane," Hazlebury in "Nuttlebury," Bridport in "Port Bredy," Maiden Newton in "Chalk Newton," a farm near Nettlecombe Tout in "Flintcomb Ash," Sherborne in "Sherton Abbas," Milton Abbey in "Middleton Abbey," Cerne Abbas in "Abbot's Cernel," Evershot in "Evershed," Taunton in "Toneborough," Bournemouth in "Sandbourne," Winchester in "Wintoncester," Oxford in "Christminster," Reading in "Aldbrickham," Newbury in "Kennetbridge," Wantage in "Alfredston," Basingstoke in "Stoke Barehills," and so on. Subject to the qualifications above given, that no detail is guaranteed,—that the portraiture of fictitiously named towns and villages was only suggested by certain real places, and wantonly wanders from inventorial descriptions of them—I do not contradict these keen hunters for the real;

I am satisfied with their statements as as least an indication of their interest in the scenes.

Thus much for the novels. Turning now to the verse—to myself the more individual part of my literary fruitage—I would say that, unlike some of the fiction, nothing interfered with the writer's freedom in respect of its form or content. Several of the poems—indeed many—were produced before novel-writing had been thought of as a pursuit; but few saw the light till all the novels had been published. The limited stage to which the majority of the latter confine their exhibitions has not been adhered to here in the same proportion, the dramatic part especially having a very broad theatre of action. It may thus relieve the circumscribed areas treated in the prose, if such relief be needed. To be sure, one might argue that by surveying Europe from a celestial point of vision—as in *The Dynasts*—that continent becomes virtually a province—a Wessex, an Attica, even a mere garden—and hence is made to conform to the principle of the novels, however far it outmeasures their region. But that may be as it will.

The few volumes filled by the verse cover a producing period of some eighteen years first and last, while the seventeen or more volumes of novels represent correspondingly about four-and-twenty years. One is reminded by this disproportion in time and result how much more concise and quintessential expression becomes when given in rhythmic form than when shaped in the language of prose.

One word on what has been called the present writer's philosophy of life, as exhibited more particularly in this metrical section of his compositions. Positive views on the Whence and the Wherefore of things have never been advanced by this pen as a consistent philosophy. Nor is it likely, indeed, that imaginative writings extending over more than forty years would exhibit a coherent scientific theory of the universe even if it had been attempted—of that universe concerning which Spencer owns to the "paralyzing thought" that possibly there exists no comprehension of it anywhere.[32] But such objectless consistency never has been attempted, and the sentiments in the following pages have been stated truly to be mere impressions of the moment, and not convictions or arguments.

That these impressions have been condemned as "pessimistic" —as if that were a very wicked adjective—shows a curious muddle-mindedness. It must be obvious that there is a higher characteristic of philosophy than pessimism, or than meliorism, or even than the optimism of these critics—which is truth. Existence is either ordered in a certain way, or it is not so ordered, and conjectures which harmonize best with experience are removed above all comparison with other conjectures which do not so harmonize. So that to say one view is worse than other views without proving it erroneous implies the possibility of a false view being better or more expedient than a true view; and no pragmatic proppings can make that *idolum specus*[33] stand on its feet, for it postulates a prescience denied to humanity.

And there is another consideration. Differing natures find their tongue in the presence of differing spectacles. Some natures become vocal at tragedy, some are made vocal by comedy, and it seems to me that to whichever of these aspects of life a writer's instinct for expression the more readily responds, to that he should allow it to respond. That before a contrasting side of things he remains undemonstrative need not be assumed to mean that he remains unperceiving.

It was my hope to add to these volumes of verse as many more as would make a fairly comprehensive cycle of the whole. I had wished that those in dramatic, ballad, and narrative form should include most of the cardinal situations which occur in social and public life, and those in lyric form a round of emotional experiences of some completeness. But

The petty done, the undone vast![34]

The more written the more seems to remain to be written; and the night cometh. I realize that these hopes and plans, except possibly to the extent of a volume or two, must remain unfulfilled.

T. H.

October 1911.

A Changed Man

[1913; Wessex Edition, XVIII, 1914]

I REPRINT in this volume, for what they may be worth, a dozen minor novels that have been published in the periodical press at various dates in the past, in order to render them accessible to readers who desire to have them in the complete series issued by my publishers.[35] For aid in reclaiming some of the narratives I express my thanks to the proprietors and editors of the newspapers and magazines in whose pages they first appeared.

T. H.

August 1913.

Late Lyrics and Earlier

[1922; Wessex Edition, Verse V, 1926]

APOLOGY

ABOUT HALF the verses that follow were written quite lately. The rest are older, having been held over in MS. when past volumes were published, on considering that these would contain a sufficient number of pages to offer readers at one time, more especially during the distractions of the war. The unusually far back poems to be found here are, however, but some that were overlooked in gathering previous collections. A freshness in them, now unattainable, seemed to make up for their inexperience and to justify their inclusion. A few are dated; the dates of others are not discoverable.

The launching of a volume of this kind in neo-Georgian days by one who began writing in mid-Victorian, and has published nothing to speak of for some years, may seem to call for a few words of excuse or explanation. Whether or no, readers may feel assured that a new book is submitted to them with great hesitation at so belated a date. Insistent practical reasons, however, among which were requests from some illustrious men of letters who are in sympathy with my productions, the accident that several of the poems have already seen the light, and that dozens of them have been lying about for years, compelled the course adopted, in spite of the natural disinclination of a writer whose works have been so frequently regarded askance by a pragmatic section here and there, to draw attention to them once more.

I do not know that it is necessary to say much on the contents of the book, even in deference to suggestions that will be mentioned presently. I believe that those readers who care for my poems at all—readers to whom no passport is required—will care for this new instalment of them, perhaps the last, as much as for any that have preceded them. Moreover, in the eyes of a less friendly class the pieces, though a very mixed collection indeed, contain, so far as I am able to see, little or nothing in technic or teaching that can be considered a Star-Chamber matter, or so much as agitating to a ladies' school; even though, to use Wordsworth's observation in his Preface to *Lyrical Ballads,* such readers may suppose "that by the act of writing in verse an author makes a formal engagement that he will gratify certain known habits of association: that he not only thus apprises the reader that certain classes of ideas and expressions will be found in his book, but that others will be carefully excluded."

It is true, nevertheless, that some grave, positive, stark delineations are interspersed among those of the passive, lighter, and traditional sort presumably nearer to stereotyped tastes. For—while I am quite aware that a thinker is not expected, and, indeed, is scarcely allowed, now more than heretofore, to state all that crosses his mind concerning existence in this universe, in his attempts to explain or excuse the presence of evil and the incongruity of penalizing the irresponsible—it must be obvious to open intelligences that, without denying the beauty and faithful service of certain venerable cults, such disallowance of "obstinate questionings" and "blank misgivings"[36] tends to a paralysed intellectual stalemate. Heine observed nearly a hundred years ago that the soul has her eternal rights; that she will not be darkened by statutes, nor lullabied by the music of bells.[37] And what is to-day, in allusions to the present author's pages, alleged to be "pessimism" is, in truth, only such "questionings" in the exploration of reality, and is the first step towards the soul's betterment, and the body's also.

If I may be forgiven for quoting my own old words, let me repeat what I printed in this relation more than twenty years ago, and wrote much earlier, in a poem entitled "In Tenebris":

> If way to the Better there be, it exacts a full look at the Worst:

that is to say, by the exploration of reality, and its frank recognition stage by stage along the survey, with an eye to the best consummation possible: briefly, evolutionary meliorism. But it is called pessimism nevertheless; under which word, expressed with condemnatory emphasis, it is regarded by many as some pernicious new thing (though so old as to underlie the Gospel scheme, and even to permeate the Greek drama); and the subject is charitably left to decent silence, as if further comment were needless.

Happily there are some who feel such Levitical passing-by[38] to be, alas, by no means a permanent dismissal of the matter; that comment on where the world stands is very much the reverse of needless in these disordered years of our prematurely afflicted century: that amendment and not madness lies that way. And looking down the future these few hold fast to the same: that whether the human and kindred animal races survive till the exhaustion or destruction of the globe, or whether these races perish and are succeeded by others before that conclusion comes, pain to all upon it, tongued or dumb, shall be kept down to a minimum by loving-kindness, operating through scientific knowledge, and actuated by the modicum of free will conjecturally possessed by organic life when the mighty necessitating forces—unconscious or other—that have "the balancings of the clouds," happen to be in equilibrium, which may or may not be often.

To conclude this question I may add that the argument of the so-called optimists is neatly summarized in a stern pronouncement against me by my friend Mr. Frederic Harrison in a late essay of his, in the words: "This view of life is not mine."[39] The solemn declaration does not seem to me to be so annihilating to the said "view" (really a series of fugitive impressions which I have never tried to co-ordinate) as is complacently assumed. Surely it embodies a too human fallacy quite familiar in logic. Next, a knowing reviewer, apparently a Roman Catholic young man, speaks, with some rather gross instances of the *suggestio falsi* in his whole article, of "Mr. Hardy refusing consolation," the "dark gravity of his ideas," and so on.[40] When a Positivist and a Romanist agree there must be something wonderful in it, which should make a poet sit up. But . . . O that 'twere possible![41]

I would not have alluded in this place or anywhere else to such casual personal criticisms—for casual and unreflecting they must be—but for the satisfaction of two or three friends in whose opinion a short answer was deemed desirable, on account of the continual repetition of these criticisms, or more precisely, quizzings. After all, the serious and truly literary inquiry in this connection is: Should a shaper of such stuff as dreams are made on disregard considerations of what is customary and expected, and apply himself to the real function of poetry, the application of ideas to life (in Matthew Arnold's familiar phrase)?[42] This bears more particularly on what has been called the "philosophy" of these poems—usually reproved as "queer." Whoever the author may be that undertakes such application of ideas in this "philosophic" direction—where it is specially required—glacial judgments must inevitably fall upon him amid opinion whose arbiters largely decry individuality, to whom *ideas* are oddities to smile at, who are moved by a yearning the reverse of that of the Athenian inquirers on Mars Hill;[43] and stiffen their features not only at sound of a new thing, but at a restatement of old things in new terms. Hence should anything of this sort in the following adumbrations seem "queer"—should any of them seem to good Panglossians to embody strange and disrespectful conceptions of this best of all possible worlds, I apologize; but cannot help it.[44]

Such divergences, which, though piquant for the nonce, it would be affectation to say are not saddening and discouraging likewise, may, to be sure, arise sometimes from superficial aspect only, writer and reader seeing the same thing at different angles. But in palpable cases of divergence they arise, as already said, whenever a serious effort is made towards that which the authority I have cited—who would now be called old-fashioned, possibly even parochial—affirmed to be what no good critic could deny as the poet's province, the application of ideas to life. One might shrewdly guess, by the by, that in such recommendation the famous writer may have overlooked the cold-shouldering results upon an enthusiastic disciple that would be pretty certain to follow his putting the high aim in practice, and have forgotten the disconcerting experience of Gil Blas with the Archbishop.[45]

To add a few more words to what has already taken up too many, there is a contingency liable to miscellanies of verse that I have never seen mentioned, so far as I can remember; I mean the chance little shocks that may be caused over a book of various character like the present and its predecessors by the juxtaposition of unrelated, even discordant, effusions; poems perhaps years apart in the making, yet facing each other. An odd result of this has been that dramatic anecdotes of a satirical and humorous intention following verse in graver voice, have been read as misfires because they raise the smile that they were intended to raise, the journalist, deaf to the sudden change of key, being unconscious that he is laughing with the author and not at him. I admit that I did not foresee such contingencies as I ought to have done, and that people might not perceive when the tone altered. But the difficulties of arranging the themes in a graduated kinship of moods would have been so great that irrelation was almost unavoidable with efforts so diverse. I must trust for right note-catching to those finely-touched spirits who can divine without half a whisper, whose intuitiveness is proof against all the accidents of inconsequence. In respect of the less alert, however, should any one's train of thought be thrown out of gear by a consecutive piping of vocal reeds in jarring tonics, without a semi-quaver's rest between, and be led thereby to miss the writer's aim and meaning in one out of two contiguous compositions, I shall deeply regret it.

Having at last, I think, finished with the personal points that I was recommended to notice, I will forsake the immediate object of this Preface; and, leaving *Late Lyrics* to whatever fate it deserves, digress for a few moments to more general considerations. The thoughts of any man of letters concerned to keep poetry alive cannot but run uncomfortably on the precarious prospects of English verse at the present day. Verily the hazards and casualties surrounding the birth and setting forth of almost every modern creation in numbers are ominously like those of one of Shelley's paper-boats on a windy lake. And a forward conjecture scarcely permits the hope of a better time, unless men's tendencies should change. So indeed of all art, literature, and "high thinking" nowadays. Whether owing to the barbarizing of taste in the younger minds by the dark madness of the late war, the unabashed cultivation of selfishness in all classes, the plethoric growth of knowledge simultaneously with the stunting of wisdom, "a degrading thirst after outrageous stimulation" (to quote Wordsworth again),[46] or from any other cause, we seem threatened with a new Dark Age.

I formerly thought, like other much exercised writers, that so far as literature was concerned a partial cause might be impotent or mischievous criticism; the satirizing of individuality, the lack of whole-seeing in contemporary estimates of poetry and kindred work, the knowingness affected by junior reviewers, the overgrowth of meticulousness in their peerings for an opinion, as if it were a cultivated habit in them to scrutinize the toolmarks and be blind to the building, to hearken for the key-creaks and be deaf to the diapason, to judge the landscape by a nocturnal exploration with a flash-lantern. In other words, to carry on the old game of sampling the poem or drama by quoting the worst line or worst passage only, in ignorance or not of Coleridge's proof that a versification of any length neither can be nor ought to be all poetry; of reading meanings into a book that its author never dreamt of writing there. I might go on interminably.

But I do not now think any such temporary obstructions to be the cause of the hazard, for these negligences and ignorances, though they may have stifled a few true poets in the run of generations, disperse like stricken leaves before the wind of next week, and are no more heard of again in the region of letters than their writers themselves. No: we may be convinced that something of the deeper sort mentioned must be the cause.

In any event poetry, pure literature in general, religion—I include religion, in its essential and undogmatic sense, because poetry and religion touch each other, or rather modulate into each other; are, indeed, often but different names for the same thing[47]—these, I say, the visible signs of mental and emotional life, must like all other things keep moving, becoming; even though at present, when belief in witches of Endor is displacing the Darwinian theory and "the truth that shall make you free,"[48] men's minds appear, as above noted, to be moving backwards rather than on. I speak somewhat sweepingly, and should except many thoughtful writers in verse and prose; also men in certain worthy but small bodies of various denominations, and perhaps in the homely quarter where advance might have been the very least expected a few years back—the English Church—if one reads it rightly as showing evidence of "removing those things that are shaken,"[49] in accordance with the wise Epistolary recommendation to the Hebrews. For since the historic and once august hierarchy of Rome some generation ago lost its chance of being the religion of the future by doing otherwise, and throwing over the little band of New Catholics who were making a struggle for continuity by applying the principle of evolution to their own faith, joining hands with modern science, and outflanking the hesitating English instinct towards liturgical restatement (a flank march which I at the time quite expected to witness, with the gathering of many millions of waiting agnostics into its fold); since then, one may ask, what other purely English establishment than the Church, of sufficient dignity and footing, with such strength of old association, such scope for transmutability, such architectural spell, is left in this country to keep the shreds of morality together?*

It may indeed be a forlorn hope, a mere dream, that of an alliance between religion, which must be retained unless the world is to perish, and complete rationality, which must come, unless also the world is to perish, by means of the interfusing effect of poetry—"the breath and finer spirit of all knowledge; the impassioned expression of science,"[50] as it was defined by an English

* However, one must not be too sanguine in reading signs, and since the above was written evidence that the Church will go far in the removal of "things that are shaken" has not been encouraging.

poet who was quite orthodox in his ideas. But if it be true, as Comte argued, that advance is never in a straight line, but in a looped orbit, we may, in the aforesaid ominous moving backward, be doing it *pour mieux sauter,* drawing back for a spring. I repeat that I forlornly hope so, notwithstanding the supercilious regard of hope by Schopenhauer, von Hartmann, and other philosophers down to Einstein who have my respect. But one dares not prophesy. Physical, chronological, and other contingencies keep me in these days from critical studies and literary circles

> Where once we held debate, a band
> Of youthful friends, on mind and art[51]

(if one may quote Tennyson in this century). Hence I cannot know how things are going so well as I used to know them, and the aforesaid limitations must quite prevent my knowing henceforward.

I have to thank the editors and owners of *The Times, Fortnightly, Mercury,* and other periodicals in which a few of the poems have appeared for kindly assenting to their being reclaimed for collected publication.

T. H.

February 1922.

[This essay, which Hardy called "energetic" in *The Life of Thomas Hardy, 1840-1928* (London, 1962), p. 415, was important not only because it revealed his continuing sensitivity to remarks about his "pessimism," but because he was hopeful, between 1920 and 1925, that rumors of a revised, more rationalistic liturgy might prove true. Nevertheless, he doubted the wisdom of publishing the "Apology" at all, and sought the friendly advice of Sydney Cockerell. Although willing to delete any and all "undesirable parts," Hardy finally settled for "two verbal suggestions" (not specified), and wrote, on February 18, 1922, "Meanwhile I am abridging the whole somewhat, in spite of your saying you would not omit a word; for I fancy it is a little long and iterative." The word "Apology" struck him as "piquant," more so than "Preface." *Friends of a Lifetime: Letters to Sydney*

Carlyle Cockerell, ed. by Viola Meynell (London, 1940), pp. 288-289. The publication of the new Prayer Book "doomed" his hopes that the bishops of the Church of England might drop "preternatural assumptions out of it" (*Life,* p. 376), "and from that time he lost all expectation of seeing the Church representative of modern thinking minds."]

Les Dynastes

[An unpublished French translation by Yvonne Salmon; *La Revue Nouvelle,* Paris, January-February, 1928, pp. 40-41]

Préface de l'Auteur pour la Traduction Française[1]

Lorsqu'on me suggéra que *Les Dynastes* étaient un drame qui paraissait particulièrement susceptible d'intéresser les lecteurs francais, je fus frappé par la vraisemblance de la suggestion; c'est pourquoi je me prêtai au projet de traduction du drame, formant tous les voeux pour que l'entreprise pût être conduite à terme, tout en redoutant que le labeur qu'elle impliquait ne fût quelque peu écrasant. En fait, il se révéla moins écrasant que je ne m'y attendais.

En y réfléchissant il m'apparut qu'il y avait une raison toute spéciale pour qu'une version de ce drame fût donnée en francais. Combien de fois, au cours des siècles, les deux pays de France et d'Angleterre n'avaient-ils pas été entraînés dans des conflits en vertu de codes ou de gouvernements irresponsables, alors que les

[1] Cette préface de Hardy pour la traduction française est inédite, et, selon toute vraisemblance, constitue par sa date le dernier des inédits de Hardy puisqu'elle est de décembre 1927. Dans l'original elle s'achève sur une phrase que la modestie de la traductrice a cru devoir supprimer, mais que je tiens à rétablir ici: "Je dois ajouter que j'ai grande confiance dans ma traductrice dont le courage, en s'attaquant à une tâche aussi difficile, mérite tous les éloges; je la félicite ici de son heureux achèvement." Mais si la traductrice a triomphé de la difficulté de sa tâche, il semble que jusqu'à présent nos éditeurs, eux, reculent devant la leur. Pour l'honneur de l'édition française il est inadmissible, qu'une traduction des *Dynastes*—traduction approuvée par Hardy, et dont par surcroît, à la veille de sa mort, il prit la peine de la présenter à notre public—demeure sans titulaire. Avis à qui de droit.—C. D. B.

peuples eux-mêmes eussent, comme de juste, préféré vaquer à leurs propres affaires! Tel fut notamment le cas à l'époque où se situe ce drame,—de 1805 à 1815. Je me disais qu'avec le recul du temps la perception de ce fait induirait les lecteurs français à affronter les événements sans passion ni parti-pris. Le spectacle entier, en vérité, peut maintenant être envisagé tant en France qu'en Angleterre, comme un phénomène singulier dans lequel, comme dans toute guerre en général, la raison humaine eut peu de part.

Une autre considération encore faisait taire toute objection, —je veux dire le cadre ou *merveilleux philosophique,* Napoléon est un personnage particulièrement adapté à etre traité par le dramaturge comme une marionnette du Destin: en fait lui-même s'est souvent regardé comme tel; et comme tel peut-être pouvons-nous lui pardonner certaines de ses erreurs et de ses ambitions, en attendant que dans l'avenir nous puissions en arriver à lui tout pardonner (ainsi qu'aux autres tempéraments combatifs!) si la theorie *moniste* des Causes et des Effets, adoptée dans ce drame, en vue de motifs principalement artistiques, comme la force de propulsion qui meut les personnages, se découvre être la vraie théorie de l'univers. Sur ce point toutefois, auquel d'ailleurs se trouve liée toute la question du libre arbitre, je n'ai point qualité pour prophétiser. En tout cas les compatriotes de Descartes sauront apprécier cette théorie comme système dramatique, même s'ils ne l'acceptent pas en tant que philosophie.

THOMAS HARDY.

Décembre 1927.

Winter Words

[1928; Wessex Edition, Verse VI, 1931]

SO FAR as I am aware, I happen to be the only English poet who has brought out a new volume of his verse on his . . . birthday, whatever may have been the case with the ancient Greeks, for it must be remembered that poets did not die young in those days.

This, however, is not the point of the present few preliminary words. My last volume of poems was pronounced wholly gloomy and pessimistic by reviewers—even by some of the more able class. My sense of the oddity of this verdict may be imagined when, in selecting them, I had been, as I thought, rather too liberal in admitting flippant, not to say farcical, pieces into the collection. However, I did not suppose that the licensed tasters had wilfully misrepresented the book, and said nothing, knowing well that they could not have read it.

As labels stick, I foresee readily enough that the same perennial inscription will be set on the following pages, and therefore take no trouble to argue on the proceeding, notwithstanding the surprises to which I could treat my critics by uncovering a place here and there to them in the volume.

This being probably my last appearance on the literary stage, I would say, more seriously, that though, alas, it would be idle to pretend that the publication of these poems can have much interest for me, the track having been adventured so many times before to-day, the pieces themselves have been prepared with reasonable care, if not quite with the zest of a young man new to print.

I also repeat what I have often stated on such occasions, that no harmonious philosophy is attempted in these pages—or in any bygone pages of mine, for that matter.

T. H.

[To this final Preface, the publisher, Macmillan & Co., Ltd., added a note: "*Winter Words,* though prepared for the press, would have undergone further revision, had the author lived to issue it on the birthday of which he left the number uninserted below."]

II.
Prefaces to the Works of Other Writers

Dorchester [Dorset] and its Surroundings, by F. R. and Sidney Heath

[Dorchester and London, 1905-1906, p. 7]

I HAVE been asked by the compiler of this guide-book to examine the topographical and historical portions of his text; and having done so, I can say without hesitation that, so far as I am able to judge, he has embodied therein a quantity of closely-packed material, rich in antiquarian and contemporaneous fact to a degree not common in so small a volume. This is particularly the case in the paragraphs which deal with the period of the Roman occupation and the mediaeval and later centuries.

On the pages which refer to certain works of fiction and poems of recent date I naturally express no opinion.

The book has the recommendation of containing a map of the town and its suburbs—a feature lacking, so far as I am aware, in all previous guides of the kind. Natives of the ancient borough may smile at the idea of any sane person losing his way in a town of ten thousand inhabitants; yet I have been credibly informed that such is frequently the case, even amongst teetotallers; and I have myself met with one gentleman—a most ingenious and intelligent person—who suffered from the same misadventure, and complained bitterly of there being no readily accessible map for his guidance. The need is now supplied.

THOMAS HARDY.

[Purdy (p. 310) notes that this book is Volume 46 of The Homeland Handbooks, and was published in October, 1905.]

Dorchester Antiquities, by H. J. Moule

[Dorchester, 1906, pp. 7-13]

H. J. M.:

Some Memories and Letters

My first distinct recollection of Henry Moule carries me back, through a long avenue of years, towards the middle of the last century. His figure emerges from the obscurity of forgotten and half-forgotten things somewhere between 1856 and 1860, when I recall him as he stood beside me while I was attempting a sketch from nature in water colours. He must have been about thirty, and had already became an adept in out-door painting. As I was but a youth, and by no means practised in that art, he criticized my performance freely.

How it happened that we were together thus I am quite unable to remember; also whether I had known him long. Possibly I had known him slightly for some time, for at this date there was a perennial discussion in progress between my father and his, the Vicar of Fordington, about a field which my father owned but had no use for, which the Vicar had a mind to take for experiments in his well-known hobby of spade husbandry. Every year the question was renewed, the field looked at, heads shaken, and the matter again shelved.

Anyhow, when I took up water-colouring, our common interest led him frequently to call at my home, to ascertain what further exercises I had been giving myself in that accomplishment. He was such an enthusiast in painting that, though he always insisted on calling himself a mere amateur, there is no doubt he would have achieved high results therein if he had chosen to make of it a profession instead of a pastime. To such a man my youthful and intermittent fancy for the same pursuit must have semed unsatisfactory enough.

At this time he used to impress me as being rather taciturn than otherwise, which may seem strange to those who knew him only as the fluent conversationalist of later years. Another difference from more recent conceptions of him lay in the fact that his interests seemed to be not especially centered in Dorset and Dorset matters—further than that the county afforded good sketching ground. This may probably be explained by his experiences immediately preceding those years. Since leaving Cambridge he had travelled over a good deal of Europe, had lived away from Dorset even when in England, and had had his attention fixed on men and affairs quite dissociated from this county. Nobody could have supposed at that time that a day would come when his interests would extend but rarely beyond it.

Change took us both far from Dorset anon; him to Scotland and elsewhere as land-agent, and me to London in the study of architecture. For a long while I heard nothing of him, except indirectly through members of his family or of mine. But a continuous residence in London of several years having begun to tell upon my health I determined to go into the country for a time. He heard of my plan, and wrote to me suggesting estate management as a change of occupation, which would give me plenty of air. The scheme did not suit me, but it had the advantage of renewing our intercourse for a brief season.

The curtain again dropped between us, and how our acquaintance was revived is a mere matter of conjecture. The vicissitudes of life carried me hither and thither between London, Dorset, Somerset, Surrey, Paris, Germany, and elsewhere; but never a line can I discover from him during this long interval. That I saw him occasionally in the seventies is however possible. Not till 1881 does my record reach firm ground. I have before me a letter received from him in the July of that year, when I was temporarily at Wimborne and he was at Weymouth, which shows that the silence between had been broken:

> Your kind invitation to visit you in your new abode has been by no means forgotten by me, and I write to make a proposal in connection with it.
>
> If all goes well I shall be present at my brother Handley's wedding at Cambridge on Aug. 16, and it has occurred to me that as I shall in any case be passing by Wimborne, it would be a capital chance for me to have the pleasure of reviving my acquaintance with you. Do tell me, then, if you shall be at home on the 17th or 18th, and if so, whether it will be convenient to you to receive me for a night. I wish I could bring Mrs. Moule with me, but unfortunately she will be obliged to remain at home.

I clearly recall the visit, and how I met him at the station on his arrival. I feared that after so many years I might not recognize him; but there was no difficulty in doing that, though he had changed of course, and so, no doubt, had I. We had a day or two of delightful intercourse, sitting up till the small hours, and one of the subjects of our conversation is alluded to in a letter from him a week or two after:

> . . . I have been thinking much of what you say as to my pencil being brought into play in conjunction with your pen. I do heartily wish that it might come to pass somehow or other. . . . If, as you think, landscape with smallish figures will do, I trust that I should be able to do you justice. . . . Then again, I take much to Mrs. Hardy's idea of a book on Dorset written by you with landscape and architectural illustrations by me. There I should be at home, I may say. . . . I shall be glad to hear from you again on these matters.

Further correspondence ensued on the subject, but nothing came of it, there being doubts "if Dorset pure and simple would pay." It must be remembered that the date was nearly a quarter of a century back, when the county was not so popular as it is now. In concluding another letter thereon (October 1881) he adds:

I am so sorry that you had such poor weather for Scotland in general and Roslin in particular. That charming wooded glen depends much on weather for its beauty. The weather in Scotland seems to have changed very locally this season. I was told on Saturday of two parties of tourists who spent August in Scotland—in different parts, it would seem; for one party had 27 wet days and four fine ones, and the other 27 fine and four wet!

After a visit to London and elsewhere, he wrote, the following March (1882):

It seems to me a very long time since last I heard from you. . . . There is one clause in your letter which ought to have been answered.

This, it appears, related to illustrations for magazines, for which he had a fancy just then, and he describes some of his experiments in wood engraving, pen-and-ink drawing, &c., concluding:

I saw the Electric Exhibition at the Crystal Palace, and thought of what you had said of electric engineering being a good field. . . . I have always (ever since) thought of it for my elder boy, who is mighty at mechanism and that sort of thing. . . . To be sure it is early days as yet. He is only 15.

It would be such a pleasure to see you both if you penetrate so far at any time. We could house you in a "prophet's chamber."

New Year's Eve, 1883, stirred the muse in him, on the subject of barrows and flint arrow-heads, whereon I had touched in *The Return of the Native,* and he sent me a production in verse. The lines are strong and lyrical, as, *e.g.,* the following. They are supposed to be said or sung by the spirit of a departed Kelt who wanders on the heath in modern times:

We sleep here lonely on the hill, and as we lie
Seasons and years and ages slowly pass us by;
And still they stand, our far-seen barrows on the heath,
But men speak not the names of us who lie beneath.
Ah! but our names were shouted loud on that brave day
When here the astonished legion saw us turn at bay,
And, shudd'ring, heard the spell poured forth in magic song
That makes the foeman weak, but Keltic tribesmen strong!

And when through helm and shield, and through close-jointed mail,
Pierc'd our death-bearing flint-points, thick as storm of hail,
Down went Centurion, Praetor, Eagle-bearer bold,
But not the Eagle—passed in death to comrade's hold!
But not the Eagle—over sullen slow retreat,
Still shining, held on high to guide unwilling feet.

* * * * * *

In purple robe his god-like state doth Caesar keep—
In purple pall 'tis meet his liegemen sleep.

The removal to Dorchester of both my friend and myself put an end to the necessity of correspondence. From such brief notes as passed between us thence onward I make a few extracts. One for painting, with Wool Bridge house[1] in the middle distance; it shows that his zest for landscape art was unabated:

It struck me as a hard problem, and I think so still. However, from an up-train on Wednesday, and a down one to-day, I looked my best to see if I could spy out a fitting spot. The result is that I have a hope —slight, however—that something might be done from a place North of a group of cottages, public house, &c., that you pass about a mile W. of Wool Station.

Later, writing about a view of the same meadows from Norris Mill,[2] he flies off to another subject—one relating to my novel of *Jude,* then being published serially:

It was a good lecture last evening on Christminster (?), and it was a good stroke of policy to have it delivered. It will, I hope, induce some of our artizan friends to attend the lectures in January on the Colonies—lectures emanating from the beautiful city with which they may now claim some acquaintance. It is a fine thing, this permeation of the land by the Universities. Here, yesterday, was Oxford Wells discoursing of Oxford grey colleges and Oxford extension work. Here, yesterday, was Cambridge C. Moule [the writer's brother][3] holding a Cambridge local examination.

Four or five more years of occasional meetings and brief notes lead up to a letter of October, 1902, which reached me when I was staying at Bath. It is about a matter of folk-lore, on which he was keen, and he plunges into it without preface:

> Have you heard, I wonder, of the hare "incident," as the French would call it?
>
> Yesterday a hare could think of nothing better to do than to run all up South Street, across Bull Stake, and up Pease Lane [the Dorchester Council, with doubtful wisdom, has obliterated these historic names].[4] At the top of the lane, opposite Miss A---'s stables, someone killed it. People who saw it, or heard of it, said that this vagary was a sure sign that there would be a fire here within a week. So certain of this was a fireman that he said he was half inclined not to go to bed last night, as it was more than possible that he should be roused before morning by the fire-bell.[5]
>
> Well, it was not so prompt a fulfilment—this prophecy—as he feared. But it is a fact that this morning there was a fire, and, of all places, at Miss A---'s stable. Soon put out it was, I believe; but some of our friends in the bottom of their hearts have, very likely, a thought that the ghost of the hare had to do with it.
>
> *Certe, post hoc; vix propter hoc.* But I can imagine you taking this very strange occurrence up, as you did South's elm-tree totem in *The Woodlanders*.[6]

It will be perceived that he still writes as zestfully as ever. But a few months more brought about a sad change. I quote from a note sent in the spring of 1903, concerning a proposition Mrs. Hardy had made that he should occupy our house while we were away in London:

> It had been a weight on my mind, the yearly giving over of our dwelling to the indefatigable charwoman. I couldn't go a long journey—I couldn't go out of hail of the doctor—and lo! you two kind friends just exactly solve the puzzle—*dei ex machinâ* indeed. . . . To an old decrepit fogey like me there will be a delight in having Conquer Barrow and the hedge-side track to Came Wood close at hand.[7]

The plan was carried out, and he derived great benefit from the change, which reflected itself in his letters to me in London. He was daily finding prospects for sketches, old associations, naturally, enhancing their artistic charm; the year, moreover, being in the very act of putting forth the beauties of leafy June.

Twenty-acres, with its far views on three sides, I can hardly keep out of. This morning I found a spot in the middle cart-road from which I mean to make three sketches without moving, except to turn west, north, and east. Yesterday I did a little bit (first outdoor sketch since January.)

It is a real satisfaction to me that you, coming from a nightingale be-sung home, should also have the glorious song here at this house. Margie heard a nightingale the night before last.

On the 16th of June he says:

My bulletin is not a confirmation of my former one, but something far exceeding it in favourable character. . . . I can hardly believe in the betterment which has taken place. I am quite a different being. *Deo gratias*. My enjoyment of your country surroundings here has increased day by day, and also my delight in sketching bits thereof. The ever-changing "distances" seen from various points, S., W., and N. from quite close, and E. from the other side of Mount Pleasant, are a never-failing joy to my heart.

I had visions of his comparative rejuvenation by occasional residence there. But little do we divine how the future means to handle us. Exactly nine months from the date of this letter I was attending his funeral. At the beginning, I think, of the March following, he was taken seriously ill. I was just starting to call at his house one day after, when news was brought by a member of his family that he was much better; and I decided to postpone my visit till the next day. Within a few hours it was too late. And thus abruptly was brought to an end a friendship of between forty and fifty years.

THOMAS HARDY.

[It is difficult to overestimate the influence of the Moule family on Hardy's life. The Reverend Henry Moule (1801-1880) was the Vicar of Fordington, Dorchester, for fully half a century. His labors during a cholera epidemic in Fordington (1849-1854) prevented the plague from spreading; his broad-ranging interests included sanitation, gardening, and literature. Hardy's mother admired him, and Matthew Arnold was impressed. Hardy himself regarded the Vicar as a very great man, although he could not accept his religious teachings in later years, and aspects of the parson in "A Changed Man" will remind many readers of their historical original.

The Vicar had eight children, one of whom died in infancy; the rest Hardy nicknamed "The Seven Brethren." George Evans Moule (1828-1912) became the first bishop of central China (1880-1906). Handley Carr Glyn Moule (1841-1920) served two decades (1901-1920) as Bishop of Durham. Charles Moule became President of Corpus Christi College, Cambridge, and inspired, at least partially, the creation of Angel Clare in *Tess of the d'Urbervilles.* Horatio Moseley Moule (1832-1873) was a talented Greek scholar, a teacher, a musician, a reviewer and leader-writer, and, as Hardy wrote in the *London Mercury* of October, 1922, "had early showed every promise of becoming a distinguished English poet. But the fates said otherwise." In 1865 Hardy read Newman's *Apologia* with "a great desire to be convinced by him, because Moule liked him so much," but found "no first link" to Newman's "excellent chain of reasoning," and gave up discouraged. Twice the counsel of Horatio changed Hardy's life: first, when he dissuaded Hardy from continuing with his classical studies (modest encouragement might have led Hardy to abandon architecture for a university career), and second, when he urged a discouraged author, in the early 1870's, "not to give up writing altogether."

This brief sketch of Henry Joseph Moule (1825-1904) consists largely of quotations from letters, but pays tribute to "a friendship of between forty and fifty years." Henry's curatorship of the Dorset County Museum, an institution in which Hardy took a deep and lasting interest, was doubtless one of the factors leading to the decision of Florence Emily Hardy to leave, by the terms of her will, most of Hardy's books and papers at Max Gate to the Museum.]

The Society of Dorset Men in London

[Year-book, 1907-1908; London, 1907, pp. 3-4]

Forewords

By the President

The Society of Dorset Men in London has entered upon the fourth year of its existence, and can no longer be regarded as a tender bantling whose every breath needs to be watched and counted, hopefully or the reverse. The idea of such a Society has become familiar to its members; and as the seasons pass, and a younger generation of exiles from the parent county duly succeeds to associateship, it will gradually cease to cross their minds that there ever was a time when "neither vell nor mark" (to use a phrase from home)[8] of such an institution was apparent in the roaring loom of London life.

If it were worth doing, I could describe to those who are now in the full vigor of their activities in this City, and in the full flush of comradeship with brethren of the Society and others, what London seemed like to a Dorset young man who plunged into it alone more than forty-five years ago, in the somewhat reckless method of becoming a Londoner that was perhaps more common then than now. I might also describe what permanent residence in town meant to such a young man—living on from year to year, strolling up and down Holborn Hill before the Viaduct was constructed, wandering in the labyrinth of Seven Dials before the new Avenues were cut, and hastening off to Drury Lane or the Princess's Theatre to see Phelps or Charles Kean in a Shakespearean tragedy. So far as I can recollect, the last thing that such a young man ever thought of was association with persons coming from his own part of England, or even discovering their existence. Though obviously (it is astonishing how obvious a thing becomes when it has been carried out) nothing tends so largely to remove that isolation which is so apt to depress, and harm—sometimes permanently—the lives of country beginners in London, as a Society like ours, at bottom it is but one symptom among many of the general growth of human altruism noticeable everywhere. I can, unhappily, recall cases in which such a Society would probably have saved from rack and ruin many a promising youth so circumstanced.

My impression is that though the members themselves are grateful to those energetic spirits who set the Society going—I can express the belief freely, since I myself had no part in doing it—those who are pre-eminently grateful do not live in London at all, or but a small minority of them. I refer to the mothers of the younger constituents of this body. The sleepless nights and anxious days that have been spent, not only by Dorset mothers, but by those of every other county, at the time of their youthful sons' first plunge into the City alone, would make a pathetic record if they could be revealed. Such anxieties—which would be intenser if all the risks were realised—can never be entirely dispelled. But I think that our County Society, young as it is, is doing as much to allay them as can be accomplished by any similar means, and will do more as it unfolds itself in future years.

T. H.

[Hardy, who began his term of office as President of a young organization (he was only its second President), helped to strengthen it by his quiet but enthusiastic support, continued throughout his life. He served two successive terms. The Society is very much in existence today, and flourishes.]

Select Poems of William Barnes, Chosen and Edited by Thomas Hardy

[London, 1908, pp. iii-xii]

THIS VOLUME of verse includes, to the best of my judgement, the greater part of that which is of the highest value in the poetry of William Barnes. I have been moved to undertake the selection by a thought that has overridden some immediate objections to such an attempt,—that I chance to be (I believe) one of the few living persons having a practical acquaintance with letters who knew familiarly the Dorset dialect when it was spoken as Barnes writes it, or, perhaps, who know it as it is spoken now. Since his death, education in the west of England as elsewhere has gone on with its silent and inevitable effacements, reducing the speech of this country to uniformity, and obliterating every year many a fine old local word. The process is always the same: the word is ridiculed by the newly taught; it gets into disgrace; it is heard in holes and corners only; it dies; and, worst of all, it leaves no synonym. In the villages that one recognizes to be the scenes of these pastorals the poet's nouns, adjectives, and idioms daily cease to be understood by the younger generation, the luxury of four demonstrative pronouns, of which he was so proud, vanishes by their compression into the two of common English, and the suffix to verbs which marks continuity of action[9] is almost everywhere shorn away.

To cull from a dead writer's whole achievement in verse portions that shall exhibit him is a task of no small difficulty, and of some temerity. There is involved, first of all, the question of right. A selector may say: These are the pieces that please me best; but he may not be entitled to hold that they are the best in themselves and for everybody. This opens the problem of equating the personality—of adjusting the idiosyncrasy of the chooser to mean pitch. If it can be done in some degree—one may doubt it

—there are to be borne in mind the continually changing taste of the times. But, assuming average critical capacity in the compiler, that he represents his own time, and that he finds it no great toil to come to a conclusion on which in his view are the highest levels and the lowest of a poet's execution, the complete field of the work examined almost always contains a large intermediate tract where the accomplishment is of nearly uniform merit throughout, selection from which must be by a process of sampling rather than of gleaning; many a poem, too, of indifferent achievement in its wholeness may contain some line, couplet, or stanza of great excellence; and contrariwise, a bad or irrelevant verse may mar the good remainder; in each case the choice is puzzled, and the balance struck by a single mind can hardly escape being questioned here and there.

A word may be said on the arrangement of the poems as "lyrical and elegiac"; "descriptive and meditative"; "humorous"; a classification which has been adopted with this author in the present volume for the first time. It is an old story that such divisions may be open to grave objection, in respect, at least, of the verse of the majority of poets, who write in the accepted language. For one thing, many fine poems that have lyric moments are not entirely lyrical; many largely narrative poems are not entirely narrative; many personal reflections or meditations in verse hover across the frontiers of lyricism. To this general opinion I would add that the same lines may be lyrical to one temperament and meditative to another; nay, lyrical and not lyrical to the same reader at different times, according to his mood and circumstance. Gray's *Elegy* may be instanced as a poem that has almost made itself notorious by claiming to be a lyric in particular humours, situations, and weathers, and waiving the claim in others.

One might, to be sure, as a smart impromptu, narrow down the definition of lyric to the safe boundary of poetry that has all its nouns in the vocative case, and so settle the question by the simple touchstone of the grammar-book, adducing the *Benedicite* as a shining example. But this qualification would be disconcerting in its stringency, and cause a fluttering of the leaves of many an accepted anthology.

A story which was told the writer by Mr. Barnes himself may be apposite here. When a pupil of his was announced in the *Times* as having come out at the top in the Indian Service examination-list of those days, the schoolmaster was overwhelmed with letters from anxious parents requesting him at any price to make their sons come out at the top also. He replied that he willingly would, but that it took two to do it. It depends, in truth, upon the other person, the reader, whether certain numbers shall be raised to lyric pitch or not; and if he does not bring to the page of these potentially lyric productions a lyrical quality of mind, they must be classed, for him, as non-lyrical.

However, to pass the niceties of this question by. In the exceptional instance of a poet like Barnes who writes in a dialect only, a new condition arises to influence considerations of assortment. Lovers of poetry who are but imperfectly acquainted with his vocabulary and idiom may yet be desirous of learning something of his message; and the most elementary guidance is of help to such students, for they are liable to mistake their author on the very threshold. For some reason or none, many persons suppose that when anything is penned in the tongue of the country-side, the primary intent is burlesque or ridicule, and this especially if the speech be one in which the sibilant has the rough sound, and is expressed by Z. Indeed, scores of thriving story-tellers and dramatists seem to believe that by transmuting the flattest conversation into a dialect that never existed, and making the talkers say "be" where they would really say "is," a Falstaffian richness is at once imparted to its qualities.

But to a person to whom a dialect is native its sounds are as consonant with moods of sorrow as with moods of mirth: there is no grotesqueness in it as such. Nor was there to Barnes. To provide an alien reader with a rough clue to the taste of the kernel that may be expected under the shell of the spelling has seemed to be worth while, and to justify a division into heads that may in some cases appear arbitrary.

In respect of the other helps—the glosses and paraphrases given on each page—it may be assumed that they are but a sorry substitute for the full significance the original words bear to those who read them without translation, and know their delicate ability to express the doings, joys and jests, troubles, sorrows, needs and sicknesses of life in the rural world as elsewhere. The Dorset dialect being—or having been—a tongue, and not a corruption, it is the old question over again, that of the translation of poetry; which, to the full, is admittedly impossible. And further; gesture and facial expression figure so largely in the speech of the husbandmen as to be speech itself; hence in the mind's eye of those who know it in its original setting each word of theirs is accompanied by the qualifying face-play which no construing can express.

It may appear strange to some, as it did to friends in his lifetime, that a man of insight who had the spirit of poesy in him should have persisted year after year in writing in a fast-perishing language, and on themes which in some not remote time would be familiar to nobody, leaving him pathetically like

> A ghostly cricket, creaking where a house was burned;[10]

—a language with the added disadvantage by comparison with other dead tongues that no master or books would be readily available for the acquisition of its finer meanings. He himself simply said that he could not help it, no doubt feeling his idylls to be an extemporization, or impulse, without prevision or power of appraisement on his own part.

Yet it seems to the present writer that Barnes, despite this, really belonged to the literary school of such poets as Tennyson, Gray, and Collins, rather than to that of the old unpremeditating singers in dialect. Primarily spontaneous, he was academic closely after; and we find him warbling his native wood-notes[11] with a watchful eye on the predetermined score, a far remove from the popular impression of him as the naif and rude bard who sings only because he must,[12] and who submits the uncouth lines of his page to us without knowing how they come there. Goethe never knew better of his; nor Milton; nor, in their rhymes, Poe; nor, in their whimsical alliterations here and there, Langland and the versifiers of the fourteenth and fifteenth centuries.

In his aim at closeness of phrase to his vision he strained at times the capacities of dialect, and went wilfully outside the dramatization of peasant talk. Such a lover of the art of expression was this penman of a dialect that had no literature, that on some occasions he would allow art to overpower spontaneity and to cripple inspiration; though, be it remembered, he never tampered with the dialect itself. His ingenious internal rhymes, his subtle juxtaposition of kindred lippings and vowel-sounds, show a fastidiousness in word-selection that is surprising in verse which professes to represent the habitual modes of language among the western peasantry. We do not find in the dialect balladists of the seventeenth century, or in Burns (with whom he has sometimes been measured), such careful finish, such verbal dexterities, such searchings for the most cunning syllables, such satisfaction with the best phrase. Had he not begun with dialect, and seen himself recognized as an adept in it before he had quite found himself as a poet, who knows that he might not have brought upon his muse the disaster that has befallen so many earnest versifiers of recent time, have become a slave to the passion for form, and have wasted all his substance in whittling at its shape.

From such, however, he was saved by the conditions of his scene, characters, and vocabulary. It may have been, indeed, that he saw this tendency in himself, and retained the dialect as a corrective to the tendency. Whether or no, by a felicitous instinct he does at times break into sudden irregularities in the midst of his subtle rhythms and measures, as if feeling rebelled against further drill. Then his self-consciousness ends, and his naturalness is saved.

But criticism is so easy, and art so hard: criticism so flimsy, and the life-seer's voice so lasting. When we consider what such appreciativeness as Arnold's could allow his prejudices to say about the highest-soaring among all our lyricists; what strange criticism Shelley himself could indulge in now and then; that the history of criticism is mainly the history of error, which has not even, as many errors have, quaintness enough to make it interesting, we may well doubt the utility of such writing on the sand.[13] What is the use of saying, as has been said of Barnes, that compound epithets like "the blue-hill'd worold," "the wide-horn'd cow," "the grey-topp'd heights of Paladore," are a high-handed enlargement of the ordinary ideas of the field-folk into whose mouths they are put? These things are justified by the art of every age when they can claim to be, as here, singularly precise and beautiful definitions of what is signified; which in these instances, too, apply with double force to the deeply tinged horizon, to the breed of kine, to the aspect of Shaftesbury Hill, characteristic of the Vale within which most of his revelations are enshrined.

Dialect, it may be added, offered another advantage to him as the writer, whatever difficulties it may have for strangers who try to follow it. Even if he often used the dramatic form of peasant speakers as a pretext for the expression of his own mind and experiences—which cannot be doubted—yet he did not always do this, and the assumed character of husbandman or hamleteer enabled him to elude in his verse those dreams and speculations that cannot leave alone the mystery of things,—possibly an unworthy mystery and disappointing if solved, though one that has a harrowing fascination for many poets,—and helped him to fall back on dramatic truth, by making his personages express the notions of life prevalent in their sphere.

As by the screen of dialect, so by the intense localization aforesaid, much is lost to the outsider who by looking into Barnes's pages only revives general recollections of country life. Yet many passages may shine into that reader's mind through the veil which partly hides them; and it is hoped and believed that, even in a superficial reading, something more of this poet's charm will be gathered from the present selection by persons to whom the Wessex R and Z are uncouth misfortunes, and the dying words those of an unlamented language that need leave behind it no grammar of its secrets and no key to its tomb.

T. H.

September 1908.

The English Poets, ed. Thomas Humphry Ward, Vol. V, *Browning to Rupert Brooke*

[London, 1918, pp. 174-176]

William Barnes

The veil of a dialect, through which except in a few cases readers have to discern whatever of real poetry there may be in William Barnes, is disconcerting to many, and to some distasteful, chiefly, one thinks, for a superficial reason which has more to do with spelling than with the dialect itself. As long as the spelling of standard English is other than phonetic it is not obvious why that of the old Wessex language should be phonetic, except in a pronouncing dictionary. We have however to deal with Barnes's verse as he chose to write it, merely premising that his aim in the exact literation of Dorset words is not necessarily to exhibit humour and grotesqueness.

It often seemed strange to lovers of Barnes that he, a man of insight and reading, should have persisted year after year to sing in a tongue which, though a regular growth and not a provincial corruption, is indubitably fast perishing. He said that he could not help it. But he may have seen the unwisdom of such self-limitation—at those times, let us suppose, when he appeared to be under an uncontrollable impulse to express his own feelings, and to convey an ampler interpretation of life than his rustic vehicle would carry unenlarged, which resulted in his putting into the mouths of husbandmen compound epithets that certainly no user of the dialect ever concocted out of his own brain, and subtle sentiments that would have astonished those husbandmen and their neighbours.

But though true dramatic artistry lies that way, the way of all who differentiate imaginative revelation from the blind transcripts of a reporter's note-book, it was probably from some misgivings on the score of permanence that now and then he would turn a lyric in "common English," and once or twice brought out a little volume so written as an experiment. As usual, the prepossessions of his cocksure critics would not allow them to tolerate what they had not been accustomed to, a new idea, and the specimens were coldly received; which seems to have discouraged him. Yet in the opinion of the present writer the ordinary language which, as a school-master, Barnes taught for nearly forty years, could soon have been moulded to verse as deftly as dialect by a man whose instinct it was to catch so readily the beat of hearts around him. I take as an example the lines (which I translate) on the husband who comes home from abroad to find his wife long dead:—

> The rose was dust that bound her brow,
>   Moth-eaten was her Sunday cape,
> Her frock was out of fashion now,
>   Her shoes were dried up out of shape—
> Those shoes that once had glittered black
> Along the upland's beaten track;

and his frequent phrases like that of the autumn sun "wandering wan," the "wide-horned cows," the "high-sunned" noons, the "hoarse cascade," the "hedgerow-bramble's swinging bow."

Barnes, in fact, surprising as it may seem to those who know him, and that but a little, as a user of dialect only, was an academic poet, akin to the school of Gray and Collins, rather than a spontaneous singer of rural songs in folk-language like Burns, or an extemporizer like the old balladists. His apparently simple unfoldings are as studied as the so-called simple Bible-narratives are studied; his rhymes and alliterations often cunningly schematic. The speech of his ploughmen and milkmaids in his *Eclogues*—his own adopted name for these pieces—is as sound in its syntax as that of the Tityrus and Meliboeus of Virgil whom he had in mind, and his characters have often been likened to the shepherds and goatherds in the idylls of Theocritus.

Recognition came with the publication of the first series of Dorset poems in 1844, though some reviewers were puzzled whether to criticize them on artistic or philological grounds; later volumes however were felt to be the poetry of profound art by Coventry Patmore, F. T. Palgrave, H. M. Moule, and others. They saw that Barnes, behind his word-screen, had a quality of the great poets, a clear perception or instinct that human emotion is the primary stuff of poetry.

Repose and content mark nearly all of Barnes's verse; he shows little or none of the spirit of revolt which we find in Burns; nothing of the revolutionary politics of Béranger. He held himself artistically aloof from the ugly side of things—or perhaps shunned it unconsciously; and we escape in his pictures the sordid miseries that are laid bare in Crabbe, often to the destruction of charm. But though he does not probe life so deeply as the other parson-poet I have named, he conserves the poetic essence more carefully, and his reach in his highest moments, as exampled by such a poignant lyric as *The Wife a-lost,* or by the emotional music of *Woak Hill,* or *The Wind at the Door,* has been matched by few singers below the best.

THOMAS HARDY.

[In this, Hardy's final comment on the value of Barnes's poetry, some remarks of the Preface to *Select Poems of William Barnes* (above, pp. 76-82) were repeated, perhaps because Hardy felt that what he had to say now came in the nature of a "paraphrase" of earlier comments. The critical introduction preceded ten poems by Barnes: "In the Spring," "Jenny out vrom Hwome," "The Wife a-lost," "Woak Hill," "The Widow's House" (last stanza omitted), "The Water Crowvoot," "Blackmwore Maidens," "The Morning Moon," and two poems from which Hardy removed "the veil of a dialect," "White and Blue" and "The Wind at the Door." See pp. 94-106.]

A Book of Remembrance

[London (1919), pp. 5-6]

THE STURDY Dorset family of the Popes, a section of which has been grouped together for memorizing in the following volume, needs no apology for a modest appearance in a privately printed record based upon the varied achievements of one household, so to speak, in the present war—a household which has been for many years among my nearest neighbours.

Upon the family name it is not necessary to dilate. It has been known hereabouts—in Stalbridge, Marnhull, Corscombe, the Tollers and, later, Chilfrome—for centuries; and it may be mentioned that when John White went from Dorchester, England, to found Dorchester, Mass., U.S.A., he took with him some Dorchester Popes, whose descendants are now noteworthy people of Massachusetts. That research might be able to trace consanguinity between the Dorset Popes and the poet Alexander has often been a conjecture of the present writer, based partly on the poet's interest in at least one corner of the county—Sherborne and its vicinity—of which, as is well known, he gives a long description in a letter to Miss Blount.[14]

The circumstances of the great conflict which, we may at least hope, is hastening to a close, differ so largely from those of the previous wars of this country, that it is impossible to infer how many, or even if any more than had already done so, of the eleven brethren here marshalled would have deliberately chosen a military or naval career in ordinary conditions. Yet to read over their actions at this point of time conveys a fancy that they would all have fallen into line naturally:

> Though war nor no known quarrel were in question;
> ... assembled and collected
> As were a war in expectation.[15]

However that may be, these chronicles, even when they become musty with age, may be interesting not only to descendants of the family but to others who are not of their blood or name. It often has happened that an account of what befell particular individuals in unusual circumstances has conveyed a more vivid picture of those circumstances than a comprehensive view of them has been able to raise.

T. H.

September 1918.

[The full title of this beautifully printed volume, issued in a limited edition of 250 copies, was *A Book of Remembrance, Being a Short Summary of the Service and Sacrifice Rendered to the Empire during the Great War by One of the Many Patriotic Families of Wessex, the Popes of Wrackleford, Co. Dorset.* The book was printed for use of the Pope family. Hardy, according to Purdy (p. 320), "read and revised the proofs of the whole volume," and was a close friend of the family of Alfred Pope.]

A Dull Day in London, by Dora Sigerson Shorter

[London (1920), pp. 7-8]

MANY YEARS ago when I chanced to be sitting by the sea in the company of the writer of the following charming sketches, I was struck by the evidences of her sympathy with the lower animal creation (as we are accustomed to call the less favoured of our fellow-mortals who are often nobler than ourselves). On opening, this week, these last pages of hers, the first thing I remark is the same sympathy further extended, till it seems to embrace all animate and inanimate nature.

Though not unfinished in execution, their brevity leads a reader to muse on what the author's achievements in the same kind on a larger scale might have been had she ever attempted such, for which her life could be supposed to have afforded her plenty of time. Whether if she had lived longer a constitutional impatience of sustained effort would always have prevented her building up her ideas on a broader artistic framework is a question that must now for ever remain unanswered.

[Clement King Shorter (1857-1926) requested a note of this nature for a posthumous collection of his wife's sketches (she had died in 1918). Shorter's activities as collector and private printer of Hardy's briefer writings bordered on the unethical, and Purdy, who traces the development of the curious relationship between the two men (pp. 349-350), believes that "there was no intimacy . . . between the two men, and at no time did Shorter enjoy Hardy's confidence."]

Wessex Worthies, by Joshua James Foster

[London, 1920-(1921), p. ix]

WESSEX—or at any rate the Dorset division of it—has not been regarded as a part of England in any way remarkable for the energy and resourcefulness of its natives. They had been supposed to pay for their advantages in point of climatic mildness, length of winter days, and nearness to the ports of fair France, by a lack of the driving power which is believed to be inherent in the folk of the northern latitudes of this island.

It is a question on which I cannot pronounce an opinion, but I venture to say that in the arts and sciences which soften manners and tend to make life tolerable the people of south-western England have certainly not been behind those at other counties.

The author of this book, who is himself Wessex born of a far-dating Wessex family, has devoted many years to the subject matter of its pages, and has had unique opportunities for his study—in especial for the discovery and exhumation of the portraits of personages which were difficult of access, and in many cases supposed not to exist at all. His painstaking in this respect has surprised me, and has brought to light many curious details. These shadows of people of importance in their day remind me of a remark of Leslie Stephen's when planning the *Dictionary of Biography*;[16] that he was making it his object to get hold of the personal appearance of his characters whenever he could do so, holding that a few words on the look of a man as he walked and talked, so far as it could be gathered from portraits and traditions, was worth a page of conjecture on his qualities. There is also a passage in Carlyle to the same effect in which he says, "In all my poor historical investigations it has been and always is, one of the most primary wants to procure a bodily likeness of the personage enquired after—a good portrait if such exists; failing that, even an indifferent if sincere one. In short, any representation made by a faithful creature of that face and figure which he saw with his eyes, and which I can never see with mine, is now valuable to me, and much better than none at all."[17]

[signed] Th. Hardy

[Joshua James Foster (1847-1923) was the son of a bookseller in Dorchester, and a boyhood friend of Hardy. He specialized in the miniatures and enamels of artists who had flourished during the seventeenth and eighteenth centuries, and was particularly knowledgeable about the Stuarts—specifically, Mary Queen of Scots. Two of his well-regarded works were *French Art from Watteau to Prud'hon* (1905-1907) and *Chats on Old Miniatures* (1908).]

III.
On Literary Matters

Dialect in Novels [1]

[*Athenaeum,* November 30, 1878, p. 688]

A SOMEWHAT vexed question is reopened in your criticism of my story, *The Return of the Native*; namely, the representation in writing of the speech of the peasantry when that writing is intended to show mainly the character of the speakers, and only to give a general idea of their linguistic peculiarities.

An author may be said to fairly convey the spirit of intelligent peasant talk if he retains the idiom, compass, and characteristic expressions, although he may not encumber the page with obsolete pronunciations of the purely English words, and with mispronunciations of those derived from Latin and Greek. In the printing of standard speech hardly any phonetic principle at all is observed; and if a writer attempts to exhibit on paper the precise accents of a rustic speaker he disturbs the proper balance of a true representation by unduly insisting upon the grotesque element; thus directing attention to a point of inferior interest, and diverting it from the speaker's meaning, which is by far the chief concern where the aim is to depict the men and their natures rather than their dialect forms.

THOMAS HARDY.

[Hardy had no reason to like any part of the review, which appeared in the *Athenaeum* of November 23, 1878, p. 654, for the critic considered *The Return of the Native* "distinctly inferior to anything of his" which he had yet read. "People talk as no people ever talked before, or perhaps we should say as no people ever talk now," the reviewer continued. "The language of his peasants may be Elizabethan, but it can hardly be Victorian. Such phrases as 'being a man of the mournfullest make, I was scared a little,' or 'he always had his great indignation ready against anything underhand,' are surprising in the mouth of the modern rustic." It perhaps is not unexpected, therefore, that the final sentences should rebuke Hardy for creating in Eustacia Vye "a type which English opinion will not allow a novelist to depict in its completeness . . . ."]

Papers of the Manchester Literary Club
Dialect in Novels [2]

[*Spectator,* October 15, 1881, p. 1308]

Sir,—In your last week's article on the "Papers of the Manchester Literary Club," there seems a slight error, which, though possibly accidental, calls for a word of correction from myself. In treating of dialect in novels, I am instanced by the writer as one of two popular novelists "whose thorough knowledge of the dialectical peculiarities of certain districts has tempted them to write whole conversations which are, to the ordinary reader, nothing but a series of linguistic puzzles." So much has my practice been the reverse of this (as a glance at my novels will show), that I have been reproved for too freely translating dialect-English into readable English, by those of your contemporaries who attach more importance to the publication of local niceties of speech than I do. The rule of scrupulously preserving the local idiom, together with the words which have no synonym among those in general use, while printing in the ordinary way most of those local expressions which are but a modified articulation of words in use elsewhere, is the rule I usually follow; and it is, I believe, generally recognised as the best, where every such rule must of necessity be a compromise, more or less unsatisfactory to lovers of form. It must, of course, be always a matter for regret that, in order to be understood, writers should be obliged thus slightingly to treat varieties of English which are intrinsically as genuine, grammatical, and worthy of the royal title as is the all-prevailing competitor which bears it; whose only fault was that they happened not to be central, and therefore were worsted in the struggle for existence, when a uniform tongue became a necessity among the advanced classes of the population.—I am, Sir, &c., THOMAS HARDY.

The Avenue, Wimborne, Dorset, October 11th.

[This letter, dealing with a subject much on Hardy's mind during the 1870's, was a response to a review of Volume VII of *Papers of the Manchester Literary Club,* published by Abel Heywood and Son, which had appeared in the *Spectator,* October 8, 1881 (pp. 1277-1279). The reviewer had quoted approvingly from W. E. A. Axon's paper, "George Eliot's Use of Dialect," in which two possible methods of using dialect were specified: scientific ("aims at the illustration of the dialect itself, with its historical associations and philological affinities"), and artistic ("uses it for the elucidation of character, and by the aid of its minute touches increases the individuality of the portrait"). Axon had praised George Eliot's restraint in contriving to give "the impression of provincial speech, without imparting any great number of unfamiliar words into the text"; and the *Spectator*'s reviewer went on to say: "These are wise words on a matter of some artistic importance, and they might with advantage be taken to heart by some deservedly popular novelists—notably, we think, by Dr. George Macdonald and Mr. Thomas Hardy, whose thorough knowledge of the dialectical peculiarities of certain districts has tempted them to write whole conversations which are, to the ordinary reader, nothing but a series of linguistic puzzles, and probably . . . not really representative of the common speech 'at any particular time or place.' "]

An Unsigned Review of *Poems of Rural Life in the Dorset Dialect*, by William Barnes

[*New Quarterly Magazine,* October, 1879, pp. 469-473]

SELDOM does a new edition come before the public with better claims to a hearty welcome than this of Mr. Barnes's Poems, which have now for the first time been all collected in one volume. Since the first instalment of these now well-known lyrics was put forth from the remote and peaceful home of their author, twenty years ago, acquaintance has been made far and wide with a writer whose exceptional knowledge of rustic life is as unquestionable as his power to cast his memories of that life in beautiful and pleasing form.

Though these poems are distinguished on the title-page by the name of the county generally from whose recesses their scenes and characters are derived, the more precise source of their inspiration is a limited district lying to the north and north-west of Dorsetshire, and having marked characteristics of its own. This fertile and sheltered tract of country, in which the fields are never brown, and the springs never dry, is bounded on the south by the bold chalk ridge that embraces the prominences of Hambledon Hill, Bulbarrow, Nettlecombe Tout, Dogbury, and High Stoy. The tourist from the coast who, after plodding for ten or fifteen miles over chalk downs and cornlands, suddenly reaches the verge of one of these escarpments, is surprised and delighted to behold extended like a map beneath him a country differing absolutely from that which he has passed through. Behind him the hills are open, the sun blazes down upon fields so large as to give an unenclosed look to the landscape, the lanes are white, the hedges low, the atmosphere colourless. Here in the valley the world seems to be constructed upon a smaller and more delicate scale; the fields are mere paddocks, so reduced that from this height their hedgerows appear like a network of dark green threads spread out upon the paler green of the grass. The atmosphere is cool, and is so tinged with azure that what artists call the middle distance partakes also of that hue, while the horizon northwards is of the deepest ultramarine. The arable land has nearly disappeared; with but few exceptions the landscape is a broad rich mass of grass and trees, swelling over minor hills and dales. The scene is one which rivals, and in many points surpasses, those much lauded views of Surrey and Buckinghamshire from Richmond Hill and the terrace at Windsor Castle. It is the Vale of Blackmore or Blackmoor; and the portion immediately beneath us—included in the triangle formed by Sherborne, Shaftesbury, and Bulbarrow—is the abiding-place of the people whose daily duties, sayings, and innermost emotions have been laid bare in these poems; the spot is also the early home of the poet himself.

The district is of historic no less than of topographical interest. The Vale was known in former times as the Forest of White Hart, from a curious legend of King Henry the Third's reign, in which the killing by a certain Thomas de la Lynd of a beautiful white hart that the king had run down and spared, was made the occasion of a heavy fine. In those days, and till comparatively recent times, the country was densely wooded. Even now traces of its earlier condition are to be found in the old oak copses and irregular belts of timber that yet survive upon its slopes, and the hollow-trunked trees that shade so many of its pastures.

Unlike the bucolic poets of old time, Mr. Barnes does not merely use the beauties of nature as a background, reserving the whole front for the rustic characters, their manners, their emotions, and their simplicities. Moved by the pervading instinct of the nineteenth century, he gives us whole poems of still life, brief and unaffected, but realistic as a Dutch picture. In these the slow green river Stour, with its deep pools whence the trout leaps to the May-fly undisturbed by anglers, is found to be the dearest river of his memories, and the inspirer of some of his happiest effusions. Its multitudinous patches of water-lilies yellow and white, its pollard willows, its heavy-headed bulrushes, are for ever haunting him; and such is the loving fidelity with which the stream is depicted, that one might almost construct a bird's-eye view of its upper course by joining together the vignettes which are given of this and that point in its length.

Mr. Barnes frequently introduces compound epithets into his descriptive passages; and though many of these show a considerable divergence from the ordinary speech of the people, they are in themselves singularly precise, and often beautiful, definitions of the thing signified. Such expressions as "the blue-hill'd worold," "the wide-horn'd cow," true as they may be in the general, apply with double force to the highly-tinged horizon which bounds the Blackmore landscape, and the breed of cow which composes its dairies. And so of single adjectives. When "the rustlèn copse" is spoken of in connection with early winter, it should be known that the particular copse signified is an oak copse, and that the dead oak leaves of young underwood linger on their branches far into the winter weather, giving out to the wind the distinctive sound of which the writer has taken note.

We pass on to those more important lyrics which are entirely concerned with human interests and human character. The incidents are those of everyday life, cottagers' sorrows and cottagers' joys, but they are tinged throughout with that golden glow—"the light that never was"[1]—which art can project upon the commonest things. They abound with touches of rare and delicate beauty; though that inequality of power which has been the misfortune of all writers and singers from Homer downwards becomes more visible among these than elsewhere. Indeed, there are some which have a questionable right to stand beside such a poem as the following, for instance, which is to our thinking of rare intensity as an expression of grief; the turn of thought in the sixth line of each stanza being particularly fine:

THE WIFE A-LOST

Since I noo mwore do zee your feäce,
  Up-steäirs or down below,
I'll zit me in the lwonesome pleäce,
  Where flat-bough'd beech do grow.
Below the beeches' bough, my love,
  Where you did never come,
An' I don't look to meet ye now,
  As I do look at hwome.

Since you noo mwore be at my zide,
  In walks in zummer het,
I'll goo alwone where mist do ride
  Drough trees a-drippèn wet:
Below the raïn-wet bough, my love,
  Where you did never come,
An' I don't grieve to miss ye now,
  As I do grieve at hwome.

Since now bezide my dinner bwoard
  Your vaïce do never sound,
I'll eat the bit I can avword,
  A-vield upon the ground;
Below the darksome bough, my love,
  Where you did never dine,
An' I don't grieve to miss ye now
  As I at hwome do pine.

Pictures of the lives of Hellenic or Sicilian fishermen and goatherds, refined into sheer severity of outline by the atmosphere of two thousand intervening years, have been reproduced by modern poets as subjects more worthy of treatment than similar ones of to-day; but they mostly lack these life-giving touches and the human interest which is present in the homely verse that flows without effort from Mr. Barnes's pen. That the life of a modern peasant is not too hopelessly ingrained in prose for poetic treatment he has plainly shown. Farm life as, regulated by the seasons, it varies from day to day through the year, is truthfully reflected;

and we are at every step indirectly reminded wherein lies that poetry which, in spite of the occasional sting of poverty, is inseparable from such a condition of life. It lies less in the peasant's residence among fields and trees than in his absolute dependence on the moods of the air, earth, and sky. Sun, rain, wind, snow, dawn, darkness, mist, are to him, now as ever, personal assistants and obstructors, masters and acquaintances, with whom he comes directly into contact, whose varying tempers must be well-considered before he can act with effect.

Unlike Burns, Béranger, and other poets of the people, Mr. Barnes never assumes the high-conventional style, and entirely leaves alone ambition, pride, despair, and other of the strong passions which move mankind, great and small. His rustics are, as a rule, happy people, and very seldom feel the painful sting of the rest of modern mankind, the disproportion between the desire for serenity and the power of obtaining it.

But we have not exhausted the various moods from grave to gay which find voice in this volume. An almost perfect expression of the Arcadian lover's ecstasy occurs in the lines called "In the Spring."

> My love is the maïd ov all maïdens,
>   Though all mid be comely,
> Her skin's lik' the jessamy blossom
>   A-spread in the Spring.
>
> . . . .
>
> O grey-leafy pinks o' the geärden,
>   Now bear her sweet blossoms;
> Now deck wi' a rwose-bud, O briar,
>   Her head in the Spring.
>
> O light-rollèn wind, blow me hither
>   The väice ov her talkèn,
> Or bring vrom her veet the light doust
>   She do tread in the Spring.

O zun, meäke the gil'cups all glitter
In goold all around her;
An' meäke o' the deäisys' white flowers
A bed in the Spring.

O whistle, gäy birds, up bezide her,
In drong-way, an' woodlands,
O zing, swingèn lark, now the clouds
Be a-vled in the Spring.

Such songs as these—the *vers de société* of the Blackmore rustic world—make us regret that Mr. Barnes has not swept that gay chord a little oftener.

Enough has been said to show how many are the passages of true poetic beauty that will reveal themselves here, even in a superficial reading by persons to whom the Dorset *r* and *z* are unknown utterances.

[Hardy's admiration of William Barnes, the Dorsetshire poet, was expressed many times in print, and the following selection, no less than this review of a book by Barnes, stresses the honesty, preciseness of utterance, and industriousness of a man whom Hardy sought to emulate. Barnes was born on February 22, 1800, to a farmer's family in the Vale of Blackmore, and received his education at Sturminster Newton. He served some time as a solicitor's pupil (in Dorchester), studied classics and organ music, made creditable progress in the art of wood-engraving, and taught school for several years in Mere, Wiltshire, and in Dorchester from 1835 to 1862. He was rector of Winterborne Came (he died there on October 7, 1886). Two interests of his led to significant accomplishments: in philology, with several original and provocative studies of Dorset dialect and Anglo-Saxon; and in poetry. The Dorset *r* and *z*, as Barnes knew and Hardy pointed out, were linguistic peculiarities that necessarily circumscribed the audience of Barnes's poetry; but Hardy believed, like Barnes, that the native dialect of Dorsetshire was, in several ways, richer than that of "correct English." Barnes's example, at any rate, was useful to Hardy's attempt to use a universalized local idiom in his novels, and to rationalize "a general idea" of linguistic peculiarities that would replace phonetic signs, footnotes, and a glossary. In "the simplicity of his [Barnes's] character, his forbearance, and the charming spurts of youthful ardour which would burst out as rays even in his latest hours," Hardy delineated the hero of his youth, indeed of his entire life. Hardy never wrote another review for publication. The remarks about the attractiveness of the landscape to the north of Dorsetshire were reproduced, with minor changes, in Chapter II of *Tess of the d'Urbervilles*, and some of his appreciation of the way in which Barnes "never assumed the high conventional style," and avoided "the grander passions" was repeated, unchanged, in the obituary Hardy wrote for the *Athenaeum* (next selection).]

The Rev. William Barnes, B. D.

[*Athenaeum*, October 16, 1886, pp. 501-502]

UNTIL within the last year or two there were few figures more familiar to the eye in the county town of Dorset on a market day than an aged clergyman, quaintly attired in caped cloak, knee-breeches, and buckled shoes, with a leather satchel slung over his shoulders, and a stout staff in his hand. He seemed usually to prefer the middle of the street to the pavement, and to be thinking of matters which had nothing to do with the scene before him. He plodded along with a broad, firm tread, notwithstanding the slight stoop occasioned by his years. Every Saturday morning he might have been seen thus trudging up the narrow South Street, his shoes coated with mud or dust according to the state of the roads between his rural home and Dorchester, and a little grey dog at his heels, till he reached the four cross ways in the centre of the town. Halting here, opposite the public clock, he would pull his old-fashioned watch from its deep fob, and set it with great precision to London time. This, the invariable first act of his market visit, having been completed to his satisfaction, he turned round and methodically proceeded about his other business.

This venerable and well-characterized man was William Barnes, the Dorsetshire poet and philologer, by whose death last week at the ripe age of eighty-six the world has lost not only a lyric writer of a high order of genius, but probably the most interesting link between present and past forms of rural life that England possessed. The date of his birth at the very beginning of the century is less explanatory of his almost unique position in this respect than the remoteness, even from contemporary provincial civilization, of the pastoral recesses in which his earlier years were passed—places with whose now obsolete customs and beliefs his mind was naturally imbued. To give one instance of the former tardiness of events in that part of the country: it was a day almost within his remembrance when, amidst the great excitement and applause of the natives, who swept the street with brooms in honour of its arrival, a stage coach made its first entry into Sturminster Newton, the little market town nearest to the hamlet of Bagbere, the home of his parents. And there used to come to a little bridge, close to his father's door, till quite recently, a conjuror or "white wizard," who cured afflicted persons by means of the toad-bag—a small piece of linen having a limb from a living toad sewn up inside, to be worn round the sufferer's neck and next his skin, the twitching movements of which limb gave, so it was said, "a turn" to the blood of the wearer, and effected a radical change in his constitution.[2]

Born so long ago as February 22nd, 1800 (1801 has been given, but I believe incorrectly),[3] amid such surroundings, a thorough son of the soil, and endowed with great retentiveness and powers of observation, it is no wonder that Barnes became a complete repertory of forgotten manners, words, and sentiments, a store which he afterwards turned to such good use in his writings on ancient British and Anglo-Saxon speech, customs, and folklore; above all, in the systematic study of his native dialect, as a result of which he has shown the world that far from being, as popularly supposed, a corruption of correct English, it is a distinct branch of Teutonic speech, regular in declension and conjugation, and richer in many classes of words than any other tongue known to him. As an instance of the latter he used to mention the pronouns with particular pride, there being no fewer than four demonstratives to set against the current English two. He would also instance any natural object, such as a tree, and show that there were double the number of names for its different parts in the Dorset dialect to those available in the standard tongue.

It was a proud day for young William Barnes when, sometime[4] in the year 1814 or 1815, a local solicitor, the late Mr. Dashwood, entered the village school and inquired if there was a boy clever enough with his pen to come and copy deeds in his office in a clerkly hand. The only lad who at all approximated to such a high description was Barnes, and the scene of testing him with the long quill pen and paper, and his selection by the lawyer, must have been one to which Mulready alone could have done justice.[5] The youth thus found himself at a solicitor's desk, and, what was more, in a position to help himself in some degree to the grammars and glossaries his soul desired, and by whose diligent perusal at odd hours through many laborious years he became familiar with an astonishing number of languages and dialects. A more notable instance of self-help has seldom been recorded, considering the date in the century, the young man's circumstances, and the remote place of his residence, for it appears that he still lived on at the hamlet, walking to and from the town—or rather townlet—every day. In later years academic scholars were sometimes found to remark upon the unsystematic character of his linguistic attainments, but it cannot be gainsaid that he was almost always ready with definite and often exclusive information on whatever slightly known form of human speech might occur to the mind of his questioner, from Persian to Welsh, from the contemporary vernaculars of India to the tongues of the ancient British tribes. Over and above these subjects, his mind was occupied after his removal to Dorchester, to judge from his letters to old local newspapers, with investigations of Roman remains, theories on the origin of Stonehenge, and kindred archaeological matters; while among his other hobbies about this time was engraving on wood and on silver, crests and initials upon old pieces of plate in the neighbourhood still remaining to testify to his skill in the art.

Though Barnes's first practical step in life had brought him to the office of a solicitor, his instincts were towards tuition; and when, some years later, he had become well settled in the county town he opened a school. As schoolmaster he was fairly successful from the first, and as time went by and he obtained, as a ten years' man, his university degree and took orders,[6] the school grew highly popular. It was during this period—from early in the forties onwards—that he wrote at intervals the first, second, and third series of those sweet rustic poems by which his name will be best remembered.

He used to tell an amusing story of his experience on relinquishing the school at Dorchester to retire to the country rectory of Winterborne Came, in which he has ended his days. About the very week of his translation, so to call it, the name of one of his pupils appeared in the *Times* and other papers at the head of the Indian examination list, a wide proportion of marks separating it from the name following. The novelty of these lists lent a keen interest to them in those days, and the next morning Mr. Barnes was deluged with letters from all parts of the country requesting him at almost any price to take innumerable sons, and produce upon them the same successful effect. "I told them it took two to do it," he would say, adding, "Thus a popularity which I had never known during the working years of my life came at almost the first moment when it was no longer of use to me."

To many readers of these pages the charming idyls known as Barnes's "Poems in the Dorset Dialect" are too familiar to need description or eulogy. Though locally distinguished on the title-page by the name of the county at large, the chief scenes of their inspiration lie more precisely in the limited district to the north and north-west of Dorsetshire, that is to say in the secluded Vale of Blackmore, whose margin formed the horizon of his boyhood, and was, as he himself sings in one of the poems, the end of the world to him then. This fertile and sheltered tract of country, where the fields are never brown and the springs never dry, is bounded on the south by the bold chalk ridge that embraces the prominences of Hambledon Hill, Bulbarrow, Nettlecombe Tout, Dogbury, and High-Stoy. The prospect northwards from each of these heights is one which rivals, and in many points surpasses, those much admired views of Surrey and Buckinghamshire from Richmond Hill and the terrace at Windsor Castle, while the portion of the landscape immediately beneath the spectator is the abiding-place of the people whose daily doings, sayings, and emotions have been crystallized in the poet's verse. Occasionally, it is true, we find among the men and women presented in Mr. Barnes's volumes some who are housed in hamlets lying nominally beyond the Vale, but to my mind these characters are in a great measure Blackmore people away from home, bearing with them still the well-marked traits which distinguish the Vale population from that of the neighbouring uplands. The same may be said of his backgrounds and scenery. Moreover, when, moved by the pervading instinct of the nineteenth century, he gives us whole poems of still life, unaffected and realistic as a Dutch picture, the slow green river Stour of the same valley, with its deep pools, whence the trout leaps to the may-fly undisturbed by anglers, is found to be the stream dearest to his memory and the inspirer of some of his happiest effusions.

Unlike Burns, Béranger, and other poets of the people, Mr. Barnes never assumed the high conventional style; and he entirely leaves alone ambition, pride, despair, defiance, and other of the grander passions which move mankind great and small. His rustics are, as a rule, happy people, and very seldom feel the sting of the rest of modern mankind—the disproportion between the desire for serenity and the power of obtaining it. One naturally thinks of Crabbe in this connexion; but though they touch at points, Crabbe goes much further than Barnes in questioning the justice of circumstance. Their pathos, after all, is the attribute upon which the poems must depend for their endurance; and the incidents which embody it are those of everyday cottage life, tinged throughout with that "light that never was,"[7] which the emotional art of the lyrist can project upon the commonest things. It is impossible to prophesy, but surely much English literature will be forgotten when "Woak Hill" is still read for its intense pathos, "Blackmore Maidens" for its blitheness, and "In the Spring" for its Arcadian ecstasy.

Notwithstanding the wide appreciation of his verse both here and in America, so largely local were the poet's interests that it may be questioned if the enthusiasm which accompanied his own readings of his works in the townhalls of the shire was not more grateful to him than the admiration of a public he had never seen. The effect, indeed, of his recitations upon an audience well acquainted with the *nuances* of the dialect—impossible to impart to outsiders by any kind of translation—can hardly be imagined by readers of his lines acquainted only with English in its customary form. The poet's own mild smile at the boisterous merriment provoked by his droll delivery of such pieces as "The Shy Man," "A Bit o' Sly Coorten," and "Dick and I" returns upon the memory as one of the most characteristic aspects of a man who was nothing if not genial; albeit that, while the tyranny of his audience demanded these broadly humorous productions, his own preferences were for the finer and more pathetic poems, such as "Wife a-lost," "Woak Hill," and "Jaäy a-past."

To those who knew Mr. Barnes in his prime it may have been a matter for conjecture why a man of his energies should not at some point or other of his career have branched off from the quiet byways of his early manhood into the turmoils of the outer world, particularly as his tastes at that time were somewhat general, and the direction of his labours was dictated in the main by his opportunities. The explanation seems to be that the poetic side of his nature, though not always dominant, was but faintly ruled by the practical at any time, that his place-attachment was strong almost to a fault, and that his cosmopolitan interests, though lively, were always subordinate to those local hobbies and solicitudes whence came alike his special powers and his limitations.

Few young people who have seen him only in latter years, since the pallor and stoop of old age overcame him, can realize the robust, upright form of his middle life, the ruddy cheek, and the bright quick eye. The last, indeed, dimmed but slightly, and even on his death-bed his zest for the subject of speech-form was strong as ever. In one of his latest conversations he became quite indignant at the word "bicycle." "Why didn't they call it 'wheel-saddle'?" he exclaimed.

Though not averse to social intercourse, his friendships extended over but a small area of society. But those who, like the present writer, knew him well and long, entertained for him a warm affection; while casual visitors from afar were speedily won to kindly regard by the simplicity of his character, his forbearance, and the charming spurts of youthful ardour which would burst out as rays even in his latest hours.

THOMAS HARDY.

Fine Passages in Verse and Prose; Selected by Living Men of Letters

[Contribution to a symposium in the *Fortnightly Review*, August, 1887, pp. 304-306]

"I SHOULD have replied sooner, but the words, 'The one passage in all poetry which seems to me the finest' quite bewildered my mind by their immensity. I should say that there is no one passage finest; that the various kinds of best poetry are not reducible to a common standard. 'There is one glory of the sun, and another glory of the moon, and another of the stars.'[8] I know that you ask 'what *seems* the finest'; but that seeming varies with the time and mood, and according to the class of poetry that is for the nonce nearest to the tone of our situation.

"I have very often felt (but not always) that one of the most beautiful of English lyrics is Shelley's *Lament*, 'O world, O life, O time'; and of descriptive poetry I do not know that anything has as yet been fairly able to oust our old friends in *Childe Harold* —*e.g.* C. III., stanzas 85 to 87.

"I know this is an old-fashioned taste; but it is a well-considered relapse on my part, for though in past years I have been very modern in this matter I begin to feel that mere intellectual subtlety will not hold its own in time to come against the straightforward expression of good feeling.

"With regard to prose the task is somewhat more practicable, and yet how hopeless! But I will go thus far: I think that the passages in Carlyle's *French Revolution* on the silent growth of the oak have never been surpassed by anything I have read, except perhaps by his sentences on night in a city, as specimens of contemplative prose (if they may be so called); and that in narrative prose the chapter of the Bible (2 Sam. xviii.) containing the death of Absalom is the finest example of its kind that I know, showing beyond its power and pathos the highest artistic cunning." The passages referred to by Mr. Hardy are, in poetry—

BYRON's *Childe Harold*

LXXXV

Clear, placid Leman! thy contrasted lake,
With the wild world I dwelt in, is a thing
Which warns me, with its stillness, to forsake
Earth's troubled waters for a purer spring.
This quiet sail is as a noiseless wing
To waft me from distraction; once I loved
Torn ocean's roar, but thy soft murmuring
Sounds sweet as if a Sister's voice reproved,
That I with stern delights should e'er have been so moved.

LXXXVI

It is the hush of night, and all between
Thy margin and the mountains, dusk, yet clear,
Mellow'd and mingling, yet distinctly seen,
Save darken'd Jura, whose capt heights appear
Precipitously steep; and drawing near,
There breathes a living fragrance from the shore,
Of flowers yet fresh with childhood; on the ear
Drops the light drip of the suspended oar,
Or chirps the grasshopper one good-night carol more;

LXXXVII

He is an evening reveller, who makes
His life an infancy, and sings his fill;
At intervals, some bird from out the brakes
Starts into voice a moment, then is still.
There seems a floating whisper on the hill,
But that is fancy, for the starlight dews
All silently their tears of love instil,
Weeping themselves away, till they infuse
Deep into Nature's breast the spirit of her hues.

In prose—

CARLYLE'S *French Revolution*

The oak grows silently, in the forest, a thousand years; only in the thousandth year, when the woodman arrives with his axe, is there heard an echoing through the solitudes; and the oak announces itself when, with far-sounding crash, it *falls*. How silent too was the planting of the acorn; scattered from the lap of some wandering wind! Nay, when our oak flowered, or put on its leaves (its glad events), what shout of proclamation could there be? Hardly from the most observant a word of recognition. These things *befell* not, they were slowly *done*; not in an hour, but through the flight of days: what was to be said of it? This hour seemed altogether as the last was, as the next would be.

It is thus everywhere that foolish Rumour babbles not of what was done, but of what was misdone or undone; and foolish History (ever, more or less, the written epitomised synopsis of Rumour) knows so little that were not as well unknown. Attila Invasions, Walter-the-

Penniless Crusades, Sicilian Vespers, Thirty-Years Wars: mere sin and misery; not work, but hindrance of work! For the Earth, all this while, was yearly green and yellow with her kind harvests; the hand of the craftsman, the mind of the thinker rested not: and so, after all, and in spite of all, we have this so glorious high-domed blossoming World; concerning which, poor History may well ask, with wonder, Whence *it* came? She knows so little of it, knows so much of what obstructed it, which would have rendered it impossible. Such, nevertheless, by necessity or foolish choice, is her rule and practice; whereby that paradox, 'Happy the people whose annals are vacant,' is not without its true side.

[Book II, The Paper Age, Chapter I, "Astraea Redux." The number of variations in spelling and punctuation from a standard text is so large that the editor has reproduced this extract directly from Thomas Carlyle's *Works*, Centenary Edition, ed. by H. D. Traill (London, 1897-1905), II, 27-28, rather than from the pages of the *Fortnightly Review.*]

Sartor Resartus

"Ach, mein Lieber!" said he once, at midnight, when we had returned from the Coffee-house in rather earnest talk, "it is a true sublimity to dwell here. These fringes of lamplight, struggling up through smoke and thousandfold exhalation, some fathoms into the ancient reign of Night, what thinks Boötes of them, as he leads his Hunting-Dogs over the Zenith in their leash of sidereal fire? That stifled hum of Midnight, when Traffic has lain down to rest; and the chariot-wheels of Vanity, still rolling here and there through distant streets, are bearing her to Halls roofed-in, and lighted to the due pitch for her; and only Vice and Misery, to prowl or to moan like nightbirds, are abroad: that hum, I say, like the stertorous, unquiet slumber of sick Life, is heard in Heaven! Oh, under that hideous coverlet of vapours and putrefactions, and unimaginable gases, what a Fermenting-vat lies simmering and hid! The joyful and the sorrowful are there; men are dying there, men are being born; men are praying,—on the other side of a brick partition, men are cursing; and around them all is the vast, void Night.

[Chapter III, "Reminiscences."]

[Frank Harris, as Editor of the *Fortnightly Review*, had written to a number of writers and critics for "the one passage in all poetry which seems the finest, and also the one passage which appears of its kind the best." Told that his request had called for too "absolute" a judgment, he modified it to request only "such passages as had lodged themselves in the memory and had afforded the most continual delight." Even this proved too much for Tennyson, Browning, Cardinal Newman, and William Morris; but enough responses came back for Harris to publish the results, beginning in August, 1887, for four consecutive issues. Among those who thought the question worth responding to: Matthew Arnold, Grant Allen, Mrs. Lynn Linton, George Meredith, A. C. Swinburne, Augustine Birrell, Wilkie Collins, Professor Dowden, Edmund Gosse, Vernon Lee, Ouida, Ernest Rhys, Olive Schreiner, John Addington Symonds, R. Y. Tyrrell, Theodore Watts, Thomas Bailey Aldrich, and Austin Dobson.]

The Profitable Reading of Fiction

[*Forum* (New York), March, 1888, pp. 57-70]

When the editor of this review courteously offered me space in his pages to formulate a few general notions upon the subject of novel reading, considered with a view to mental profit, I could not help being struck with the timeliness of the theme; for in these days the demand for novels has risen so high, in proportion to that for other kinds of literature, as to attract the attention of all persons interested in education. But I was by no means persuaded that one whose own writings have largely consisted in books of this class was in a position to say anything on the matter, even if he might be supposed to have anything to say. The field, however, is so wide and varied that there is plenty of room for impersonal points of regard; and I may as well premise that the remarks which follow, where not exclusively suggested by a consideration of the works of dead authors, are mere generalizations from a cursory survey, and no detailed analysis, of those of to-day.

If we speak of deriving good from a story, we usually mean something more than the gain of pleasure during the hours of its perusal. Nevertheless, to get pleasure out of a book is a beneficial and profitable thing, if the pleasure be of a kind which, while doing no moral injury, affords relaxation and relief when the mind is overstrained or sick of itself. The prime remedy in such cases is change of scene, by which, change of the material scene is not necessarily implied. A sudden shifting of the mental perspective into a fictitious world, combined with rest, is well known to be often as efficacious for renovation as a corporeal journey afar.

In such a case the shifting of scene should manifestly be as complete as if the reader had taken the hind seat on a witch's broomstick. The town man finds what he seeks in novels of the country, the countryman in novels of society, the indoor class generally in outdoor novels, the villager in novels of the mansion, the aristocrat in novels of the cottage.

The narrative must be of a somewhat absorbing kind, if not absolutely fascinating. To discover a book or books which shall possess, in addition to the special scenery, the special action required, may be a matter of some difficulty, though not always of such difficulty as to be insuperable; and it may be asserted that after every variety of spiritual fatigue there is to be found refreshment, if not restoration, in some antithetic realm of ideas which lies waiting in the pages of romance.

In reading for such hygienic purposes it is, of course, of the first consequence that the reader be not too critical. In other words, his author should be swallowed whole, like any other alterative pill. He should be believed in slavishly, implicitly. However profusely he may pour out his coincidences, his marvelous juxtapositions, his catastrophes, his conversions of bad people into good people at a stroke, and *vice versâ*, let him never be doubted for a moment. When he exhibits people going out of their way and spending their money on purpose to act consistently, or taking a great deal of trouble to move in a curious and roundabout manner when a plain, straight course lies open to them; when he shows that heroes are never faithless in love, and that the unheroic always are so, there should arise a conviction that this is precisely according to personal experience. Let the invalid reverse the attitude of a certain class of critics—now happily becoming less numerous—who only allow themselves to be interested in a novel by the defeat of every attempt to the contrary. The aim should be the exercise of a generous imaginativeness, which shall find in a tale not only all that was put there by the author, put he it never so awkwardly, but which shall find there what was never inserted by him, never foreseen, never contemplated. Sometimes these additions which are woven around a work of fiction by the intensitive power of the reader's own imagination are the finest parts of the scenery.

It is not altogether necessary to this tonic purpose that the stories chosen should be "of most disastrous chances, of moving accidents by flood and field."[9] As stated above, the aim should be contrast. Directly the circumstances begin to resemble those of the reader, a personal connection, an interest other than an imaginative one, is set up, which results in an intellectual stir that is not in the present case to be desired. It sets his serious thoughts at work, and he does not want them stimulated just now; he wants to dream.

So much may be said initially upon alleviating the effects of over-work and carking care by a course of imaginative reading. But I will assume that benefit of this sort is not that which is primarily contemplated when we speak of getting good out of novels, but intellectual or moral profit to active and undulled spirits.

It is obvious that choice in this case, though more limited than in the former, is by no means limited to compositions which touch the highest level in the essential constituents of a novel—those without which it would be no novel at all—the plot and the characters. Not only may the book be read for these main features—the presentation, as they may collectively be called—but for the accidents and appendages of narrative; and such are of more kinds than one. Excursions into various philosophies, which vary or delay narrative proper, may have more attraction than the regular course of the enactment; the judicious inquirer may be on the look-out for didactic reflection, such as is found in large lumps in *Rasselas*; he may be a picker-up of trifles of useful knowledge, statistics, queer historic fact, such as sometimes occur in the pages of Hugo; he may search for specimens of the manners of good or bad society, such as are to be obtained from the fashionable writers; or he may even wish to brush up his knowledge of quotations from ancient and other authors by studying some chapters of *Pelham* and the disquisitions of Parson Adams in *Joseph Andrews*.

Many of the works which abound in appurtenances of this or a kindred sort are excellent as narrative, excellent as portraiture, even if in spite rather than in consequence of their presence. But they are the exception. Directly we descend from the highest levels we find that the majority are not effectual in their ostensible undertaking, that of giving us a picture of life in action; they exhibit a machinery which often works awkwardly, and at the instigation of unlikely beings. Yet, being packed with thoughts of some solidity, or more probably sprinkled with smart observations on men and society, they may be read with advantage even by the critical, who, for what they bring, can forgive the audible workings of the wheels and wires and carpentry, heard behind the performance, as the wires and trackers of a badly constructed organ are heard under its tones.

Novels of the latter class—formerly more numerous than now—are the product of cleverness rather than of intuition; and in taking them up—bearing in mind that profit, and not amusement, is the student's aim—his manifest course is to escape from the personages and their deeds, gathering the author's wit or wisdom nearly as it would have presented itself if he had cast his thoughts in the shape of an essay.

But though we are bound to consider by-motives like these for reading fiction as praiseworthy enough where practicable, they are by their nature of an illegitimate character, more or less, and apart from the ruling interest of the genuine investigator of this department of literature. Such ingredients can be had elsewhere in more convenient parcels. Our true object is a lesson in life, mental enlargement from elements essential to the narratives themselves and from the reflections they engender.

Among the qualities which appertain to representations of life, construed, though not distorted, by the light of imagination—qualities which are seldom shared by views *about* life, however profound—is that of self-proof or obviousness. A representation is less susceptible of error than a disquisition; the teaching, depending as it does upon intuitive conviction, and not upon logical reasoning, is not likely to lend itself to sophistry. If endowed with ordinary intelligence, the reader can discern, in delineative art professing to be natural, any stroke greatly at variance with nature, which, in the form of moral essay, *pensée*, or epigram, may be so wrapped up as to escape him.

Good fiction may be defined here as that kind of imaginative writing which lies nearest to the epic, dramatic, or narrative masterpieces of the past. One fact is certain: in fiction there can be no intrinsically new thing at this stage of the world's history. New methods and plans may arise and come into fashion, as we see them do; but the general theme can neither be changed, nor (what is less obvious) can the relative importance of its various particulars be greatly interfered with. The higher passions must ever rank above the inferior—intellectual tendencies above animal, and moral above intellectual—whatever the treatment, realistic or ideal. Any system of inversion which should attach more importance to the delineation of man's appetites than to the delineation of his aspirations, affections, or humors, would condemn the old masters of imaginative creation from Æschylus to Shakespeare. Whether we hold the arts which depict mankind to be, in the words of Mr. Matthew Arnold, a criticism of life,[10] or, in those of Mr. Addington Symonds, a revelation of life,[11] the material remains the same, with its sublimities, its beauties, its uglinesses, as the case may be. The finer manifestations must precede in importance the meaner, without such a radical change in human nature as we can hardly conceive as pertaining to an even remote future of decline, and certainly do not recognize now.

In pursuance of his quest for a true exhibition of man, the reader will naturally consider whether he feels himself under the guidance of a mind who sees further into life than he himself has seen; or, at least, who can throw a stronger irradiation over subjects already within his ken than he has been able to do unaided. The new light needs not to be set off by a finish of phraseology or incisive sentences of subtle definition. The treatment may be baldly incidental, without inference or commentary. Many elaborate reflections, for example, have been composed by moralizing chroniclers on the effect of prosperity in blunting men's recollection of those to whom they have sworn friendship when they shared a hard lot in common. But the writer in Genesis who tells his legend of certain friends in such adverse circumstances, one of whom, a chief butler, afterward came to good fortune, and ends the account of this good fortune with the simple words, "Now the chief butler did not remember Joseph, but forgat him,"[12] brings out a dramatic sequence on ground prepared for assent, shows us the general principle in the particular case, and hence writes with a force beyond that of aphorism or argument. It is the force of an appeal to the emotional reason rather than to the logical reason; for by their emotions men are acted upon, and act upon others.

If it be true, as is frequently asserted, that young people nowadays go to novels for their sentiments, their religion, and their morals, the question as to the wisdom or folly of those young people hangs upon their methods of acquisition in each case. A deduction from what these works exemplify by action that bears evidence of being a counterpart of life, has a distinct educational value; but an imitation of what may be called the philosophy of the personages—the doctrines of the actors, as shown in their conversation—may lead to surprising results. They should be informed that a writer whose story is not a tract in disguise has as his main object that of characterizing the people of his little world. A philosophy which appears between the inverted commas of a dialogue may, with propriety, be as full of holes as a sieve if the person or persons who advance it gain any reality of humanity thereby.

These considerations only bring us back again to the vital question how to discriminate the best in fiction. Unfortunately the two hundred years or so of the modern novel's development have not left the world so full of fine examples as to make it particularly easy to light upon them when the first obvious list has been run through. The, at first sight, high-piled granary sifts down to a very small measure of genuine corn. The conclusion cannot be resisted, notwithstanding what has been stated to the contrary in so many places, that the scarcity of perfect novels in any language is because the art of writing them is as yet in its youth, if not in its infancy. Narrative art is neither mature in its artistic aspect, nor in its ethical or philosophical aspect; neither in form nor in substance. To me, at least, the difficulties of perfect presentation in both these kinds appear of such magnitude that the utmost which each generation can be expected to do is to add one or two strokes toward the selection and shaping of a possible ultimate perfection.

In this scarcity of excellence in novels as wholes the reader must content himself with excellence in parts; and his estimate of the degree to which any given modern instance approximates to greatness will, of course, depend not only upon the proportion that the finer characteristics bear to the mass, but upon the figure cut by those finer characteristics beside those of the admitted masterpieces as yet. In this process he will go with the professed critic so far as to inquire whether the story forms a regular structure of incident, accompanied by an equally regular development of character—a composition based on faithful imagination, less the transcript than the similitude of material fact. But the appreciative, perspicacious reader will do more than this. He will see what his author is aiming at, and by affording full scope to his own insight, catch the vision which the writer has in his eye, and is endeavoring to project upon the paper, even while it half eludes him.

He will almost invariably discover that, however numerous the writer's excellencies, he is what is called unequal; he has a specialty. This especial gift being discovered, he fixes his regard more particularly thereupon. It is frequently not that feature in an author's work which common repute has given him credit for; more often it is, while co-existent with his popular attribute, overshadowed by it lurking like a violet in the shade of the more obvious, possibly more vulgar, talent, but for which it might have received high attention. Behind the broad humor of one popular pen he discerns startling touches of weirdness; amid the colossal fancies of another he sees strokes of the most exquisite tenderness; and the unobtrusive quality may grow to have more charm for him than the palpable one.

It must always be borne in mind, despite the claims of realism, that the best fiction, like the highest artistic expression in other modes, is more true, so to put it, then history or nature can be.[13] In history occur from time to time monstrosities of human action and character explicable by no known law which appertains to sane beings; hitches in the machinery of existence, wherein we have not yet discovered a principle, which the artist is therefore bound to regard as accidents, hinderances to clearness of presentation, and, hence, weakeners of the effect. To take an example from sculpture: no real gladiator ever died in such perfect harmony with normal nature as is represented in the well-known Capitoline marble. There was always a jar somewhere, a jot or tittle[14] of something foreign in the real death-scene, which did not essentially appertain to the situation, and tended toward neutralizing its pathos; but this the sculptor omitted, and so consecrated his theme. In drama likewise. Observe the characters of any sterling play. No dozen persons who were capable of being animated by the profound reasons and truths thrown broadcast over *Hamlet* or *Othello,* of feeling the pulse of life[15] so accurately, ever met together in one place in this world to shape an end. And, to come to fiction, nobody ever met an Uncle Toby who was Uncle Toby all round; no historian's Queen Elizabeth was ever so perfectly a woman as the fictitious Elizabeth of *Kenilworth.* What is called the idealization of characters is, in truth, the making of them too real to be possible.

It may seem something of a paradox to assert that the novels which most conduce to moral profit are likely to be among those written without a moral purpose. But the truth of the statement may be realized if we consider that the didactic novel is so generally devoid of *vraisemblance* as to teach nothing but the impossibility of tampering with natural truth to advance dogmatic opinions. Those, on the other hand, which impress the reader with the inevitableness of character and environment in working out destiny, whether that destiny be just or unjust, enviable or cruel, must have a sound effect, if not what is called a good effect, upon a healthy mind.

Of the effects of such sincere presentation on weak minds, when the courses of the characters are not exemplary, and the rewards and punishments ill adjusted to deserts, it is not our duty to consider too closely. A novel which does moral injury to a dozen imbeciles, and has bracing results upon a thousand intellects of normal vigor, can justify its existence; and probably a novel was never written by the purest-minded author for which there could not be found some moral invalid or other whom it was capable of harming.

To distinguish truths which are temporary from truths which are eternal, the accidental from the essential, accuracies as to custom and ceremony from accuracies as to the perennial procedure of humanity, is of vital importance in our attempts to read for something more than amusement. There are certain novels, both among the works of living and the works of deceased writers, which give convincing proof of much exceptional fidelity, and yet they do not rank as great productions; for what they are faithful in is life garniture and not life. You are fully persuaded that the personages are clothed precisely as you see them clothed in the street, in the drawing-room, at the assembly. Even the trifling accidents of their costume are rendered by the honest narrator. They use the phrases of the season, present or past, with absolute accuracy as to idiom, expletive, slang. They lift their tea-cups or fan themselves to date. But what of it, after our first sense of its photographic curiousness is past? In aiming at the trivial and the ephemeral they have almost surely missed better things. A living French critic goes even further concerning the novelists of social minutiae. "They are far removed," says he, "from the great imaginations which create and transform. They renounce free invention; they narrow themselves to scrupulous exactness; they paint clothes and places with endless detail."[16]

But we must not, as inquiring readers, fail to understand that attention to accessories has its virtues when the nature of its regard does not involve blindness to higher things; still more when it conduces to the elucidation of higher things. The writer who describes his type of a jeweled leader of society by saying baldly how much her diamonds cost at So-and-So's, what the largest of them weighed and measured, how it was cut and set, the particular style in which she wore her hair, cannot convey much profit to any class of readers save two—those bent on making a purchase of the like ornaments or of adorning themselves in the same fashion; and, a century hence, those who are studying the costumes and expenditure of the period. But, supposing the subject to be the same, let the writer be one who takes less of a broker's view of his heroine and her adornments; he may be worth listening to, though his simplicity be quite childlike. It is immaterial that our example is in verse:

Be you not proud of that rich hair
Which wantons with the love-sick air;
Whenas that ruby which you wear,
Sunk from the tip of your soft ear,
Will last to be a precious stone
When all your world of beauty's gone.—*Herrick*.[17]

And thus we are led to the conclusion that, in respect of our present object, our concern is less with the subject treated than with its treatment. There have been writers of fiction, as of poetry, who can gather grapes of thorns and figs of thistles.[18]

Closely connected with the humanizing education found in fictitious narrative which reaches to the level of an illuminant of life, is the aesthetic training insensibly given by familiarity with story which, presenting nothing exceptional in other respects, has the merit of being well and artistically constructed. To profit of this kind, from this especial source, very little attention has hitherto been paid, though volumes have been written upon the development of the aesthetic sense by the study of painting and sculpture, and thus adding to the means of enjoyment. Probably few of the general body denominated the reading public consider, in their hurried perusal of novel after novel, that, to a masterpiece in story there appertains a beauty of shape, no less than to a masterpiece in pictorial or plastic art, capable of giving to the trained mind an equal pleasure. To recognize this quality clearly when present, the construction of the plot, or fable, as it used to be called, is to be more particularly observed than either in a reading for sentiments and opinions, or in a reading merely to discover the fates of the chief characters. For however real the persons, however profound, witty, or humorous the observations, as soon as the book comes to be regarded as an exemplification of the art of story-telling, the story naturally takes the first place, and the example is not noteworthy as such unless the telling be artistically carried on.

The distinguishing feature of a well-rounded tale has been defined in various ways, but the general reader need not be burdened with many definitions. Briefly, a story should be an organism. To use the words applied to the epic by Addison, whose artistic feeling in this kind was of the subtlest, "nothing should go before it, be intermixed with it, or follow after it, that is not related to it."[19] Tested by such considerations as these there are obviously many volumes of fiction remarkable, and even great, in their character-drawing, their feeling, their philosophy, which are quite second-rate in their structural quality as narratives. Instances will occur to every one's mind; but instead of dwelling upon these it is more interesting to name some which most nearly fulfill the conditions. Their fewness is remarkable, and bears out the opinion expressed earlier in this essay, that the art of novel-writing is as yet in its tentative stage only. Among them *Tom Jones* is usually pointed out as a near approach to perfection in this as in some other characteristics; though, speaking for myself, I do not perceive its great superiority in artistic form over some other novels of lower reputation. *The Bride of Lammermoor* is an almost perfect specimen of form, which is the more remarkable in that Scott, as a rule, depends more upon episode, dialogue, and description, for exciting interest, than upon the well-knit interdependence of parts. And the first thirty chapters of *Vanity Fair* may be instanced as well-nigh complete in artistic presentation, along with their other magnificent qualities.

Herein lies Richardson's real if only claim to be placed on a level with Fielding: the artist spirit that he everywhere displays in the structural parts of his work and in the interaction of the personages, notably those of *Clarissa Harlowe*. However cold, even artificial, we may, at times, deem the heroine and her companions in the pages of that excellent tale, however numerous the twitches of unreality in their movements across the scene beside those in the figures animated by Fielding, we feel, nevertheless, that we are under the guidance of a hand which has consummate skill in evolving a graceful, well-balanced set of conjectures, forming altogether one of those circumstantial wholes which, when approached by events in real life, cause the observer to pause and reflect, and say, "What a striking history!" We should look generously upon his deficiency in the robuster touches of nature, for it is the deficiency of an author whose artistic sense of form was developed at the expense of his accuracy of observation as regards substance. No person who has a due perception of the constructive art shown in Greek tragic drama can be blind to the constructive art of Richardson.

I have dwelt the more particularly upon this species of excellence, not because I consider it to rank in quality beside truth of feeling and action, but because it is one which so few nonprofessional readers enjoy and appreciate without some kind of preliminary direction. It is usually the latest to be discerned by the novel consumer, and it is often never discerned by him or her at all. Every intelligent reader with a little experience of life can perceive truth to nature in some degree; but a great reduction must be made for those who can trace in narrative the quality which makes the Apollo and the Aphrodite a charm in marble. Thoughtful readers are continually met with who have no intuition that such an attribute can be claimed by fiction, except in so far as it is included in style.

The indefinite word style may be made to express almost any characteristic of story-telling other than subject and plot, and it is too commonly viewed as being some independent, extraneous virtue or varnish with which the substance of a narrative is artificially overlaid. Style, as far as the word is meant to express something more than literary finish, can only be treatment, and treatment depends upon the mental attitude of the novelist; thus entering into the very substance of a narrative, as into that of any other kind of literature. A writer who is not a mere imitator looks upon the world with his personal eyes, and in his peculiar moods; thence grows up his style, in the full sense of the term.

Cui lecta potenter erit res,
Nec facundia deseret hunc, nec lucidus ordo.*[20]

Those who would profit from the study of style should formulate an opinion of what it consists in by the aid of their own educated understanding, their perception of natural fitness, true and high feeling, sincerity, unhampered by considerations of nice collocation and balance of sentences, still less by conventionally accepted examples. They will make the discovery that certain names have, by some accident or other, grown to be regarded as of high, if not of supreme merit in the catalogue of exemplars, which have no essential claims, in this respect, to be rated higher than hundreds of the rank and file of literature who are never mentioned by critic or considered by reader in that connection. An author who has once acquired a reputation for style may write English down to the depths of slovenliness if he choose, without losing his character as a master; and this probably because, as before observed, the quality of style is so vague and inapprehensible as a distinct ingredient that it may always be supposed to be something else than what the reader perceives to be indifferent.

Considerations as to the rank or station in life from which characters are drawn can have but little value in regulating the choice of novels for literary reasons, and the reader may leave thus much to the mood of the moment. I remember reading a lecture on novels by a young and ingenious, though not very profound, critic, some years ago, in which the theory was propounded that novels which depict life in the upper walks of society must, in the nature of things, be better reading than those which exhibit the life of any lower class, for the reason that the subjects of the former represent a higher stage of development than their less fortunate brethren. At the first blush this was a plausible theory; but when practically tested it is found to be based on such a totally erroneous conception of what a novel is, and where it comes from,

* Hor. "De Arte Poetica," 40.

as not to be worth a moment's consideration. It proceeds from the assumption that a novel is the thing, and not a view of the thing. It forgets that the characters, however they may differ, express mainly the author, his largeness of heart or otherwise, his culture, his insight, and very little of any other living person, except in such an inferior kind of procedure as might occasionally be applied to dialogue, and would take the narrative out of the category of fiction; *i.e.*, verbatim reporting without selective judgment.

But there is another reason, disconnected entirely from methods of construction, why the physical condition of the characters rules nothing of itself one way or the other. All persons who have thoughtfully compared class with class—and the wider their experience the more pronounced their opinion—are convinced that education has as yet but little broken or modified the waves of human impulse on which deeds and words depend. So that in the portraiture of scenes in any way emotional or dramatic—the highest province of fiction—the peer and the peasant stand on much the same level; the woman who makes the satin train and the woman who wears it. In the lapse of countless ages, no doubt, improved systems of moral education will considerably and appreciably elevate even the involuntary instincts of human nature; but at present culture has only affected the surface of those lives with which it has come in contact, binding down the passions of those predisposed to turmoil as by a silken thread only, which the first ebullition suffices to break. With regard to what may be termed the minor key of action and speech—the unemotional, every-day doings of men—social refinement operates upon character in a way which is oftener than not prejudicial to vigorous portraiture, by making the exteriors of men their screen rather than their index, as with untutored mankind. Contrasts are disguised by the crust of conventionality, picturesqueness obliterated, and a subjective system of description necessitated for the differentiation of character. In the one case the author's word has to be taken as to the nerves and muscles of his figures; in the other they can be seen as in an *écorché*.[21]

The foregoing are a few imperfect indications how, to the best of my judgment, to discriminate fiction which will be the most desirable reading for the average man or woman of leisure, who does not wish the occupation to be wholly barren of results except in so far as it may administer to the pleasure of the hour. But, as with the horse and the stream in the proverb,[22] no outside power can compel or even help a reader to gain good from such reading unless he has some natural eye for the finer qualities in the best productions of this class. It is unfortunately quite possible to read the most elevating works of imagination in our own or any language, and, by fixing the regard on the wrong sides of the subject, to gather not a grain of wisdom from them, nay, sometimes positive harm. What author has not had his experience of such readers?—the mentally and morally warped ones of both sexes, who will, where practicable, so twist plain and obvious meanings as to see in an honest picture of human nature an attack on religion, morals, or institutions. Truly has it been observed that "the eye sees that which it brings with it the means of seeing."[23]

THOMAS HARDY.

Candour in English Fiction

[Contribution to a symposium in the *New Review*, January, 1890, pp. 15-21]

EVEN IMAGINATION is the slave of stolid circumstance; and the unending flow of inventiveness which finds expression in the literature of Fiction is no exception to the general law. It is conditioned by its surroundings like a river-stream. The varying character and strength of literary creation at different times may, indeed, at first sight seem to be the symptoms of some inherent, arbitrary, and mysterious variation; but if it were possible to compute, as in mechanics, the units of power or faculty, revealed and unrevealed, that exist in the world at stated intervals, an approximately even supply would probably be disclosed. At least there is no valid reason for a contrary supposition. Yet of the inequality in its realisations there can be no question; and the discrepancy would seem to lie in contingencies which, at one period, doom high expression to dumbness and encourage the lower forms, and at another call forth the best in expression and silence triviality.

That something of this is true has indeed been pretty generally admitted in relation to art-products of various other kinds. But when observers and critics remark, as they often do remark, that the great bulk of English fiction of the present day is characterised by its lack of sincerity, they usually omit to trace this serious defect to external, or even eccentric causes. They connect it with an assumption that the attributes of insight, conceptive power, imaginative emotion, are distinctly weaker nowadays than at particular epochs of earlier date. This may or may not be the case to some degree; but, on considering the conditions under which our popular fiction is produced, imaginative deterioration can hardly be deemed the sole or even chief explanation why such an undue proportion of this sort of literature is in England a literature of quackery.

By a sincere school of Fiction we may understand a Fiction that expresses truly the views of life prevalent in its time, by means of a selected chain of action best suited for their exhibition. What are the prevalent views of life just now is a question upon which it is not necessary to enter further than to suggest that the most natural method of presenting them, the method most in accordance with the views themselves, seems to be by a procedure mainly impassive in its tone and tragic in its developments.

Things move in cycles; dormant principles renew themselves, and exhausted principles are thrust by. There is a revival of the artistic instincts towards great dramatic motives—setting forth that "collision between the individual and the general"—formerly worked out with such force by the Periclean and Elizabethan dramatists, to name no other. More than this, the periodicity which marks the course of taste in civilised countries does not take the form of a true cycle of repetition, but what Comte, in speaking of general progress, happily characterises as "a looped orbit":[24] not a movement of revolution but—to use the current word—evolution. Hence, in perceiving that taste is arriving anew at the point of high tragedy, writers are conscious that its revived presentation demands enrichment by further truths—in other words, original treatment: treatment which seeks to show Nature's unconsciousness not of essential laws, but of those laws framed merely as social expedients by humanity, without a basis in the heart of things; treatment which expresses the triumph of the crowd over the hero, of the commonplace majority over the exceptional few.

But originality makes scores of failures for one final success, precisely because its essence is to acknowledge no immediate precursor or guide. It is probably to these inevitable conditions of further acquisition that may be attributed some developments of naturalism in French novelists of the present day, and certain crude results from meritorious attempts in the same direction by intellectual adventurers here and there among our own authors.

Anyhow, conscientious fiction alone it is which can excite a reflective and abiding interest in the minds of thoughtful readers of mature age, who are weary of puerile inventions and famishing for accuracy; who consider that, in representations of the world, the passions ought to be proportioned as in the world itself. This is the interest which was excited in the minds of the Athenians by their immortal tragedies, and in the minds of Londoners at the first performance of the finer plays of three hundred years ago. They reflected life, revealed life, criticised life. Life being a physiological fact, its honest portrayal must be largely concerned with, for one thing, the relations of the sexes, and the substitution for such catastrophes as favour the false colouring best expressed by the regulation finish that "they married and were happy ever after," of catastrophes based upon sexual relations as it is. To this expansion English society opposes a well-nigh insuperable bar.

The popular vehicles for the introduction of a novel to the public have grown to be, from one cause and another, the magazine and the circulating library; and the object of the magazine and circulating library is not upward advance but lateral advance; to suit themselves to what is called household reading, which means, or is made to mean, the reading either of the majority in a household or of the household collectively. The number of adults, even in a large household, being normally two, and these being the members which, as a rule, have least time on their hands to bestow on current literature, the taste of the majority can hardly be, and seldom is, tempered by the ripe judgment which desires fidelity. However, the immature members of a household often keep an open mind, and they might, and no doubt would, take sincere fiction with the rest but for another condition, almost generally co-existent: which is that adults who would desire true views for their own reading insist, for a plausible but questionable reason, upon false views for the reading of their young people.

As a consequence, the magazine in particular and the circulating library in general do not foster the growth of the novel which reflects and reveals life. They directly tend to exterminate it by monopolising all literary space. Cause and effect were never more clearly conjoined, though commentators upon the result, both French and English, seem seldom if ever to trace their connection. A sincere and comprehensive sequence of the ruling passions, however moral in its ultimate bearings, must not be put on paper as the foundation of imaginative works, which have to claim notice through the above-named channels, though it is extensively welcomed in the form of newspaper reports. That the magazine and library have arrogated to themselves the dispensation of fiction is not the fault of the authors, but of circumstances over which they, as representatives of Grub Street, have no control.

What this practically amounts to is that the patrons of literature—no longer Peers with a taste—acting under the censorship of prudery, rigorously exclude from the pages they regulate subjects that have been made, by general approval of the best judges, the bases of the finest imaginative compositions since literature rose to the dignity of an art. The crash of broken commandments is as necessary an accompaniment to the catastrophe of a tragedy as the noise of drum and cymbals to a triumphal march. But the crash of broken commandments shall not be heard; or, if at all, but gently, like the roaring of Bottom—gently as any sucking dove, or as 'twere any nightingale, lest we should fright the ladies out of their wits.[25] More precisely, an arbitrary proclamation has gone forth that certain picked commandments of the ten shall be preserved intact—to wit, the first, third, and seventh; that the ninth shall be infringed but gingerly; the sixth only as much as necessary; and the remainder alone as much as you please, in a genteel manner.[26]

It is in the self-consciousness engendered by interference with spontaneity, and in aims at a compromise to square with circumstances, that the real secret lies of the charlatanry pervading so much of English fiction. It may be urged that abundance of great and profound novels might be written which should require no compromising, contain not an episode deemed questionable by prudes. This I venture to doubt. In a ramification of the profounder passions the treatment of which makes the great style, something "unsuitable" is sure to arise; and then comes the struggle with the literary conscience. The opening scenes of the would-be great story may, in a rash moment, have been printed in some popular magazine before the remainder is written; as it advances month by month the situations develop, and the writer asks himself, what will his characters do next? What would probably happen to them, given such beginnings? On his life and conscience, though he had not foreseen the thing, only one event could possibly happen, and that therefore he should narrate, as he calls himself a faithful artist. But, though pointing a fine moral, it is just one of those issues which are not to be mentioned in respectable magazines and select libraries. The dilemma then confronts him, he must either whip and scourge those characters into doing something contrary to their natures, to produce the spurious effect of their being in harmony with social forms and ordinances, or, by leaving them alone to act as they will, he must bring down the thunders of respectability upon his head, not to say ruin his editor, his publisher, and himself.

What he often does, indeed can scarcely help doing in such a strait, is, belie his literary conscience, do despite to his best imaginative instincts by arranging a *dénouement* which he knows to be indescribably unreal and meretricious, but dear to the Grundyist and subscriber. If the true artist ever weeps it probably is then, when he first discovers the fearful price that he has to pay for the privilege of writing in the English language—no less a price than the complete extinction, in the mind of every mature and penetrating reader, of sympathetic belief in his personages.

To say that few of the old dramatic masterpieces, if newly published as a novel (the form which, experts tell us, they would have taken in modern conditions), would be tolerated in English magazines and libraries is a ludicrous understatement. Fancy a brazen young Shakespeare of our time—*Othello, Hamlet,* or *Antony and Cleopatra* never having yet appeared—sending up one of those creations in narrative form to the editor of a London magazine, with the author's compliments, and his hope that the story will be found acceptable to the editor's pages; suppose him, further, to have the temerity to ask for the candid remarks of the accomplished editor upon his manuscript. One can imagine the answer that young William would get for his mad supposition of such fitness from any one of the gentlemen who so correctly conduct that branch of the periodical Press.*

* It is, indeed, curious to consider what great works of the past the notions of the present day would aim to exclude from circulation, if not from publication, if they were issued as new fiction. In addition to those

Were the objections of the scrupulous limited to a prurient treatment of the relations of the sexes, or to any view of vice calculated to undermine the essential principles of social order, all honest lovers of literature would be in accord with them. All really true literature directly or indirectly sounds as its refrain the words in the *Agamemnon:* "Chant Ælinon, Ælinon! but may the good prevail."[27] But the writer may print the *not* of his broken commandment in capitals of flame; it makes no difference. A question which should be wholly a question of treatment is confusedly regarded as a question of subject.

Why the ancient classic and old English tragedy can be regarded thus deeply, both by young people in their teens and by old people in their moralities, and the modern novel cannot be so regarded; why the honest and uncompromising delineation which makes the old stories and dramas lessons in life must make of the modern novel, following humbly on the same lines, a lesson in iniquity, is to some thinkers a mystery inadequately accounted for by the difference between old and new.

Whether minors should read unvarnished fiction based on the deeper passions, should listen to the eternal verities in the form of narrative, is somewhat a different question from whether the novel ought to be exclusively addressed to those minors. The first consideration is one which must be passed over here; but it will be conceded by most friends of literature that all fiction should not be shackled by conventions concerning budding womanhood, which may be altogether false. It behoves us then to inquire how best to

---

mentioned, think of the *King Œdipus* of Sophocles, the *Agamemnon* of Æeschylus, Goethe's *Faust* and *Wilhelm Meister*, the *Prometheus* of Æschylus, Milton's *Paradise Lost.* The "unpleasant subjects" of the two first-named compositions, the "unsuitableness" of the next two, would be deemed equalled only by the profanity of the last two; for Milton, as it is hardly necessary to remind the reader, handles as his puppets the Christian divinities and fiends quite as freely as the Pagan divinities were handled by the Greek and Latin imaginative authors.

circumvent the present lording of nonage over maturity, and permit the explicit novel to be more generally written.

That the existing magazine and book-lending system will admit of any great modification is scarcely likely. As far as the magazine is concerned it has long been obvious that as a vehicle for fiction dealing with human feeling on a comprehensive scale it is tottering to its fall; and it will probably in the course of time take up openly the position that it already covertly occupies, that of a purveyor of tales for the youth of both sexes, as it assumes that tales for those rather numerous members of society ought to be written.

There remain three courses by which the adult may find deliverance. The first would be a system of publication under which books could be bought and not borrowed, when they would naturally resolve themselves into classes instead of being, as now, made to wear a common livery in style and subject, enforced by their supposed necessities in addressing indiscriminately a general audience.

But it is scarcely likely to be convenient to either authors or publishers that the periodical form of publication for the candid story should be entirely forbidden, and in retaining the old system thus far, yet ensuring that the emancipated serial novel should meet the eyes of those for whom it is intended, the plan of publication as a *feuilleton* in newspapers read mainly by adults might be more generally followed, as in France. In default of this, or coexistent with it, there might be adopted what, upon the whole, would perhaps find more favour than any with those who have artistic interests at heart, and that is, magazines for adults; exclusively for adults, if necessary. As an offshoot there might be at least one magazine for the middle-aged and old.

There is no foretelling; but this (since the magazine form of publication is so firmly rooted) is at least a promising remedy, if English prudery be really, as we hope, only a parental anxiety. There should be no mistaking the matter, no half measures. *La dignité de la pensée,* in the words of Pascal,[28] might then grow to be recognised in the treatment of fiction as in other things, and untrammelled adult opinion on conduct and theology might be axiomatically assumed and dramatically appealed to. Nothing in such literature should for a moment exhibit lax views of that purity of life upon which the well-being of society depends; but the position of man and woman in nature, and the position of belief in the minds of man and woman—things which everybody is thinking but nobody is saying—might be taken up and treated frankly.

[Hardy's bleak assessment is, in part, an outgrowth of the difficulties he had been having with *Tess of the d'Urbervilles.* (Mary Ellen Chase has reviewed the changes that Hardy felt constrained to make because of the objections raised by magazine editors, book publishers, and readers; these changes affected incident, plot, characterization, and setting, as well as diction, grammar, and sentence structure. See *Thomas Hardy from Serial to Novel* [Minneapolis, 1927], pp. 69-112.)

Hardy's contribution was the third and final essay in a gathering published in this same issue of the *New Review.* Both Walter Besant (1836-1901) and Mrs. E. Lynn Linton (1822-1898) deplored, in their articles, "the barriers set up by Mrs. Grundy" which prevented novelists from venturing "into the forbidden Garden of Roses"; but Hardy took much the sternest view of the pernicious consequences that such conditions exerted on the quality of English fiction. Besant admitted that "Average Opinion" is generally "a Philistine," but argued that it could not be resisted; defended the purity of the nation against those who levied the charge of hypocrisy ("And as for the women—those above a certain level—*there is never any closed chapter at all in their lives*"); and even went so far as to say that "Love free and disobedient" was best treated by the French. Mrs. Linton concerned herself primarily with the question, "To whom ought Fiction to be addressed?" She concluded that there was a place for fiction that would treat serious themes for adult readers "who know life," no less than for fiction aimed at "the Young Person," but added her vote of approval for a "locked bookcase for greater security."]

The Science of Fiction

[Contribution to a symposium in the *New Review*,
April, 1891, pp. 315-319]

SINCE ART is science with an addition, since some science underlies all Art, there is seemingly no paradox in the use of such a phrase as "the Science of Fiction." One concludes it to mean that comprehensive and accurate knowledge of realities which must be sought for, or intuitively possessed, to some extent, before anything deserving the name of an artistic performance in narrative can be produced.

The particulars of this science are the generals of almost all others. The materials of Fiction being human nature and circumstances, the science thereof may be dignified by calling it the codified law of things as they really are. No single pen can treat exhaustively of this. The Science of Fiction is contained in that large work, the cyclopaedia of life.

In no proper sense can the term "science" be applied to other than this fundamental matter. It can have no part or share in the construction of a story, however recent speculations may have favoured such an application. We may assume with certainty that directly the constructive stage is entered upon, Art—high or low—begins to exist.

The most devoted apostle of realism, the sheerest naturalist, cannot escape, any more than the withered old gossip over her fire, the exercise of Art in his labour or pleasure of telling a tale. Not until he becomes an automatic reproducer of all impressions whatsoever can he be called purely scientific, or even a manufacturer on scientific principles. If in the exercise of his reason he select or omit, with an eye to being more truthful than truth (the just aim of Art), he transforms himself into a technicist at a move.

As this theory of the need for the exercise of the Dædalian faculty for selection and cunning manipulation has been disputed, it may be worth while to examine the contrary proposition. That it should ever have been maintained by such a romancer as M. Zola, in his work on the *Roman Expérimental,* seems to reveal an obtuseness to the disproof conveyed in his own novels which, in a French writer, is singular indeed. To be sure that author—whose powers in story-telling, rightfully and wrongfully exercised, may be partly owing to the fact that he is not a critic—does in a measure concede something in the qualified counsel that the novel should keep as close to reality *as it can;* a remark which may be interpreted with infinite latitude, and would no doubt have been cheerfully accepted by Dumas *père* or Mrs. Radcliffe. It implies discriminative choice; and if we grant that we grant all. But to maintain in theory what he abandons in practice, to subscribe to rules and to work by instinct, is a proceeding not confined to the author of *Germinal* and *La Faute de l'Abbé Mouret.*

The reasons that make against such conformation of storywriting to scientific processes have been set forth so many times in examining the theories of the realist, that it is not necessary to recapitulate them here. Admitting the desirability, the impossibility of reproducing in its entirety the phantasmagoria of experience with infinite and atomic truth, without shadow, relevancy, or subordination, is not the least of them. The fallacy appears to owe its origin to the just perception that with our widened knowledge of the universe and its forces, and man's position therein, narrative, to be artistically convincing, must adjust itself to the new alignment, as would also artistic works in form and colour, if further spectacles in their sphere could be presented. Nothing but the illusion of truth can permanently please, and when the old illusions begin to be penetrated, a more natural magic has to be supplied.

Creativeness in its full and ancient sense—the making a thing or situation out of nothing that ever was before—is apparently ceasing to satisfy a world which no longer believes in the abnormal—ceasing at least to satisfy the van-couriers of taste; and creative fancy has accordingly to give more and more place to realism, that is, to an artificiality distilled from the fruits of closest observation.

This is the meaning deducible from the work of the realists, however stringently they themselves may define realism in terms. Realism is an unfortunate, an ambiguous word, which has been taken up by literary society like a view-halloo, and has been assumed in some places to mean copyism, and in others pruriency, and has led to two classes of delineators being included in one condemnation.

Just as bad a word is one used to express a consequence of this development, namely "brutality," a term which, first applied by French critics, has since spread over the English school like the other. It aptly hits off the immediate impression of the thing meant; but it has the disadvantage of defining impartiality as a passion, and a plan as a caprice. It certainly is very far from truly expressing the aims and methods of conscientious and well-intentioned authors who, notwithstanding their excesses, errors, and rickety theories, attempt to narrate the *vérité vraie*.

To return for a moment to the theories of the scientific realists. Every friend to the novel should and must be in sympathy with their error, even while distinctly perceiving it. Though not true, it is well founded. To advance realism as complete copyism, to call the idle trade of story-telling a science, is the hyperbolic flight of an admirable enthusiasm, the exaggerated cry of an honest reaction from the false, in which the truth has been impetuously approached and overleapt in fault of lighted on.

Possibly, if we only wait, the third something, akin to perfection, will exhibit itself on its due pedestal. How that third something may be induced to hasten its presence, who shall say? Hardly the English critic.

But this appertains to the Art of novel-writing, and is outside the immediate subject. To return to the "science." . . . Yet what is the use? Its very comprehensiveness renders the attempt to dwell upon it a futility. Being an observative responsiveness to everything within the cycle of the suns that has to do with actual life, it is easier to say what it is not than to categorise its *summa genera.* It is not, for example, the paying of a great regard to adventitious externals to the neglect of vital qualities, not a precision about the outside of the platter and an obtuseness to the contents. An accomplished lady once confessed to the writer that she could never be in a room two minutes without knowing every article of furniture it contained and every detail in the attire of the inmates, and, when she left, remembering every remark. Here was a person, one might feel for the moment, who could prime herself to an unlimited extent and at the briefest notice in the scientific data of fiction; one who, assuming her to have some slight artistic power, was a born novelist. To explain why such a keen eye to the superficial does not imply a sensitiveness to the intrinsic is a psychological matter beyond the scope of these notes; but that a blindness to material particulars often accompanies a quick perception of the more ethereal characteristics of humanity, experience continually shows.

A sight for the finer qualities of existence, an ear for the "still sad music of humanity,"[29] are not to be acquired by the outer senses alone, close as their powers in photography may be. What cannot be discerned by eye and ear, what may be apprehended only by the mental tactility that comes from a sympathetic appreciativeness of life in all of its manifestations, this is the gift which renders its possessor a more accurate delineator of human nature than many another with twice his powers and means of external observation, but without that sympathy. To see in half and quarter views the whole picture, to catch from a few bars the whole tune, is the intuitive power that supplies the would-be storywriter with the scientific bases for his pursuit. He may not count the dishes at a feast, or accurately estimate the value of the jewels in a lady's diadem; but through the smoke of those dishes, and the rays from these jewels, he sees written on the wall:—

> We are such stuff
> As dreams are made of, and our little life
> Is rounded with a sleep.[30]

Thus, as aforesaid, an attempt to set forth the Science of Fiction in calculable pages is futility; it is to write a whole library of human philosophy, with instructions how to feel.

Once in a crowd a listener heard a needy and illiterate woman saying of another poor and haggard woman who had lost her little son years before: "You can see the ghost of that child in her face even now."

That speaker was one who, though she could probably neither read nor write, had the true means towards the "Science" of Fiction innate within her; a power of observation informed by a living heart. Had she been trained in the technicalities, she might have fashioned her view of mortality with good effect; a reflection which leads to a conjecture that, perhaps, true novelists, like poets, are born, not made.

[Hardy's essay, like "Candour in English Fiction," appeared as the third and last in a symposium printed in a single issue of the *New Review*. Paul Bourget (1852-1935) and Walter Besant (1836-1901) preceded him. Bourget rejected as pedantic quibbling the supposed objectivity of Flaubert's art, and preferred the writer (for example, Stendhal or Balzac) who explained what his characters were while delineating them. For Bourget the most powerful novel was the novel of character; the analytical novel, the novel of manners, and the novel of intrigue were "less complete varieties." Besant spent most of his time deploring the mediocrity of contemporary English fiction, and attributed it to the low quality of reviewing; he believed that the art of fiction could be taught; and he emphasized the value of "technique" properly passed on through analysis and imitation in some sort of "School." Hardy's comments did not respond directly to those of the other contributors, each of whom wrote independently; but their interest rests partly in the fact that Hardy took direct notice of the disparity between theory and practice in Zola's case, and in the emphasis on an artist's ability "to see in half and quarter views the whole picture, to catch from a few bars the whole tune. . . ."]

Why I Don't Write Plays

[Contribution to a symposium in the *Pall Mall Gazette*,
August 31, 1892, p. 1]

1. Inimical to the best interests of the stage: no injury to literature.

2. Have occasionally had a desire to produce a play, and have, in fact, written the skeletons of several. Have no such desire in any special sense just now.

3. Because, in general, the novel affords scope for getting nearer to the heart and meaning of things than does the play: in particular, the play as nowadays conditioned, when parts have to be moulded to actors, not actors to parts; when managers will not risk a truly original play; when scenes have to be arranged in a constrained and arbitrary fashion to suit the exigencies of scene-building, although spectators are absolutely indifferent to order and succession provided they can have set before them a developing thread of interest. The reason of this arbitrary arrangement would seem to be that the presentation of human passions is subordinated to the presentation of mountains, cities, clothes, furniture, plate, jewels, and other real and sham-real appurtenances, to the neglect of the principle that the material stage should be a conventional or figurative arena, in which accessories are kept down to the plane of mere suggestions of place and time, so as not to interfere with the required high-relief of the action and emotions.

[Hardy, along with other writers of fiction, had been asked to answer in such form as he might think fit, the following questions: "(1) Whether you regard the present divorce of fiction from the drama as beneficial or inimical to the best interests of literature and of the stage; (2) Whether you, yourself, have at any time had, or now have, any desire to exercise your gifts in the production of plays as well as of novels; and, if not, (3) Why you consider the novel the better or more convenient means for bringing your ideas before the public whom you address."]

British Authors on French Literature

[Contribution to a symposium in the *Morning Post*, February 11, 1899, p. 5]

YOUR QUESTION is a difficult one to answer in a brief letter owing to the manysidedness of that genius, the variety of lights given out by the innumerable facets into which French genius has shaped itself. My reading in your literature, moreover, has not been extensive. But I should say that the fewest names it would be possible to include in the list of these immortals are those of Rabelais, Descartes, Corneille, Pascal, Molière, Montesquieu, Voltaire, Diderot, J. J. Rousseau, Béranger, Victor Hugo, Auguste Comte, George Sand, and H. de Balzac. I should also like to add Gautier and Dumas, father and son. Not one of those typical writers could have been born of another nation, and not one of them can be regarded as the echo of a predecessor. And why not also add Villon, Racine, La Fontaine, Madame de Sévigné, Bossuet, Le Sage, Chateaubriand, De Musset, and Baudelaire? Each is characteristic. But one might go too far, and I send my selection for what it may be worth.

[Hardy was answering the question, posed by *Le Gaulois du dimanche*, Paris, "Which French authors now dead best represented in their works the distinctive genius of France?" The answers, contributed by several English authors, appeared in the "Supplément hebdomadaire littéraire et illustré" published by *Le Gaulois*, on February 11-12, 1899, p. 1, and in the *Morning Post* on February 11, 1899, p. 5. The clipping in Thomas Hardy's personal notebook is from the *St. James's Gazette*, where it appeared under the headline, "British Writers on French Authors."]

The Dynasts: A Rejoinder [1]

[*The Times Literary Supplement*, February 5, 1904, pp. 36-37]

To the Editor of *The Times:*

Sir, The objections raised by your dramatic critic to the stage-form adopted in *The Dynasts* for presenting a rapid mental vision of the Napoleonic wars—objections which I had in some degree anticipated in the preface to the book—seem to demand a reply, inasmuch as they involve a question of literary art that is of far wider importance than as it affects a single volume. I regret that in the space of a letter I shall only be able to touch upon it briefly.

Your critic is as absolute as the gravedigger in *Hamlet.* I understand his contention to be that to give a panoramic poem (which *The Dynasts* may perhaps be called) the form of a stage-drama—even a conventionalized form—or to give such a form to anything whatever that is intended for the study only, is false in principle. Whether the aim of *The Dynasts* was to dumbfound the worthy burgher (as your critic surmises in the French tongue) or not, his theory certainly does dumbfound, or, as he would say, *épate,* the present writer. According to it one must conclude that such productions as Shelley's *Prometheus Unbound,* Byron's *Cain,* and many other unactable play-like poems are a waste of means, and, in his own words, "may be read just as, *faute de mieux,* shoe-leather may be used as an article of diet."

His view would seem to be based on an assumption that in no circumstances must an art borrow the methods of a neighbour art. Yet if there is one thing needful to the vitality of any art it is the freedom of the worker therein from the restraint of such scientific reasoning as would lay down this law, freedom from the *rationale* of every development that he adopts. The artistic spirit is at bottom a spirit of caprice, and in some of its finest productions in the past it could have given no clear reason why they were run in this or that particular mould, and not in some more obvious one. And if it could be proved that in *The Dynasts* nothing is gained, but much lost, by its form, that attempt would still have been legitimate.

Nevertheless, if your reviewer's statement that the stage-form is inherently an unnatural one for reading, a waste of available means, were strictly accurate, I would concede to him the expediency, though not the obligation, of avoiding it in a book. But why, one asks, is it bad for reading? Because, I understand him to answer, it was invented for the stage. He might as well assert that bitter ale is bad drinking for England because it was invented for India. His critical hand is, indeed, subdued to what it works in when he pens such a theory. It surely ought to have occurred to him that this play-shape is essentially, if not quite literally, at one with the instinctive, primitive, narrative shape. In legends and old ballads, in the telling of "an owre true tale" by country-folks on winter nights over a dying fire, the place and time are briefly indicated at the beginning in almost all cases; and then the body of the story follows as what he said and what she said, the action being often suggested by the speeches alone. This likeness between the order of natural recital and the order of theatrical utility may be accidental; but there it is; and to write Scene so-and-so, Time so-and-so, instead of Once upon a time, At such a place, is a trifling variation that makes no difference to the mental images raised. Of half-a-dozen people I have spoken to about reading plays, four say that they can imagine the enactment in a read play better than in a read novel or epic poem. It is a matter of idiosyncrasy.

The methods of a book and the methods of a play, which he says are so different, are fundamentally similar. It must be remembered that the printed story is not a representation, but, like the printed play, a means of producing a representation, which is done in the one case by sheer imaginativeness, in the other by imaginativeness pieced out with material helps. Why, then, should not a somewhat idealized semblance of the latter means be used in the former case?

For a rather digressive reason your reviewer drags in the art of architecture. In mercy to his own argument he should have left architecture alone. Like those of a play for reading, its features are continually determined by no mechanical, material, or methodic necessities (which are confused together by your critic). As for mechanical necessities, that purest relic of Greek architecture, the Parthenon, is a conventionalized representation of the necessities of a timber house, many of which are not necessities in stone, such as the imitations of wood rafter-ends, beam-ends, and ceiling-joists. As for necessities of purpose, medieval architects constructed church-parapets with the embrasures of those of a fortress, and on the Continent planned the eastern ends of their Cathedrals in resemblance of a Roman Hall of Justice. In respect of necessities of method, that art, throughout its history, has capriciously subdued to its service, in sheer waywardness, the necessities of other arts, so that one can find in it a very magazine of examples of my own procedure in *The Dynasts*. Capitals, cornices, bosses, and scores of other details, instead of confining their shapes to those strictly demanded by their office, borrow from the art of sculpture without scruple and without reason. Sculptured human figures are boldly taken, and, by the name of caryatids, are used as columns. In sculpture itself we find the painter's "necessity" borrowed—a superficies—and used for bas-reliefs, even though shapes are misrepresented by so doing. And if we turn to poetry we find that rhythm and rhyme are a non-necessitous presentation of language under conditions that in strictness appertain only to music.

But analogies between the arts are apt to be misleading, and having said thus much in defence of the form chosen, even supposing another to have been available, I have no room left for more than a bare assertion that there was available no such other form that would readily allow of the necessary compression of space and time. I believe that any one who should sit down and consider at leisure how to present so wide a subject within reasonable compass would decide that this was, broadly speaking, the only way.

Before concluding I should like to correct a misapprehension of your critic's, and of others, that I have "hankerings after actual performance" of *The Dynasts.* My hankerings, if any, do not lie that way. But I fancy his do. His laborious search in cyclopaedias for some means of performing it plainly betray that he is dying to see the show; which is flattering. But if he will look again at the last paragraph of the preface he will perceive that my remarks on performance refer to old English dramas only.

Your obedient servant,

Max Gate, Dorset, Feb. 2. THOMAS HARDY.

[Arthur Bingham Walkley (1855-1926), who served as literary and dramatic critic on *The Times* from 1900 to 1926, wrote an unsigned article, "*The Dynasts:* A Suggestion," which appeared in *The Times Literary Supplement* on January 29, 1904. Noting that "these Napoleons and Pitts and Nelsons are puppets, blind parts of the Immanent Will," Walkley recommended that Hardy's epic-drama be staged as a puppet-show. Hardy immediately took umbrage at the "suggestion," and wrote the above letter, to which Walkley responded in a partly humorous article on February 12, "*The Dynasts* and the Puppets," in which he insisted that he, for one, *was* "dying to see the show." Hardy thereupon wrote a second letter (see the next selection), in which he insisted on the historical bases of the concept of Immanent Will.]

The Dynasts: A Postscript [2]

[*The Times Literary Supplement*, February 19, 1904, p. 53]

TO THE EDITOR OF *The Times:*

SIR,—YOUR CRITIC has humorously conducted his discourse away from his original charge against *The Dynasts* into the quaint and unexpected channel of real performance by means of fantoccini, Chinese shadows, and other startling apparatus. This is highly creditable to his ingenious mind; yet we must remember that the whole fabric of his vision[31] arose only out of his altruistic desire to provide me with a means of escape from what he holds to be an untenable position. But I still absolutely deny it to be such, though

I may seem ungrateful. I think I have shown that an attempt to write a spectacular poem (if he will allow me to use the expression for want of a better), more or less resembling a stage-play, though not one, has full artistic justification and is not "false in principle," as he stated. He naturally continues to think the other way; and there I fear the matter must remain.

But the truth seems to be—if I may say a final word here on a point outside the immediate discussion—that the real offence of *The Dynasts* lies, not in its form as such, but in the philosophy which gave rise to the form. This is revealed by symptoms in various quarters, even (if I am not mistaken) by your critic's own faint tendency to harden his heart against the "Immanent Will." Worthy British Philistia, unlike that ancient Athens it professes to admire, not only does not ask for a new thing, but even shies at that which merely appears at first sight to be a new thing. As with a certain King, the reverse of worthy, in the case of another play, some people ask, "Have you read the argument? Is there no offence in't?"[32] There can hardly be, assuredly, on a fair examination. The philosophy of *The Dynasts,* under various titles and phases, is almost as old as civilization. Its fundamental principle, under the name of Predestination, was preached by St. Paul. "Being predestinated"—says the author of the Epistle to the Ephesians, "Being predestinated according to the purpose of Him who worketh all things after the counsel of His own Will";[33] and much more to the same effect, the only difference being that externality is assumed by the Apostle rather than immanence. It has run through the history of the Christian Church ever since. St. Augustine held it vaguely, Calvin held it fiercely, and, if our English Church and its Nonconformist contemporaries have now almost abandoned it to our men of science (among whom determinism is a commonplace), it was formerly taught by Evangelical divines of the finest character and conduct. I should own in fairness that I think this has been shrewdly recognized in some quarters whose orthodoxy is unimpeachable, where the philosophy of *The Dynasts* has been handled as sanely and as calmly as I could wish.

Nevertheless, as was said in the Preface, I have used the philosophy as a plausible theory only. Though, for that matter, I am convinced that, whether we uphold this or any other conjecture on the cause of things, men's lives and actions will be little affected thereby, these being less dependent on abstract reasonings than on the involuntary inter-social emotions, which would more probably be strengthened than weakened by a sense that humanity and other animal life (roughly, though not accurately, definable as puppetry) forms the conscious extremity of a pervading urgence, or will.

Your obedient servant,

Max Gate, Dorset, Feb. 16. THOMAS HARDY.

A Plea for Pure English

[Hardy's speech as reported in *The Times*, June 4, 1912, p. 7]

IN THANKING the Royal Society of Literature and the Academic Committee very warmly for the interesting and valuable gift I need hardly say that the offer of it came quite as a surprise to myself, of which the Committee will be aware. I am, to be sure, rather an old boy to receive a medal, and am particularly unfortunate in having no younger boy to whom I can hand it on; so that, without undervaluing the receipt of it—rather, indeed, because I value it so highly—I have been thinking whether prizes of some kind could not be offered by the society to makers of literature earlier in life to urge them to further efforts.

There is no doubt that any sort of incentive to the cultivation and production of pure literature is of immense value in these latter days, and awards by the Royal Society of Literature should be among the strongest. An appreciation of what is real literature, and efforts to keep real literature alive, have, in truth, become imperative, if the taste for it is not to be entirely lost, and, with the loss of that taste, its longer life in the English language. While millions have lately been learning to read, few of them have been learning to discriminate; and the result is an appalling increase every day in slipshod writing that would not have been tolerated for one moment a hundred years ago.

I don't quite like to say so, but I fear that the vast increase of hurried descriptive reporting in the newspapers is largely responsible for this in England; writing done by men, and still more by women, who are utterly incapable of, and unconscious of, that "grin of delight" which, William Morris assured us, comes over the real artist either in letters or in other forms of art at a close approximation to, if not an exact achievement of, his ideal.[34] Then the increasing influx of American journals, fearfully and wonderfully worded, helps on the indifference to literary form. Their influence has been strongly apparent of late years in our English newspapers, where one often now meets with headlines in staring capitals that are phrases of no language whatever, and often incomprehensible at a casual glance. Every kind of reward, prize, or grant, therefore, which urges omnivorous readers and incipient writers towards appreciating the splendours of "English undefiled, and the desire"[35] of producing such for themselves, is of immense value.

For my own part I think—though all writers may not agree with me—that the shortest way to good prose is by the route of good verse. The apparent paradox—I cannot remember who first expressed it—that the best poetry is the best prose ceases on examination to be a paradox and becomes a truism. Anybody may test it for himself by taking any fine lines in verse and, casting off the fetters of metre and rhyme that seem to bind the poet, trying to express the same ideas more freely and accurately in prose. He will find that it cannot be done: the words of the verse—fettered as he thought them—are the only words that will convey the ideas that were intended to be conveyed.

I know that it is said in Fleet-street that poetry is dead. But this only means that it is dead in Fleet-street. Poetry itself cannot die, as George Sand once eloquently wrote in her novel called *André*. I cannot do better than wind up these rambling remarks with some of her words on this question:—"Poesy cannot die. Should she find for refuge but the brain of a single man she would yet have centuries of life, for she would leap out of it like the lava from Vesuvius and mark out a way for herself among the most prosaic realities. Despite her overturned temples and the false gods adored among their ruins, she is immortal as the perfume of the flowers and the splendour of the skies."[36]

[Hardy received on his seventy-second birthday the gold medal of the Royal Society of Literature, awarded to him personally by Sir Henry Newbolt and William Butler Yeats, who were staying with him at Max Gate, Dorchester, for the occasion. They reminded Hardy, at the time of the presentation, that the gold medal, highest of the Society's awards, had been bestowed upon some fifteen authors in all since the founding charter of 1823, and that among these fifteen had been Walter Scott, Washington Irving, and George Meredith. Hardy's reply was in the form of a speech.]

What Is the Best Short Poem in English?

[A contribution to a symposium in the *New York Times*, July 5, 1914, Section 5, p. 1]

Max Gate, Dorchester.

TO THE EDITOR OF THE *New York Times:*

In answer to your question of which is the best short poem I have read in the English language I can only say that I fail to see how there can be a "best" poem, long or short; that is, one best in all circumstances. This attempt to appraise by comparison is, if you will allow me to say so, one of the literary vices of the time, only a little above the inquiry who is the biggest poet, novelist, or prizefighter, although not quite so low down as that deepest deep of literary valuation, "who is the biggest seller."

THOMAS HARDY

[Hardy's note, in answer to a question sent to twenty-five poets, is reminiscent of his response to the same kind of inquiry sent out by the *Fortnightly Review* in 1887 (see pp. 106-107).]

Wessex Scenes from The Dynasts

[A speech as reported in *The Times*, December 9, 1916, p. 11]

THE CONTRAST in point of humanity, honour and chivalry between our enemies in the present struggle, and those in the struggle with Napoleon a hundred years ago, does not show to the advantage of our modern methods of warfare and modern magnanimity. It is, indeed, no less than extraordinary that an additional centenary of civilization and moral effort have resulted in greater barbarities by far than any of those the much abused Bonaparte ever put in force against us. Heaven grant that all this scientific slaughter may soon cease, and that a sense of its folly will ensure its disappearance for ever.

[Hardy's comment, reprinted in part here, was read as a prologue to performances by the "Hardy Players," of the Dorchester Debating and Dramatic Society, of *Wessex Scenes from The Dynasts*, given in Dorchester on December 6 and 7, 1916.]

Robert Louis Stevenson

[*I Can Remember Robert Louis Stevenson*, ed. Rosaline Masson, Edinburgh and London, 1922, pp. 214-216]

THE MEMORIES I have of Louis Stevenson are very meagre, as I saw him but a few times. I met him once—possibly on the first occasion—at Mr. (now Sir) Sidney Colvin's house at the British Museum. There were no other guests, and I can recall no particulars of the meeting further than that he said he liked wandering about the precincts of the Museum. A more distinct image of him accompanies my recollections of the first and last visit he paid me at Dorchester, in August, 1885. He came out to my house unexpectedly from the King's Arms Hotel in the town, where he was staying for a day or two with Mrs. Stevenson, her son, and a lady who was Louis's cousin. He said that they were on their way to Dartmoor, the air of which he had been told would benefit him. He appeared in a velveteen jacket, with one hand in a sling. I asked him why he wore the sling, as there seemed nothing the matter with his hand: his answer (I am almost certain) was that he had been advised to do it to lessen the effort of his heart in its beats. He particularly wanted to see the room I wrote in, but as I had come into the house quite recently I had not settled into any definite writing-place, and could only show him a temporary corner I used. My wife and I went the next day to call on them at the hotel just before they left, where we bade them good-bye, expecting next to hear of them from Dartmoor. To our great surprise and regret a letter from Mrs. Stevenson arrived about three weeks later, dated from an hotel in Exeter, and informing us that Louis had been taken ill on reaching that city, and could get no further; and that they were coming back to Bournemouth immediately he was well enough to travel.

From this point my mind is a blank, excepting as to one fact—that shortly after the publication of *The Mayor of Casterbridge* in the May of the following year, he wrote to ask if I would permit him to dramatise it, as he had read the story, and thought Henchard "a great fellow," adding that he himself was keeping unusually well. I wrote back my ready permission; and there the matter ended. I heard no more about the play; and I think I may say that to my vision he dropped into utter darkness from that date: I recall no further sight of or communication from him, though I used to hear of him in a roundabout way from friends of his and mine. I should add that some years later I read an interview with him that had been published in the newspapers, in which he stated that he disapproved of the morals of *Tess of the d'Urbervilles,* which had appeared in the interim, and probably had led to his silence.[37]

[Hardy's memories of Stevenson are also recorded in the *Life,* pp. 175, 179-180, 181, 246. They are slight, but in the autobiography one item of dry humor turns up that Hardy omitted from his reminiscence in Rosaline Masson's anthology. Henry James had written to R. L. S., shortly after the appearance of *Tess of the d'Urbervilles,* "Oh, yes, dear Louis: [it] is vile. The pretence of sexuality is only equalled by the absence of it (?), and the abomination of the language by the author's reputation for style" (p. 246). Hardy, who liked his "good-natured friends" James and Stevenson, called them afterwards "the Polonius and the Osric of novelists."]

G. M.: A Reminiscence

[*Nineteenth Century and After,* February, 1928, pp. 146-148]

On the centenary of the birth of George Meredith it has been thought appropriate that I should say what few words I can say about so exceptional a man; and I have assented, not because I am well qualified to speak of one of such individual and brilliant achievement—indeed, far from it—but because I chanced to encounter him at a date that has now become very remote, and when he can probably have been known to few persons still alive who met him for purely literary reasons as I did, and not as members of his family or domestic friends.

Meredith is so modern that it may surprise his younger readers who have not given much thought to the matter to be reminded that he was living for four years as a juvenile contemporary of Sir Walter Scott, who at his birth had not published *The Fair Maid of Perth, Anne of Geierstein,* or *Count Robert;* that for six years he was a contemporary of Lamb and Coleridge, for fifteen years of Southey, and for twenty-two years of Wordsworth; and that *The Ordeal of Richard Feverel* was finished before Darwin settled the question of the Origin of Species.

It is hopeless to attempt to get back all the way from effects to causes in terrestrial affairs as in celestial, but at any rate a proximate cause of my knowledge of Meredith was the late Mr. Alexander Macmillan. He had been the first to read the manuscript of my first novel—if it could be called a novel (though I had dabbled in verse for years)—and, being apparently in some doubt about it, suggested that I should let it be seen by Messrs. Chapman & Hall, to which firm of publishers he gave me an introduction. He may have had it in his mind that by sending me there the troublesome manuscript would be read by Meredith, but he did not tell me so. Anyway, thither I went, left the novel, and some weeks later received a letter from the firm, asking me if I could "meet the gentleman who has read your MS., as he would like to speak to you about it."

Hence it happened that on a wintry afternoon hard upon sixty years ago—to be precise, in January 1869—I was shown into a back room of Messrs. Chapman & Hall's premises in Piccadilly, and found Meredith awaiting me there. I felt that he was an unusual sort of man to discover in a back office in London, though I knew nothing about his personality, Mr. Frederick Chapman, who presented me to him, not having told me his name.

He must have been then about forty years of age, and was quite in the prime of life. At that time he had by no means escaped the shots of reviewers who were out to suppress anything like originality. The criticisms bestowed upon his writings were, indeed, as various probably as those upon any author before or since whose treatment by the press can be remembered. Only six or seven years earlier the *Spectator*'s pronouncement was, "Mr. Meredith may be a very clever man, but he is not a genius," or words to that effect, which provoked Swinburne into writing an expostulatory letter to that paper, the editor, I must add, honestly printing the letter intact, despite his own opinion.[38] And about five years before—though I cannot quite remember the exact sequence of events—the

Saturday Review treated Meredith's volume entitled *Modern Love, and Poems of the English Roadside,* in this fashion:

> His strong thought and quaint expression remind us here and there—though at a considerable interval—of Robert Browning. . . . However, a perusal of Mr. George Meredith's more ambitious productions, and especially of *Modern Love*, leads one reluctantly to the conclusion that he has entirely mistaken his powers, and has utterly marred what might have been a rare and successful volume. . . . It is, as we have said, bad enough that a writer of real ability and skill should allow himself to associate this kind of fustian with poems of worth and merit. But Mr. George Meredith's descent from his "roadside" style of thought and composition to his lyrical mood is, we regret to say, only trifling compared with the change which he undergoes in an elaborate analysis of a loathsome series of phenomena which he is pleased to call "Modern Love," . . . a choice of subject involving a mistake so grave as utterly to disqualify the chooser from achieving any great and worthy result in art.[39]

Thus we see that the two leading weekly reviews of that mid-Victorian decade during which I made his acquaintance were practically in accord about Meredith, and doubtless they were strong enough to put a damper on the circulation of *Modern Love* till years after.

However, as above stated, I was not aware that my adviser at the interview was the man who had undergone these bludgeonings, and was just then emerging from them triumphantly. Unfortunately I made no note of our conversation; in those days people did not usually write down everything as they do now for the concoction of reminiscences, the only words of his that I remember being, "Don't nail your colours to the mast just yet." But I well recall his appearance—a handsome man with hair and beard not at all grey, and wearing a frock coat buttoned at the waist and loose above.

Many years were to elapse before I saw him again—this time as himself, and not "as the gentleman who has read your MS."—when he had been accepted and had become familiar to those who could enjoy his writings as "chaos illuminated by flashes of lightning," full of epigrams of thought and beauty. Our meetings were then continued at irregular intervals that covered a long span of time, till there came a last, of which I can only recall one trifling incident. A literary lady of rank had asked me if I would take her to see him, which she said she was dying to do. I did not wish to take her, but I put the question to him as I was leaving. To his warm invitation to me to come again soon, which I promised to do, he added drily: "But don't bring the lady."

As is so often the case with such intentions, before I had gone again I was confronted one afternoon by a newspaper placard—almost close to the spot in Piccadilly where I had first met him forty years before—announcing in large capitals: "DEATH OF MR. GEORGE MEREDITH."

I am not able to say what influence Meredith may be exercising over the writings of the present generation. Some of his later contemporaries and immediate successors certainly bear marks of his style and outlook, particularly in respect of *The Comic Spirit,* most of them forgetting, as he did not forget (though he often conveniently veiled his perception of it), that, as I think Ruskin remarks, "Comedy is Tragedy if you only look deep enough."[40] The likelihood is that, after some years have passed, what was best in his achievement—at present partly submerged by its other characteristics—will rise still more distinctly to the surface than it has done already. Then he will not only be regarded as a writer who said finest and profoundest things often in a tantalising way, but as one whose work remains as an essential portion of the vast universal volume which enshrines as contributors all those that have adequately recorded their reading of life.

[Meredith's son and the editor of the *Nineteenth Century and After* solicited this article, which Hardy completed only a few months before his death, and which he regarded as "a poor thing." The "reminiscence" appeared posthumously. Hardy met Meredith in March, 1869 (rather than January), and a fuller, more interesting account of that interview may be found in the *Life*, pp. 60-62.]

IV.
Reminiscences and Personal Views

How I Built Myself a House

[Unsigned sketch in *Chambers's Journal,* March 18, 1865, pp. 161-164]

MY wife Sophia, myself, and the beginning of a happy line, formerly lived in the suburbs of London, in the sort of house called a Highly-Desirable Semi-detached Villa. But in reality our residence was the opposite of what we wished it to be. We had no room for our friends when they visited us, and we were obliged to keep our coals out of doors in a heap against the back-wall. If we managed to squeeze a few acquaintances round our table to dinner, there was very great difficulty in serving it; and on such occasions the maid, for want of sideboard room, would take to putting the dishes in the staircase, or on stools and chairs in the passage, so that if anybody else came after we had sat down, he usually went away again, disgusted at seeing the remains of what we had already got through standing in these places, and perhaps the celery waiting in a corner hard by. It was therefore only natural that on wet days, chimney-sweepings, and those cleaning times when chairs may be seen with their legs upwards, a tub blocking a doorway, and yourself walking about edgeways among the things, we called the villa hard names, and that we resolved to escape from it as soon as it would be politic, in a monetary sense, to carry out a notion which had long been in our minds.

This notion was to build a house of our own a little further out of town than where we had hitherto lived. The new residence was to be right and proper in every respect. It was to be of some mysterious size and proportion, which would make us both peculiarly happy ever afterwards—that had always been a settled thing. It was neither to cost too much nor too little, but just enough to fitly inaugurate the new happiness. Its situation was to be in a healthy spot, on a stratum of dry gravel, about ninety feet above the springs. There were to be trees to the north, and a pretty view to the south. It was also to be easily accessible by rail.

Eighteen months ago, a third baby being our latest blessing, we began to put the above-mentioned ideas into practice. As the house itself, rather than its position, is what I wish particularly to speak of, I will not dwell upon the innumerable difficulties that were to be overcome before a suitable spot could be found. Maps marked out in little pink and green oblongs clinging to a winding road, became as familiar to my eyes as my own hand. I learned, too, all about the coloured plans of Land to be Let for Building Purposes, which are exhibited at railway stations and in agents' windows—that sketches of cabbages in rows, or artistically irregular, meant large trees that would afford a cooling shade when they had been planted and had grown up—that patches of blue shewed fishponds and fountains; and that a wide straight road to the edge of the map was the way to the station, a corner of which was occasionally shewn, as if it would come within a convenient distance, disguise the fact as the owners might.

After a considerable time had been spent in these studies, I began to see that some of our intentions in the matter of site must be given up. The trees to the north went first. After a short struggle, they were followed by the ninety feet above the springs. Sophia, with all wifely tenacity, stuck to the pretty view long after I was beaten about the gravel subsoil. In the end, we decided upon a place imagined to be rather convenient, and rather healthy, but possessing no other advantage worth mentioning. I took it on a lease for the established period, ninety-nine years.

We next thought about an architect. A friend of mine, who

sometimes sends a paper on art and science to the magazines, strongly recommended a Mr. Penny, a gentleman whom he considered to have architectural talent of every kind, but if he was a trifle more skilful in any one branch of his profession than in another, it was in designing excellent houses for families of moderate means. I at once proposed to Sophia that we should think over some arrangement of rooms which would be likely to suit us, and then call upon the architect, that he might put our plan into proper shape.

I made my sketch, and my wife made hers. Her drawing and dining rooms were very large, nearly twice the size of mine, though her doors and windows shewed sound judgment. We soon found that there was no such thing as fitting our ideas together, do what we would. When we had come to no conclusion at all, we called at Mr. Penny's office. I began telling him my business, upon which he took a sheet of foolscap, and made numerous imposing notes, with large brackets and dashes to them. Sitting there with him in his office, surrounded by rolls of paper, circles, squares, triangles, compasses, and many other of the inventions which have been sought out by men from time to time, and perceiving that all these were the realities which had been faintly shadowed forth to me by Euclid some years before, it is no wonder that I became a puppet in his hands. He settled everything in a miraculous way. We were told the only possible size we could have the rooms, the only way we should be allowed to go upstairs, and the exact quantity of wine we might order at once, so as to fit the wine-cellar he had in his head. His professional opinions, propelled by his facts, seemed to float into my mind whether I wished to receive them or not. I thought at the time that Sophia, from her silence, was in the same helpless state; but she has since told me it was quite otherwise, and that she was only a little tired.

I had been very anxious all along that the stipulated cost, eighteen hundred pounds, should not be exceeded, and I impressed this again upon Mr. Penny.

"I will give you an approximate estimate for the sort of thing we are thinking of," he said. "Linem." (This was the clerk.)

"Did you speak, sir?"

"Forty-nine by fifty-four by twenty-eight, twice fourteen by thirty-one by eleven, and several small items which we will call one hundred and sixty."

"Eighty-two thousand four hundred,"——

"But eighteen hundred at the very outside," I began, "is what"——

"Feet, my dear sir—feet, cubic feet," said Mr. Penny. "Put it down at sixpence a foot, Linem, remainders not an object."

"Two thousand two hundred pounds." This was too much.

"Well, try it at something less, leaving out all below hundreds, Linem."

"About eighteen hundred and seventy pounds."

"Very satisfactory, in my opinion," said Mr. Penny turning to me. "What do you think?"

"You are so particular, John," interrupted my wife. "I am sure it is exceedingly moderate: elegance and extreme cheapness never do go together."

(It may be here remarked that Sophia never calls me "my dear" before strangers. She considers that, like the ancient practice in besieged cities of throwing loaves over the walls, it really denotes a want rather than an abundance of them within.)

I did not trouble the architect any further, and we rose to leave.

"Be sure you make a nice conservatory, Mr. Penny," said my wife; "something that has character about it. If it could only be in the Chinese style, with beautiful ornaments at the corners, like Mrs. Smith's, only better," she continued, turning to me with a glance in which a broken tenth commandment might have been seen.[1]

"Some sketches shall be forwarded, which I think will suit you," answered Mr. Penny pleasantly, looking as if he had possessed for some years a complete guide to the minds of all people who intended to build.

It is needless to go through the whole history of the plan-making. A builder had been chosen, and the house marked out, when we went down to the place one morning to see how the foundations looked.

It is a strange fact, that a person's new house drawn in outline on the ground where it is to stand, looks ridiculously and inconveniently small. The notion it gives one is, that any portion of one's after-life spent within such boundaries must of necessity be rendered wretched on account of bruises daily received by running against the partitions, doorposts, and fireplaces. In my case, the lines shewing sitting-rooms seemed to denote cells; the kitchen looked as if it might develop into a large box; whilst the study appeared to consist chiefly of a fireplace and a door. We were told that houses always looked so; but Sophia's disgust at the sight of such a diminutive drawing-room was not to be lessened by any scientific reasoning. Six feet longer—four feet then—three it must be, she argued; and the room was accordingly lengthened. I felt rather relieved when at last I got her off the ground, and on the road home.

The building gradually crept upwards, and put forth chimneys. We were standing beside it one day, looking at the men at work on the top, when the builder's foreman came toward us.

"Being your own house, sir, and as we are finishing the last chimney, you would perhaps like to go up," he said.

"I am sure I should much, if I were a man," was my wife's observation to me. "The landscape must appear so lovely from that height."

This remark placed me in something of a dilemma, for it must be confessed that I am not given to climbing. The sight of cliffs, roofs, scaffoldings, and elevated places in general, which have no sides to keep people from slipping off, always causes me to feel how infinitely preferable a position at the bottom is to a position at the top of them. But as my house was by no means lofty, and it was but for once, I said I would go up.

My knees felt a good deal in the way as I ascended the ladder; but that was not as disagreeable as the thrill which passed through me as I followed my guide along two narrow planks, one bending beneath each foot. However, having once started, I kept on, and next climbed another ladder, thin and weak-looking, and not tied at the top. I could not help thinking, as I viewed the horizon between the steps, what a shocking thing it would be if any part should break; and to get rid of the thought, I adopted the device of mentally criticising the leading articles in that morning's *Times;* but as the plan did not answer, I tried to fancy that, though strangely enough it seemed otherwise, I was only four feet from the ground. This was a failure too; and just as I had commenced upon an idea that great quantities of feather-beds were spread below, I reached the top scaffold.

"Rather high," I said to the foreman, trying, but failing to appear unconcerned.

"Well, no," he answered; "nothing to what it is sometimes (I'll just trouble you not to step upon the end of that plank there, as it will turn over); though you may as well fall from here as from the top of the Monument for the matter of life being quite extinct when they pick you up," he continued, looking around at the weather and the crops, as it were.

Then a workman, with a load of bricks, stamped along the boards, and overturned them at my feet, causing me to shake up and down like the little servant-men behind private cabs. I asked, in trepidation, if the bricks were not dangerously heavy, thinking of a newspaper paragraph headed "Frightful Accident from an Overloaded Scaffold."

"Just what I was going to say. Dan has certainly too many there," answered the man. "But it won't break down if we walk without springing, and don't sneeze, though the mortar-boy's hooping-cough was strong enough in my poor brother Jim's case," he continued abstractly, as if he himself possessed several necks, and could afford to break one or two.

My wife was picking daisies a little distance off, apparently in a state of complete indifference as to whether I was on the scaffold, at the foot of it, or in St. George's Hospital; so I roused myself for a descent, and tried the small ladder. I cannot accurately say how I did get down; but during that performance, my body seemed perforated by holes, through which breezes blew in all directions. As I got nearer the earth, they went away. It may be supposed that my wife's notion of the height differed considerably from my own, and she inquired particularly for the landscape, which I had quite forgotten; but the discovery of that fact did not cause me to break a resolution not to trouble my chimneys again.

Beyond a continual anxiety and frequent journeyings along the sides of a triangle, of which the old house, the new house, and the architect's office were the corners, nothing worth mentioning happened till the building was nearly finished. Sophia's ardour in the business, which at the beginning was so intense, had nearly burned itself out, so I was left pretty much to myself in getting over the later difficulties. Amongst them was the question of a porch. I had often been annoyed whilst waiting outside a door on a wet day at being exposed to the wind and rain, and it was my favourite notion that I would have a model porch whenever I should build a house. Thus it was very vexing to recollect, just as the workmen were finishing off, that I had never mentioned the subject to Mr. Penny, and that he had not suggested anything about one to me.

"A porch or no porch is entirely a matter of personal feeling and taste," was his remark, in answer to a complaint from me; "so, of course, I did not put one without its being mentioned. But it happens that in this case it would be an improvement—a feature, in fact. There is this objection, that the roof will close up the window of the little place on the landing; but we may get ventilation by making an opening higher up, if you don't mind a trifling darkness, or rather gloom."

My first thought was that this might tend to reduce myself and family to a state of chronic melancholy; but remembering there were reflectors advertised to throw sunlight into any nook almost, I agreed to the inconvenience, for the sake of the porch, though I found afterwards that the gloom was for all time, the patent reflector, naturally enough, sending its spot of light against the opposite wall, where it was not wanted, and leaving none about the landing, where it was.

In getting a house built for a specified sum by contract with a builder, there is a certain pit-fall into which unwary people are sure to step—this accident is technically termed "getting into extras." It is evident that the only way to get out again without making a town-talk about yourself, is to pay the builder a large sum of money over and above the contract amount—the value of course of the extras. In the present case, I knew very well that the perceptible additions would have to be paid for. Common sense, and Mr. Penny himself, perhaps, should have told me a little more distinctly that I must pay if I said "yes" to questions whether I preferred one window a trifle larger than it was originally intended, another a trifle smaller, second thoughts as to where a doorway should be, and so on. Then came a host of things "not included" —a sink in the scullery, a rain-water tank and a pump, a trap-door into the roof, a scraper, a weather-cock and four letters, ventilators in the nursery, same in the kitchen, all of which worked vigorously enough, but the wrong way; patent remarkable bell-pulls; a royal letters extraordinary kitchen-range, which it would cost exactly threepence three-farthings to keep a fire in for twelve hours, and yet cook any joint in any way, warm up what was left yesterday, boil the vegetables, and do the ironing. But not keeping a strict account of all these expenses, and thinking myself safe in Mr. Penny's hands from any enormous increase, I was astounded to find that the additions altogether came to some hundreds of pounds. I could almost go through the worry of building another house, to shew how carefully I would avoid getting into extras again.

Then they have to be wound up. A surveyor is called in from somewhere, and, by a fiction, his heart's desire is supposed to be that you shall not be overcharged one halfpenny by the builder for the additions. The builder names a certain sum as the value of a portion—say double its worth, the surveyor then names a sum, about half its true value. Then they fight it out by word of mouth, and gradually bringing their valuations nearer and nearer together, at last meet in the middle. All my accounts underwent this operation.

A Families-removing van carried our furniture and effects to the new building without giving us much trouble; but a number of vexing little incidents occurred on our settling down, which I should have felt more deeply had not a sort of Martinmas summer of Sophia's interest in the affair now set in, and lightened them considerably. Smoke was one of our nuisances. On lighting the study-fire, every particle of smoke came curling into the room. In our trouble, we sent for the architect, who immediately asked if we had tried the plan of opening the register to cure it. We had not, but we did so, and the smoke ascended at once. The last thing I remember was Sophia jumping up one night and frightening me out of my senses with the exclamation: "O that builder! Not a single bar of any sort is there to the nursery-windows. John, some day those poor little children will tumble out in their innocence—how should they know better?—and be dashed to pieces. Why *did* you put the nursery on the second floor?" And you may be sure that some bars were put up the very next morning.

[This charming sketch, which has been reprinted several times, was in large measure the natural outgrowth of the mixed lessons in architecture and literature which Hardy provided the younger pupils of Arthur Blomfield (the architect with whom Hardy served his own apprenticeship in London between 1862 and 1867). Hence, it originally had some pedagogical value. It earned Hardy the sum of £3.15*s*., and retains the distinction of being the first published work of his long career. Hardy in later years called it a "*jeu d'esprit*," "a trifle," and "unrepresentative"; but its acceptance by a respectable journal, as he admitted, may well have turned his mind "in the direction of prose." The writing of *The Poor Man and the Lady*, his first novel, took place in 1867, less than two years later, according to the first Mrs. Hardy. The name of the architect, "Mr. Penny," evidently appealed to Hardy, for he used it again in *Under the Greenwood Tree*.]

The Dorsetshire Labourer

[*Longman's Magazine*, July, 1883, pp. 252-269]

It seldom happens that a nickname which affects to portray a class is honestly indicative of the individuals composing that class. The few features distinguishing them from other bodies of men have been seized on and exaggerated, while the incomparably more numerous features common to all humanity have been ignored. In the great world this wild colouring of so-called typical portraits is clearly enough recognised. Nationalities, the aristocracy, the plutocracy, the citizen class, and many others have their allegorical representatives, which are received with due allowance for flights of imagination in the direction of burlesque.

But when the class lies somewhat out of the ken of ordinary society the caricature begins to be taken as truth. Moreover, the original is held to be an actual unit of the multitude signified. He ceases to be an abstract figure and becomes a sample. Thus when we arrive at the farm-labouring community we find it to be seriously personified by the pitiable picture known as Hodge; not only so, but the community is assumed to be a uniform collection of concrete Hodges.

This supposed real but highly conventional Hodge is a degraded being of uncouth manner and aspect, stolid understanding, and snail-like movement. His speech is such a chaotic corruption of regular language that few persons of progressive aims consider it worth while to enquire what views, if any, of life, of nature, or of society are conveyed in these utterances. Hodge hangs his head or looks sheepish when spoken to, and thinks Lunnon[2] a place paved with gold. Misery and fever lurk in his cottage, while, to paraphrase the words of a recent writer on the labouring classes, in his future there are only the workhouse and the grave. He hardly dares to think at all. He has few thoughts of joy, and little hope of rest. His life slopes into a darkness not "quieted by hope."[3]

If one of the many thoughtful persons who hold this view were to go by rail to Dorset, where Hodge in his most unmitigated form is supposed to reside, and seek out a retired district, he might by and by certainly meet a man who, at first contact with an intelligence fresh from the contrasting world of London, would seem to exhibit some of the above-mentioned qualities. The latter items in the list, the mental miseries, the visitor might hardly look for in their fulness, since it would have become perceptible to him as an explorer, and to any but the chamber theorist, that no uneducated community, rich or poor, bond or free, possessing average health and personal liberty, could exist in an unchangeable slough of despond,[4] or that it would for many months if it could. Its members, like the accursed swine,[5] would rush down a steep place and be choked in the waters. He would have learnt that wherever a mode of supporting life is neither noxious nor absolutely inadequate, there springs up happiness, and will spring up happiness, of some sort or other. Indeed, it is among such communities as these that happiness will find her last refuge on earth, since it is among them that a perfect insight into the conditions of existence will be longest postponed.

That in their future there are only the workhouse and the grave is no more and no less true than that in the future of the average well-to-do householder there are only the invalid chair and the brick vault.

Waiving these points, however, the investigator would insist that the man he had encountered exhibited a suspicious blankness of gaze, a great uncouthness and inactivity; and he might truly approach the unintelligible if addressed by a stranger on any but the commonest subject. But suppose that, by some accident, the visitor were obliged to go home with this man, take pot-luck with him and his, as one of the family. For the nonce the very sitting down would seem an undignified performance, and at first, the ideas, the modes, and the surroundings generally, would be puzzling—even impenetrable; or if in a measurable penetrable, would seem to have but little meaning. But living on there for a few days the sojourner would become conscious of a new aspect in the life around him. He would find that, without any objective change whatever, variety had taken the place of monotony; that the man who had brought him home—the typical Hodge, as he conjectured—was somehow not typical of anyone but himself. His host's brothers, uncles, and neighbours, as they became personally known, would appear as different from his host himself as one member of a club, or inhabitant of a city street, from another. As, to the eye of a diver, contrasting colours shine out by degrees from what has originally painted itself of an unrelieved earthy hue, so would shine out the characters, capacities, and interests of these people to him. He would, for one thing, find that the language, instead of being a vile corruption of cultivated speech, was a tongue with grammatical inflection rarely disregarded by his entertainer, though his entertainer's children would occasionally make a sad hash of their talk. Having attended the National School they would mix the printed tongue as taught therein with the unwritten, dying, Wessex English that they had learnt of their parents, the result of this transitional state of theirs being a composite language without rule or harmony.

Six months pass, and our gentleman leaves the cottage, bidding his friends good-bye with genuine regret. The great change in his perception is that Hodge, the dull, unvarying, joyless one, has ceased to exist for him. He has become disintegrated into a number of dissimilar fellow-creatures, men of many minds, infinite in difference; some happy, many serene, a few depressed; some clever, even to genius, some stupid, some wanton, some austere; some mutely Miltonic, some Cromwellian;[6] into men who have private views of each other, as he has of his friends; who applaud or condemn each other; amuse or sadden themselves by the contemplation of each other's foibles or vices; and each of whom walks in his own way the road to dusty death.[7] Dick the carter, Bob the shepherd, and Sam the ploughman, are, it is true, alike in the narrowness of their means and their general open-air life; but they cannot be rolled together again into such a Hodge as he dreamt of, by any possible enchantment. And should time and distance render an abstract being, representing the field labourer, possible again to the mind of the inquirer (a questionable possibility) he will find that the Hodge of current conception no longer sums up the capacities of the class so defined.

The pleasures enjoyed by the Dorset labourer may be far from pleasures of the highest kind desirable for him. They may be pleasures of the wrong shade. And the inevitable glooms of a straitened hard-working life occasionally enwrap him from such pleasures as he has; and in times of special storm and stress the "Complaint of Piers the Ploughman" is still echoed in his heart. But even Piers had his flights of merriment and humour; and ploughmen as a rule do not give sufficient thought to the morrow[8] to be miserable when not in physical pain. Drudgery in the slums and alleys of a city, too long pursued, and accompanied as it too often is by indifferent health, may induce a mood of despondency which is well-nigh permanent; but the same degree of drudgery in the fields results at worst in a mood of painless passivity. A pure atmosphere and a pastoral environment are a very appreciable portion of the sustenance which tends to produce the sound mind and body, and thus much sustenance is, at least, the labourer's birthright.

If it were possible to gauge the average sufferings of classes, the probability is that in Dorsetshire the figure would be lower with the regular farmer's labourers—"workfolk" as they call themselves

—than with the adjoining class, the unattached labourers, approximating to the free labourers of the middle ages, who are to be found in the larger villages and small towns of the county—many of them, no doubt, descendants of the old copyholders[9] who were ousted from their little plots when the system of leasing large farms grew general. They are, what the regular labourer is not, out of sight of patronage; and to be out of sight is to be out of mind when misfortune arises, and pride or sensitiveness leads them to conceal their privations.

The happiness of a class can rarely be estimated aright by philosophers who look down upon that class from the Olympian heights of society. Nothing, for instance, is more common than for some philanthropic lady to burst in upon a family, be struck by the apparent squalor of the scene, and to straightway mark down that household in her note-book as a frightful example of the misery of the labouring classes. There are two distinct probabilities of error in forming any such estimate. The first is that the apparent squalor is no squalor at all. I am credibly informed that the conclusion is nearly always based on *colour*. A cottage in which the walls, the furniture, and the dress of the inmates reflect the brighter rays of the solar spectrum is read by these amiable visitors as a cleanly, happy home while one whose prevailing hue happens to be dingy russet, or a quaint old leather tint, or any of the numerous varieties of mud colour, is thought necessarily the abode of filth and Giant Despair.[10] "I always kip a white apron behind the door to slip on when the gentlefolk knock, for if so be they see a white apron they think ye be clane," said an honest woman one day, whose bedroom floors could have been scraped with as much advantage as a pigeon-loft; but who, by a judicious use of high lights, shone as a pattern of neatness in her patrons' eyes.

There was another woman who had long nourished an unreasoning passion for burnt umber, and at last acquired a pot of the same from a friendly young carpenter. With this pigment she covered every surface in her residence to which paint is usually applied, and having more left, and feeling that to waste it would be a pity as times go, she went on to cover other surfaces till the whole was consumed. Her dress and that of the children were mostly of faded snuff-colour, her natural thrift inducing her to cut up and re-make a quantity of old stuffs that had been her mother's; and to add to the misery the floor of her cottage was of Mayne brick—a material which has the complexion of gravy mottled with cinders. Notwithstanding that the bed-linen and underclothes of this unfortunate woman's family were like the driven snow, and that the insides of her cooking utensils were concave mirrors, she was used with great effect as the frightful example of slovenliness for many years in that neighbourhood.

The second probability arises from the error of supposing that actual slovenliness is always accompanied by unhappiness. If it were so, a windfall of any kind would be utilised in most cases in improving the surroundings. But the money always goes in the acquisition of something new, and not in the removal of what there is already too much of, dirt. And most frequently the grimiest families are not the poorest; nay, paradoxical as it may seem, external neglect in a household implies something above the lowest level of poverty. Copyholders, cottage freeholders, and the like, are as a rule less trim and neat, more muddling in their ways, than the dependent labourer; and yet there is no more comfortable or serene being than the cottager who is sure of his roof. An instance of probable error through inability to see below the surface of things occurred the other day in an article by a lady on the peasant proprietors of Auvergne. She states that she discovered these persons living on an earth floor, mixed up with onions, dirty clothes, and the "indescribable remnants of never stirred rubbish"; while one of the houses had no staircase, the owners of the premises reaching their bedrooms by climbing up a bank, and stepping in at the higher level.[11] This was an inconvenient way of getting upstairs; but we must guard against the inference that because these peasant proprietors are in a slovenly condition, and certain English peasants who are not proprietors live in model cottages copied out of a book by the squire, the latter are so much happier than the former as the dignity of their architecture is greater. It were idle to deny that, other things being equal, the family which dwells in a cleanly and spacious cottage has the probability of a more cheerful existence than a family narrowly housed and draggletailed. It has guarantees for health which the other has not. But it must be remembered that melancholy among the rural poor arises primarily from a sense of incertitude and precariousness of their position. Like Burns's field mouse,[12] they are overawed and timorous lest those who can wrong them should be inclined to exercise their power. When we know that the Damocles' sword[13] of the poor is the fear of being turned out of their houses by the farmer or squire, we may wonder how many scrupulously clean English labourers would not be glad with half-an-acre of the complaint that afflicts these unhappy freeholders of Auvergne.

It is not at all uncommon to find among the workfolk philosophers who recognise, as clearly as Lord Palmerston did, that dirt is only matter in the wrong place. A worthy man holding these wide views had put his clean shirt on a gooseberry bush one Sunday morning, to be aired in the sun, whence it blew off into the mud, and was much soiled. His wife would have got him another, but "No," he said, "the shirt shall wear his week. 'Tis fresh dirt, anyhow, and starch is no more."

On the other hand, true poverty—that is, the actual want of necessaries—is constantly trying to be decent, and one of the clearest signs of deserving poverty is the effort it makes to appear otherwise by scrupulous neatness.

To see the Dorset labourer at his worst and saddest time, he should be viewed when attending a wet hiring-fair at Candlemas, in search of a new master.[14] His natural cheerfulness bravely struggles against the weather and the incertitude; but as the day passes on, and his clothes get wet through, and he is still unhired, there does appear a factitiousness in the smile which, with a self-repressing mannerliness hardly to be found among any other class, he yet has ready when he encounters and talks with friends who have been more fortunate. In youth and manhood, this disappointment occurs but seldom; but at threescore and over, it is frequently the lot of those who have no sons and daughters to fall back upon, or whose children are ingrates, or far away.

Here, at the corner of the street, in this aforesaid wet hiring-fair, stands an old shepherd. He is evidently a lonely man. The battle of life has always been a sharp one with him, for, to begin with, he is a man of small frame. He is now so bowed by hard work and years that, approaching from behind, you can scarcely see his head. He has planted the stem of his crook in the gutter, and rests upon the bow, which is polished to silver brightness by the long friction of his hands. He has quite forgotten where he is and what he has come for, his eyes being bent on the ground. "There's work in en," says one farmer to another, as they look dubiously across; "there's work left in en still; but not so much as I want for my acreage." "You'd get en cheap," says the other. The shepherd does not hear them, and there seem to be passing through his mind pleasant visions of the hiring successes of his prime—when his skill in ovine surgery laid open any farm to him for the asking, and his employer would say uneasily in the early days of February, "You don't mean to leave us this year?"

But the hale and strong have not to wait thus, and having secured places in the morning, the day passes merrily enough with them.

The hiring-fair of recent years presents an appearance unlike that of former times. A glance up the high street of the town on a Candlemas-fair day twenty or thirty years ago revealed a crowd whose general colour was whity-brown flecked with white. Black was almost absent, the few farmers who wore that shade hardly discernible. Now the crowd is as dark as a London crowd. This change is owing to the rage for cloth clothes which possesses the labourers of to-day. Formerly they came in smock-frocks and gaiters, the shepherds with their crooks, the carters with a zone of whipcord round their hats, thatchers with a straw tucked into the brim, and so on. Now, with the exception of the crook in the hands of an occasional old shepherd, there is no mark of speciality in the groups, who might be tailors or undertakers' men, for what they exhibit externally. Out of a group of eight, for example, who talk together in the middle of the road, only one wears corduroy trousers. Two wear cloth pilot-coats and black trousers, two patterned tweed suits with black canvas overalls, the remaining four suits being of faded broadcloth. To a great extent these are their Sunday suits; but the genuine white smock-frock of Russia duck and the whity-brown one of drabbet, are rarely seen now afield, except on the shoulders of old men. Where smocks are worn by the young and middle-aged, they are of blue material. The mechanic's "slop" has also been adopted; but a mangy old cloth coat is preferred; so that often a group of these honest fellows on the arable has the aspect of a body of tramps up to some mischief in the field, rather than its natural tillers at work there.

That peculiarity of the English urban poor (which M. Taine ridicules, and unfavorably contrasts with the taste of the Continental working-people)[15]—their preference for the cast-off clothes of a richer class to a special attire of their own—has, in fact, reached the Dorset farm folk. Like the men, the women are, pictorially, less interesting than they used to be. Instead of the wing bonnet like the tilt of a waggon, cotton gown, bright-hued neckerchief, and strong flat boots and shoes, they (the younger ones at least) wear shabby millinery bonnets and hats with beads and feathers, "material" dresses, and boot-heels almost as foolishly shaped as those of ladies of highest education.

Having "agreed for a place," as it is called, either at the fair, or (occasionally) by private intelligence, or (with growing frequency) by advertisement in the penny local papers, the terms are usually reduced to writing: though formerly a written agreement was unknown, and is now, as a rule, avoided by the farmer if the labourer does not insist upon one. It is signed by both, and a shilling is passed to bind the bargain. The business is then settled, and the man returns to his place of work, to do no more in the matter till Lady Day, Old Style—April 6.[16]

Of all the days in the year, people who love the rural poor of the south-west should pray for a fine day then. Dwellers near the highways of the country are reminded of the anniversary surely enough. They are conscious of a disturbance of their night's rest by noises beginning in the small hours of darkness, and intermittently continuing till daylight—noises as certain to recur on that particular night of the month as the voice of the cuckoo on the third or fourth week of the same. The day of fulfilment has come, and the labourers are on the point of being fetched from the old farm by the carters of the new. For it is always by the waggon and horses of the farmer who requires his services that the hired man is conveyed to his destination; and that this may be accomplished within the day is the reason that the noises begin so soon after midnight. Suppose the distance to be an ordinary one of a dozen or fifteen miles. The carter at the prospective place rises "when Charles's Wain is over the new chimney,"[17] harnesses his team of three horses by lantern light, and proceeds to the present home of his coming comrade. It is the passing of these empty waggons in all directions that is heard breaking the stillness of the hours before dawn. The aim is usually to be at the door of the removing household by six o'clock, when the loading of goods at once begins; and at nine or ten the start to the new home is made. From this hour till one or two in the day, when the other family arrives at the old house, the cottage is empty, and it is only in that short interval that the interior can be in any way cleaned and lime-whitened for the new comers, however dirty it may have become, or whatever sickness may have prevailed among members of the departed family.

Should the migrant himself be a carter there is a slight modification in the arrangement, for carters do not fetch carters, as they fetch shepherds and general hands. In this case the man has to transfer himself. He relinquishes charge of the horses of the old farm in the afternoon of April 5, and starts on foot the same afternoon for the new place. There he makes the acquaintance of the horses which are to be under his care for the ensuing year, and passes the night sometimes on a bundle of clean straw in the stable, for he is as yet a stranger here, and too indifferent to the comforts of a bed on this particular evening to take much trouble to secure one. From this couch he uncurls himself about two o'clock, a.m. (for the distance we have assumed), and, harnessing his new charges, moves off with them to his old home, where, on his arrival, the packing is already advanced by the wife, and loading goes on as before mentioned.

The goods are built up on the waggon to a well-nigh unvarying pattern, which is probably as peculiar to the country labourer as the hexagon to the bee.[18] The dresser, with its finger-marks and domestic evidences thick upon it, stands importantly in front, over the backs of the shaft horses, in its erect and natural position, like some Ark of the Covenant, which must not be handled slightingly or overturned.[19] The hive of bees is slung up to the axle of the waggon, and alongside it the cooking pot or crock, within which are stowed the roots of garden flowers. Barrels are largely used for crockery, and budding gooseberry bushes are suspended by the roots; while on the top of the furniture a circular nest is made of the bed and bedding for the matron and children, who sit there through the journey. If there is no infant in arms, the woman holds the head of the clock, which at any exceptional lurch of the waggon strikes one, in thin tones. The other object of solicitude is the looking-glass, usually held in the lap of the eldest girl. It is emphatically spoken of as *the* looking-glass, there being but one in the house, except possibly a small shaving-glass for the husband. But labouring men are not much dependent upon mirrors for a clean chin. I have seen many men shaving in the chimney corner, looking into the fire; or, in summer, in the garden, with their eyes fixed upon a gooseberry-bush, gazing as steadfastly as if there were a perfect reflection of their image—from which it would seem that the concentrated look of shavers in general was originally demanded rather by the mind than by the eye. On the other hand, I knew a man who used to walk about the room all the time he was engaged in the operation, and how he escaped cutting himself was a marvel. Certain luxurious dandies of the furrow, who could not do without a reflected image of themselves when using the razor, obtained it till quite recently by placing the crown of an old hat outside the window-pane, then confronting it inside the room and falling to—a contrivance which formed a very clear reflection of a face in high light.

The day of removal, if fine, wears an aspect of jollity, and the whole proceeding is a blithe one. A bundle of provisions for the journey is usually hung up at the side of the vehicle, together with a three-pint stone jar of extra strong ale; for it is as impossible to move house without beer as without horses. Roadside inns, too, are patronized, where, during the halt, a mug is seen ascending and descending through the air to and from the feminine portion of the household at the top of the waggon. The drinking at these times is, however, moderate, the beer supplied to travelling labourers being of a preternaturally small brew; as was illustrated by a dialogue which took place on such an occasion quite recently. The liquor was not quite to the taste of the male travellers, and they complained. But the landlady upheld its merits. " 'Tis our own brewing, and there is nothing in it but malt and hops," she said, with rectitude. "Yes, there is," said the traveller. "There's water." "Oh! I forgot the water," the landlady replied. "I'm d——d if you did, mis'ess," replied the man; "for there's hardly anything else in the cup."

Ten or a dozen of these families, with their goods, may be seen halting simultaneously at an out-of-the-way inn, and it is not possible to walk a mile on any of the high roads this day without meeting several. This annual migration from farm to farm is much in excess of what it was formerly. For example, on a particular farm where, a generation ago, not more than one cottage on an average changed occupants yearly, and where the majority remained all their lifetime, the whole number of tenants were changed at Lady Day just past, and this though nearly all of them had been new arrivals on the previous Lady Day. Dorset labourers now look upon an annual removal as the most natural thing in the world, and it becomes with the younger families a pleasant excitement. Change is also a certain sort of education. Many advantages accrue to the labourers from the varied experience it brings, apart from the discovery of the best market for their abilities. They have become shrewder and sharper men of the world, and have learnt how to hold their own with firmness and judgment. Whenever the habitually-removing man comes into contact with one of the old-fashioned stationary sort, who are still to be found, it is impossible not to perceive that the former is much more wide awake than his fellow-worker, astonishing him with stories of the wide world comprised in a twenty-mile radius from their homes.

They are also losing their peculiarities as a class; hence the humorous simplicity which formerly characterised the men and the unsophisticated modesty of the women are rapidly disappearing or lessening, under the constant attrition of lives mildly approximating to those of workers in a manufacturing town. It is the common remark of villagers above the labouring class, who know the latter well as personal acquaintances, that "there are no nice homely workfolk now as there used to be." There may be, and is, some exaggeration in this, but it is only natural that, now different districts of them are shaken together once a year and redistributed, like a shuffled pack of cards, they have ceased to be so local in feeling or manner as formerly, and have entered on the condition of inter-social citizens, "whose city stretches the whole county over." Their brains are less frequently than they once were "as dry as the remainder biscuit after a voyage,"[20] and they vent less often the result of their own observations than what they have heard to be the current ideas of smart chaps in towns. The women have, in many districts, acquired the rollicking air of factory hands. That seclusion and immutability, which was so bad for their pockets, was an unrivalled fosterer of their personal charm in the eyes of those whose experiences had been less limited. But the artistic merit of their old condition is scarcely a reason why they should have continued in it when other communities were marching on so vigorously towards uniformity and mental equality. It is only the old story that progress and picturesqueness do not harmonise. They are losing their individuality, but they are widening the range of their ideas, and gaining in freedom. It is too much to expect them to remain stagnant and old-fashioned for the pleasure of romantic spectators.

But, picturesqueness apart, a result of this increasing nomadic habit of the labourer is naturally a less intimate and kindly relation with the land he tills than existed before enlightenment enabled him to rise above the condition of a serf who lived and died on a particular plot, like a tree. During the centuries of serfdom, of copyholding tenants, and down to twenty or thirty years ago, before the power of unlimited migration had been clearly realised, the husbandman of either class had the interest of long personal association with his farm. The fields were those he had ploughed and sown from boyhood, and it was impossible for him, in such circumstances, to sink altogether the character of natural guardian in that of hireling. Not so very many years ago, the landowner, if he were good for anything, stood as a court of final appeal in cases of the harsh dismissal of a man by the farmer. "I'll go to my lord" was a threat which overbearing farmers respected, for "my lord" had often personally known the labourer long before he knew the labourer's master. But such arbitrament is rarely practicable now. The landlord does not know by sight, if even by name, half the men who preserve his acres from the curse of Eden. They come and go yearly, like birds of passage, nobody thinks whence or whither. This dissociation is favoured by the customary system of letting the cottages with the land, so that, far from having a guarantee of a holding to keep him fixed, the labourer has not even the stability of a landlord's tenant; he is only tenant of a tenant, the latter possibly a new comer, who takes strictly commercial views of his man and cannot afford to waste a penny on sentimental considerations.

Thus, while their pecuniary condition in the prime of life is bettered, and their freedom enlarged, they have lost touch with their environment, and that sense of long local participancy which is one of the pleasures of age. The old *casus conscientiae*[21] of those in power—whether the weak tillage of an enfeebled hand ought not to be put up with in fields which have had the benefit of that hand's strength—arises less frequently now that the strength has often been expended elsewhere. The sojourning existence of the town masses is more and more the existence of the rural masses, with its corresponding benefits and disadvantages. With uncertainty of residence often comes a laxer morality, and more cynical views of the duties of life. Domestic stability is a factor in conduct which nothing else can equal. On the other hand, new varieties of happiness evolve themselves like new varieties of plants, and new charms may have arisen among the classes who have been driven to adopt the remedy of locomotion for the evils of oppression and poverty—charms which compensate in some measure for the lost sense of home.

A practical injury which this wandering entails on the children of the labourers should be mentioned here. In shifting from school to school, their education cannot possibly progress with that regularity which is essential to their getting the best knowledge in the short time available to them. It is the remark of village schoolteachers of experience, that the children of the vagrant workfolk form the mass of those who fail to reach the ordinary standard of knowledge expected of their age. The rural schoolmaster or mistress enters the schoolroom on the morning of the sixth of April, and finds that a whole flock of the brightest young people has suddenly flown away. In a village school which may be taken as a fair average specimen, containing seventy-five scholars,[22] thirty-three vanished thus on the Lady Day of the present year. Some weeks elapse before the new comers drop in, and a longer time passes before they take root in the school, their dazed, unaccustomed mood rendering immediate progress impossible; while the original bright ones have by this time themselves degenerated into the dazed strangers of other districts.

That the labourers of the country are more independent since their awakening to the sense of an outer world cannot be disputed. It was once common enough on inferior farms to hear a farmer, as he sat on horseback amid a field of workers, address them with a contemptuousness which could not have been greatly exceeded in the days when the thralls of Cedric[23] wore their collars of brass. Usually no answer was returned to these tirades; they were received as an accident of the land on which the listeners had happened to be born, calling for no more resentment than the blows of the wind and rain. But now, no longer fearing to avail himself of his privilege of flitting, these acts of contumely have ceased to be regarded as inevitable by the peasant. And while men do not of their own accord leave a farm without a grievance, very little fault-finding is often deemed a sufficient one among the younger and stronger. Such ticklish relations are the natural result of generations of unfairness on one side, and on the other an increase of knowledge, which has been kindled into activity by the exertions of Mr. Joseph Arch.[24]

Nobody who saw and heard Mr. Arch in his early tours through Dorsetshire will ever forget him and the influence his presence exercised over the crowds he drew. He hailed from Shakespeare's county, where the humours of the peasantry have a marked family relationship with those of Dorset men; and it was this touch of nature,[25] as much as his logic, which afforded him such ready access to the minds and hearts of the labourers here. It was impossible to hear and observe the speaker for more than a few minutes without perceiving that he was a humourist—moreover, a man by no means carried away by an idea beyond the bounds of common sense. Like his renowned fellow-dalesman Corin, he virtually confessed that he was never in court,[26] and might, with that eminent shepherd, have truly described himself as a "natural philosopher," who had discovered that "he that wants money, means, and content, is without three good friends."[27]

"Content" may for a moment seem a word not exactly explanatory of Mr. Arch's views; but on the single occasion, several years ago, on which the present writer numbered himself among those who assembled to listen to that agitator, there was a remarkable moderation in his tone, and an exhortation to contentment with a reasonable amelioration, which, to an impartial auditor, went a long way in the argument. His views showed him to be rather the social evolutionist—what M. Émile de Laveleye would call a "Possibilist"[28]— than the anarchic irreconcilable. The picture he drew of a comfortable cottage life as it should be, was so cosy, so well within the grasp of his listeners' imagination, that an old labourer in the crowd held up a coin between his finger and thumb exclaiming, "Here's zixpence towards that, please God!" "Towards what?" said a bystander. "Faith, I don't know that I can spak the name o't, but I know 'tis a good thing," he replied.

The result of the agitation, so far, upon the income of the labourers, has been testified by independent witnesses with a unanimity which leaves no reasonable doubt of its accuracy. It amounts to an average rise of three shillings a week in wages nearly all over the county. The absolute number of added shillings seems small; but the increase is considerable when we remember that it is three shillings on eight or nine—*i.e.,* between thirty and forty per cent. And the reflection is forced upon everyone who thinks of the matter, that if a farmer can afford to pay thirty per cent. more wages in times of agricultural depression than he paid in times of agricultural prosperity, and yet live, and keep a carriage, while the landlord still thrives on the reduced rent which has resulted, the labourer must have been greatly wronged in those prosperous times. That the maximum of wage has been reached for the present is, however, pretty clear; and indeed it should be added that on several farms the labourers have submitted to a slight reduction during the past year, under stress of representations which have appeared reasonable.

It is hardly necessary to observe that the quoted wages never represent the labourer's actual income. Beyond the weekly payment—now standing at eleven or twelve shillings—he invariably receives a lump sum of 2*l.* or 3*l.* for harvest work. A cottage and garden is almost as invariably provided, free of rent, with, sometimes, an extra piece of ground for potatoes in some field near at hand. Fuel, too, is frequently furnished, in the form of wood faggots. At springtime, on good farms, the shepherd receives a shilling for every twin reared, while a carter gets what is called journey-money, that is, a small sum, mostly a shilling, for every journey taken beyond the bounds of the farm. Where all these supplementary trifles are enjoyed together, the weekly wage in no case exceeds eleven shillings at the present time.

The question of enough or not enough often depends less upon the difference of two or three shillings a week in the earnings of the head of a family than upon the nature of his household. With a family of half a dozen children, the eldest of them delicate girls, nothing that he can hope to receive for the labour of his one pair of hands can save him from many hardships during a few years. But with a family of strong boys, of ages from twelve to seventeen or eighteen, he enjoys a season of prosperity. The very manner of the farmer towards him is deferential; for home-living boys, who in many cases can do men's work at half the wages, and without requiring the perquisites of house, garden-land, and so on, are treasures to the employer of agricultural labour. These precious lads are, according to the testimony of several respectable labourers, a more frequent cause of contention between employer and man than any other item in their reckonings. As the boys grow, the father asks for a like growth in their earnings; and disputes arise which frequently end in the proprietor of the valuables taking himself off to a farm where he and his will be better appreciated. The mother of the same goodly row of sons can afford to despise the farmer's request for female labour; she stays genteelly at home, and looks with some superciliousness upon wives who, having no useful children, are obliged to work in the fields like their husbands. A triumphant family of the former class, which recently came under notice, may be instanced. The father and eldest son were paid eleven shillings a week each, the younger son ten shillings, three nearly grown-up daughters four shillings a week each, the mother the same when she chose to go out, and all the women two shillings a week additional at harvest; the men, of course, receiving their additional harvest-money as previously stated, with house, garden, and allotment free of charge. And since *"sine prole"*[29] would not frequently be written of the Dorset labourer if his pedigree were recorded in the local history like that of the other county families, such cases as the above are not uncommon.

Women's labour, too, is highly in request, for a woman who, like a boy, fills the place of a man at half the wages, can be better depended on for steadiness. Thus where a boy is useful in driving a cart or a plough, a woman is invaluable in work which, though somewhat lighter, demands thought. In winter and spring a farmwoman's occupation is often "turnip-hacking"—that is, picking out from the land the stumps of turnips which have been eaten off by the sheep—or feeding the threshing-machine, clearing away straw from the same, and standing on the rick to hand forward the sheaves. In mid-spring and early summer her services are required for weeding wheat and barley (cutting up thistles and other noxious plants with a spud), and clearing weeds from pasture-land in like manner. In later summer her time is entirely engrossed by haymaking—quite a science, though it appears the easiest thing in the world to toss hay about in the sun. The length to which a skilful raker will work and retain command over her rake without moving her feet is dependent largely upon practice, and quite astonishing to the uninitiated.

Haymaking is no sooner over than the women are hurried off to the harvest-field. This is a lively time. The bonus in wages during these few weeks, the cleanliness of the occupation, the heat, the cider and ale, influence to facetiousness and vocal strains. Quite the reverse do these lively women feel in the occupation which may be said to stand, emotionally, at the opposite pole to gathering in corn: that is, threshing it. Not a woman in the county but hates the threshing machine. The dust, the din, the sustained exertion demanded to keep up with the steam tyrant, are distasteful to all women but the coarsest. I am not sure whether, at the present time, women are employed to feed the machine, but some years ago a woman had frequently to stand just above the whizzing wire drum, and feed from morning to night—a performance for which she was quite unfitted, and many were the manœuvres to escape that responsible position. A thin saucer-eyed woman of fifty-five, who had been feeding the machine all day, declared on one occasion that in crossing a field on her way home in the fog after dusk, she was so dizzy from the work as to be unable to find the opposite gate, and there she walked round and round the field, bewildered and terrified, till three o'clock in the morning, before she could get out. The farmer said that the ale had got into her head, but she maintained that it was the spinning of the machine. The point was never clearly settled between them; and the poor woman is now dead and buried.

To be just, however, to the farmers, they do not enforce the letter of the Candlemas agreement in relation to the woman, if she makes any reasonable excuse for breaking it; and indeed, many a nervous farmer is put to flight by a matron who has a tongue with a tang, and who chooses to assert, without giving any reason whatever, that, though she had made fifty agreements, "be cust if she will come out unless she is minded"—possibly terrifying him with accusations of brutality at asking her, when he knows "how she is just now." A farmer of the present essayist's acquaintance, who has a tendency to blush in the presence of beauty, and is in other respects a bashful man for his years, says that when the ladies of his farm are all together in the field, and he is the single one of the male sex present, he would as soon put his head into a hornet's nest as utter a word of complaint, or even a request beyond the commonest.

The changes which are so increasingly discernible in village life by no means originate entirely with the agricultural unrest. A depopulation is going on which in some quarters is truly alarming. Villages used to contain, in addition to the agricultural inhabitants, an interesting and better-informed class, ranking distinctly above those—the blacksmith, the carpenter, the shoemaker, the small higgler, the shopkeeper (whose stock-in-trade consisted of a couple of loaves, a pound of candles, a bottle of brandy-balls and lumps of delight, three or four scrubbing-brushes, and a frying-pan), together with nondescript-workers other than farm-labourers, who had remained in the houses where they were born for no especial reason beyond an instinct of association with the spot. Many of these families had been life-holders, who built at their own expense the cottages they occupied, and as the lives dropped, and the property fell in they would have been glad to remain as weekly or monthly tenants of the owner. But the policy of all but some few philanthropic landowners is to disapprove of these petty tenants who are not in the estate's employ, and to pull down each cottage as it falls in, leaving standing a sufficient number for the use of the farmer's men and no more. The occupants who formed the backbone of the village life have to seek refuge in the boroughs. This process, which is designated by statisticians as "the tendency of the rural population towards the large towns," is really the tendency of water to flow uphill when forced. The poignant regret of those who are thus obliged to forsake the old nest can only be realised by people who have witnessed it—concealed as it often is under a mask of indifference. It is anomalous that landowners who are showing unprecedented activity in the erection of comfortable cottages for their farm labourers, should see no reason for benefiting in the same way these unattached natives of the village who are nobody's care. They might often expostulate in the words addressed to King Henry the Fourth by his fallen subject:—

> Our house, my sovereign liege, little deserves
> The scourge of greatness to be used on it;
> And that same greatness, too, which our own hands
> Have holp to make so portly.[30]

The system is much to be deplored, for every one of these banished people imbibes a sworn enmity to the existing order of things, and not a few of them, far from becoming merely honest Radicals, degenerate into Anarchists, waiters on chance, to whom danger to the State, the town—nay, the street they live in, is a welcomed opportunity.

A reason frequently advanced for dismissing these families from the villages where they have lived for centuries is that it is done in the interests of morality; and it is quite true that some of the "liviers" (as these half-independent villagers used to be called) were not always shining examples of churchgoing, temperance, and quiet walking. But a natural tendency to evil, which develops to unlawful action when excited by contact with others like-minded, would often have remained latent amid the simple isolated experiences of a village life. The cause of morality cannot be served by compelling a population hitherto evenly distributed over the country to concentrate in a few towns, with the inevitable results of overcrowding and want of regular employment. But the question of the Dorset cottager here merges in that of all the houseless and landless poor, and the vast topic of the Rights of Man, to consider which is beyond the scope of a merely descriptive article.

[Purdy's note on the bibliographical mystery surrounding the pamphlet *The Dorset Farm Labourer Past and Present*, supposedly imprinted at Dorchester in 1884, is judiciously phrased: "A tentative conclusion suggests that Hardy authorized the pamphlet, that it was printed but for some reason never circulated, that in later years he forgot the affair completely, and that in 1931 a cache of copies, mostly imperfect, was discovered, from which the copies here described were salvaged" (p. 50). The text of that pamphlet varies slightly from that of the article printed in *Longman's Magazine*; the title has been changed; and the title-page refers to an organization that did not exist in 1884, the "Dorset Agricultural Workers' Union." Five copies exist, and all appeared in 1931 or later.

Important sections of this essay turn up in *Tess of the d'Urbervilles*, where, for example, Angel Clare's residence at Talbothays as "a student of kine" leads him to take a greater delight in the speech and manners of the real rustic behind the newspaper stereotype known as Hodge (pp. 151-153); and where the ceremony of Old Lady-Day, with its picturesque movements from one farm to the next, is described in Chapter LI (Phase the Sixth). "The Egypt of one family was the Land of Promise to the family who saw it from a distance, till by residence there it became in turn their Egypt also; and so they changed and changed" (p. 449).

Hardy's regret for a world that was changing in a way that could never be reversed, although quite marked in this essay, deepened as time passed. By 1895, in his Preface to *The Mayor of Casterbridge*, Hardy found it necessary to explain to his readers who had "not yet arrived at middle age" that "the home Corn Trade, on which so much of the action turns, had an importance that can hardly be realized by those accustomed to the sixpenny loaf of the present date, and to the present indifference of the public to harvest weather." Although he himself had been a small boy when the Corn Laws were repealed (1846), this essay commemorates a way of living and thinking that was truer of Hardy's youth than of 1883.

The remark that the rustics of Dorset were "also losing their peculiarities as a class" might well be compared with the melancholy remarks made in the speech which he delivered when he received the freedom of the Borough of Dorchester (November 16, 1910). Dorchester, in destroying its ancient buildings, was losing its individuality. A London suburb could never have the charm of the old Dorchester, with its now-vanished castle, churches, and medieval mansions. "Old All-Saints was, I believe, demolished because its buttresses projected too far into the pavement. What a reason for destroying a record of 500 years in stone! I knew the architect who did it; a milder-mannered man never scuttled a sacred edifice." Toward the end of his life Hardy knew that he had outlived the Dorchester he loved best, and that his friends lay buried under "a slope of green access" across the railway-bridge and the Weymouth Road (*Life*, pp. 351-353). Dorchester no longer looked like Casterbridge, and he was pleased to be told that his Casterbridge was "a place more Dorchester than Dorchester itself." His art had salvaged something from the past. But there was no question that it had become the past. In 1909, when he sketched a design for the improvement of Holy Trinity Church in Dorchester, he added wistfully, "The church is sadly deficient in external dignity at present, and no stranger in passing realises that such a large church stands there."

At any rate, the interest of "The Dorsetshire Labourer" is much larger than simply its consideration of either agricultural or architectural matters.]

Some Romano-British Relics Found at Max Gate, Dorchester

[Dorchester, 1890; a speech read at the Dorchester Meeting of the Dorset Natural History and Antiquarian Field Club in 1884, but omitted from the volume of that date]

I HAVE been asked to give an account of a few relics of antiquity lately uncovered in digging the foundations of a house at Max Gate, in Fordington Field. But, as the subject of archaeology is one to a great extent foreign to my experience, my sole right to speak upon it at all, in the presence of the professed antiquarians around, lies in the fact that I am one of the only two persons who saw most of the remains *in situ,* just as they were laid bare, and before they were lifted up from their rest of, I suppose, fifteen hundred years. Such brief notes as I have made can be given in a few words. Leaving the town by the south-eastern or Wareham Road we come first, as I need hardly observe, to the site of the presumably great Romano-British cemetery upon Fordington Hill. Proceeding along this road to a further distance of half-a-mile, we reach the spot on which the relics lay. It is about fifty yards back from the roadside, and practically a level, bearing no immediate evidence that the natural contour of the surface has ever been disturbed more deeply than by the plough. But though no barrow or other eminence rises there it should, perhaps, be remarked that about three hundred yards due east from the spot stands the fine and commanding tumulus called Conquer Barrow (the name of which, by the way, seems to be a corruption of some earlier word). On this comparatively level ground we discovered, about three feet below the surface, three human skeletons in separate and distinct graves. Each grave was, as nearly as possible, an ellipse in plan, about 4 ft. long and 2½ ft. wide, cut vertically into the solid chalk. The remains bore marks of careful interment. In two of the graves, and, I believe, in the third, a body lay on its right side, the knees being drawn up to the chest, and the arms extended straight downwards, so that the hands rested against the ankles. Each body was fitted with, one may almost say, perfect accuracy into the oval hole, the crown of the head touching the maiden chalk at one end and the toes at the other, the tight-fitting situation being strongly suggestive of the chicken in the egg shell. The closest examination failed to detect any enclosure for the remains, and the natural inference was that, save their possible cerements, they were deposited bare in the earth. On the head of one of these, between the top of the forehead and the crown, rested a fibula or clasp of bronze and iron, the front having apparently been gilt. That is, I believe, a somewhat unusual position for this kind of fastening, which seemed to have sustained a fillet for the hair.

In the second grave a similar one was found, but as it was taken away without my knowledge I am unable to give its exact position when unearthed. In the third grave nothing of the sort was discovered after a careful search.

In the first grave a bottle of white clay, nearly globular, with a handle, stood close to the breast of the skeleton, the interior being stained as if by some dark liquid. The bottle, unfortunately, fell into fragments on attempting to remove it. In the same cavity, touching the shin bones of the occupant, were two urns of the material known as grey ware, and of a design commonly supposed to be characteristic of Roman work of the third or fourth century. It is somewhat remarkable that beside them was half, and only a half, a third urn, with a filmy substance like black cobweb adhering to the inner surface.

In the second cavity were four urns, standing nearly upright like the others, two being of ordinary size, and two quite small. They stood touching each other, and close to the breast of the skeleton; these, like the former, were empty, except of the chalk which had settled into them by lapse of time; moreover, the unstained white chalk being in immediate contact with the inner surface of the vessels was nearly a proof that nothing solid had originally intervened. In the third grave two other urns of like description were disclosed.

Two yards south from these graves a circular hole in the native chalk was uncovered, measuring about two feet in diameter and five feet deep. At the bottom was a small flagstone; above this was the horn, apparently of a bull, together with teeth and bones of the same animal. The horn was stumpy and curved, altogether much after the modern shorthorn type, and it has been conjectured that the remains were possibly those of the wild ox formerly inhabiting this island. Pieces of a black bituminous substance were mixed in with these, and also numerous flints, forming a packing to the whole. A few pieces of tile, and brick of the thin Roman kind, with some fragments of iridescent glass were also found about the spot.

There was naturally no systematic orientation in the interments—the head in one case being westward, in the other eastward, and in the third, I believe, south-west. It should be mentioned that the surface soil has been cleared away to a distance extending 50 ft. south and west from where these remains were disinterred; but no further graves or cavities have been uncovered —the natural chalk lying level and compact—which seems to signify that the site was no portion of a regular Golgotha,[31] but an isolated resting-place reserved to a family, set, or staff; such outlying tombs having been common along the roadsides near towns in those far-off days—a humble Colonial imitation, possibly, of the system of sepulture along the Appian Way.

In spite of the numerous vestiges that have been discovered from time to time of the Roman city which formerly stood on the site of modern Dorchester, and which are still being unearthed daily by our local Schliemann, one is struck with the fact that little has been done towards piecing together and reconstructing these evidences into an unmutilated whole—such as has been done, for instance, with the evidences of Pompeian life—a whole which should represent Dorchester in particular and not merely the general character of a Roman station in this country—composing a true picture by which the uninformed could mentally realise the ancient scene with some completeness.

It would be a worthy attempt to rehabilitate, on paper, the living Durnovaria[32] of fourteen or fifteen hundred years ago—as it actually appeared to the eyes of the then Dorchester men and women, under the rays of the same morning and evening sun which rises and sets over it now. Standing, for instance, on the elevated ground near where the South-Western Station is at present, or at the top of Slyer's Lane, or at any other commanding point, we may ask what kind of object did Dorchester then form in the summer landscape as viewed from such a point; where stood the large buildings, were they small, how did the roofs group themselves, what were the gardens like, if any, what social character had the streets, what were the customary noises, what sort of exterior was exhibited by these hybrid Romano-British people, apart from the soldiery? Were the passengers up and down the ways few in number, or did they ever form a busy throng such as we now see on a market day? These are merely the curious questions of an outsider to initiated students of the period. When we consider the vagueness of our mental answers to such inquiries as the above, we perceive that much is still left of this fascinating investigation which may well occupy the attention of the Club in future days.

[Hardy's home, named after a toll-gate once tended by a man named Mack (hence, Mack's Gate), was built on a site purchased from the Duchy of Cornwall after some pleasant negotiations with the Duchy's agent, Mr. Herriott. It took twenty months to construct, from October, 1883, to June, 1885, and, as Carl Weber has written in *Hardy of Wessex: His Life and Literary Career* (Hamden, Connecticut, 1962), p. 98, when Hardy moved into his new home, "the native had returned to stay." The speech reprinted here, which Hardy read to members of the Dorset Natural History and Antiquarian Field Club, meeting in Dorchester, communicates the excitement that Hardy experienced over an archaeological discovery. He spoke to Sir Lawrence Alma-Tadema (1836-1912) about them, and the painter, in turn, became "much excited, as he was painting, or about to paint, a picture expressing the art of that date" (*Life*, p. 164). Oddly enough, the text was not printed in the *Proceedings* for seven years, although the *Dorset County Chronicle* reported it on May 15, 1884. The relics described by Hardy are today in the Dorset County Museum. Hardy told William Archer that the heads of "five Roman soldiers, or colonists" had been accidentally decapitated by the workmen who were moving earth in order to construct a drive at Max Gate (*Real Conversations*, London, 1904, p. 38). Details of this essay, and of "Maumbury Ring" (pp. 225-232), are used again, without much change in the wording, in Chapter XI of *The Mayor of Casterbridge*, which describes Henchard's meeting with Susan in the ruins of The Ring at Casterbridge. For a brief description of Hardy's interest in the ancient past, see Evelyn Hardy's *Thomas Hardy: A Critical Biography* (London, 1954), pp. 194-196.]

Shall Stonehenge Go?

[An interview reported in the *Daily Chronicle*, August 24, 1899, p. 3]

YESTERDAY I went down into Wessex to ask Mr. Thomas Hardy what he thought about Stonehenge. That mysterious relic belongs to all England, but is the hub of olden Wessex.

As his friends know, the great novelist of Wessex is most timorous of appearing in any public way, except through his writings. Had I sallied south to lionise Mr. Hardy himself I should, almost surely, have had no luck. It was different to have for my subject Stonehenge—Stonehenge in the market.

"On such an occasion," Mr. Hardy admitted, "one may fairly enough be called upon to speak, only I am not entitled to give any authoritative opinion in regard to Stonehenge and its future, as I have no more knowledge of the monument than is common to, or obtainable by anybody who chooses to visit it."

Well, to say nothing more, Mr. Hardy added to its fame when he wrote that fine scene in *Tess of the d'Urbervilles*. He made special visits to Stonehenge to get his lights for the chapter; and, broadly, to use his own homely phrase, he lives within a bicycle ride of it. At Max Gate, his house on a brow of ground overlooking Dorchester, I found him in cycling costume. It was a badge of the good health which shone in his face and found expression in his alert walk as he led the way across his garden to a summer-house.

"Here," he said, "we have both shade and the open air, two grateful things." The sun burned hot—had done so all the road from London, though indeed you whirled through the pines, by stretches of sea, past beds of red heather, all giving freshness to the day. Wessex was drowsy under the sun's rays, but looking out upon it Mr. Hardy was all eagerness for its unique Stonehenge.

"The intimation that the relic is for sale," he went on, "has quite taken me by surprise. That is the more so because I used to hear that the late Sir Edmund Antrobus would not have a stone turned, even for research, lest the monument might by any chance be injured. I believe that a well-known antiquarian asked him for permission to conduct two days' digging in the vicinity of the relic, but was refused, for the reason I have mentioned."

"Of course, the object of the inquiry would have been to settle, if that were possible, the history of Stonehenge?"

"Just so. There are many theories, but the smallest amount of evidence, yielded by remains which might be discovered, would be most valuable. Now, if the statements which have appeared in the papers are to be accepted, we practically have Stonehenge put up for auction to any bidder at home or abroad. Frankly, I cannot realise the possibility of Stonehenge being carted out of the country, say, by the rich American who is rumored to have made an offer for it. No, no; nobody would think of that in any sort of circumstances."

"You feel that Stonehenge, while it may be private property, is nevertheless, and above all, a national possession?"

"Yes; and here a general statement may be made. A nation like our own ought to have what may be called a final guardianship over any monument or relic which is of value to it as a page of history, even though the hieroglyphics of such monument or relic cannot be deciphered as yet. I don't know how this is to be brought about—it is not for myself to make any suggestion—but that the thing is desirable and right there cannot, I fancy, be two opinions. In fact, we assume that the owner of property on which there happens to be a national relic, is in the larger sense the custodian for the nation of that relic. It is possible to conceive circumstances wherein this might be an individual hardship, only there it is. But to return, it is evident that the case of Stonehenge will not wait, and therefore has to be treated by itself."

"And in your view what should be done?"

"I assume that in all events Stonehenge must remain the wonder of Salisbury Plain, and of England, which it has been for so many centuries—a sacred possession. Why, merely give two thoughts to the bare idea of anything else. Suppose, for argument's sake—nothing more—that you carry the stones to America and re-erect them there. What happens? They lose all interest, because they would not form Stonehenge; and the same with the Stonehenge which was left. The relics being gone the associations of the place would be broken, all the sentiments would have evaporated. Altogether, it would be as if King Solomon had cut the child in two, leaving no child at all."

"We return to the line for the people and for Government?"

"Emphatically Stonehenge should be purchased by the nation, since apparently it is to be sold. More, I welcome the chance, because I have never liked the idea of its being private property. The essential condition is that it should be obtainable for a fair price, such as might be agreed upon after due investigation. Inquiry and arbitration—that is what I would suggest; and until then there is little use in speaking of figures. It seems to me, however, that there is no call for the nation to purchase all the land that has been offered along with Stonehenge. A certain area—shall we put it at 2,000 acres?—must be bought as securing control of the surroundings of the monument. It derives much from its site —the freedom, the feeling of Salisbury Plain—and that element must be safeguarded. It would never do for somebody to get a plot of ground near by, and on it, given the humor, erect a building."

"Your advice is this—that the nation should buy Stonehenge and its immediate surroundings, paying a fair price, and no more, as arbitration might fix."

"That's it, the last word always being the supremacy of the nation. It ought to be possible to name a price which any reasonable man would be willing to accept. What should next be done, or if anything else should be done, is a more difficult question."

"You mean the condition of the ruins and the best means of preserving them?"

"What strikes a visitor accustomed to observe the effect of years and weather on ruins so exposed as these, is that the dilapidation in progress is not so insignificant as may be cursorily imagined. Wet weather and frost are, as all know, the destructive factors in the case, and to the best of my recollection it is on the south-west face of the ruin that decay goes on most rapidly. On this south-west side time nibbles year after year, and it is only owing to the shelter afforded by the south-west walls to the rest of the structure, that any of the columns are erect—all these being the ones to the north-east. Indeed, to those persons who have had the misfortune to be on Salisbury Plain in a piercing downpour, and have noticed, or rather have felt, how the drops pass into them like arrows, it is a matter of wonder that the erection has stood so long."

"Is the wet the chief enemy?"

"Well, you see, apart from the effect of the water on the stones themselves, they are gradually undermined by the trickling down of the rain they intercept, forming pools on the ground, so that the foundation sinks on the wettest side till the stone topples over. There are only three architraves now remaining supported on their proper pillars, and as these decline the architraves will slip off. The only way of protecting the ruin from driving rains which will ultimately abrade and overthrow them, would be by a belt of plantations."

"But the landscape?"

"Yes, against such planting there is to be urged that most people consider the gaunt nakedness of its situation to be a great part of the solemnity and fascination of Stonehenge. It is by no means certain, however, that the country immediately round it was originally bare and open on all sides, and if it were enclosed by a wood approaching no nearer than, say, ten chains to the bank of earth surrounding the stone circle, the force of these disastrous winds and rains would be broken by the trees, and the duration of the ruin lengthened far beyond its possible duration now. As cultivation and agricultural buildings have latterly advanced over the plain, till they are quite near the spot and interfere with its loneliness, the objection to such planting would be less in that the trees would shut out these incongruities."

"You, who know Stonehenge intimately, have perhaps got impressions there which don't occur to the mere visitor?"

"The size of the whole structure is considerably dwarfed to the eye by the openness of the place, as with all such erections, and a strong light detracts from its impressiveness. In the brilliant noonday sunlight, in which most visitors repair thither, and surrounded by bicycles and sandwich papers, the scene is not to my mind attractive, but garish and depressing. In dull, threatening weather, however, and in the dusk of the evening its charm is indescribable. On a day of heavy cloud the sky seems almost to form a natural roof touching the pillars, and colors are revealed on the surfaces of the stones whose presence would not be suspected on a fine day. And if a gale of wind is blowing the strange musical hum emitted by Stonehenge can never be forgotten. To say that on moonlight nights it is at its finest is a commonplace."

"Have you any personal opinion as to the probable origin of Stonehenge?"

"All one can say is that the building was probably erected after the barrow period of interment in these islands, from the fact that one or two barrows seem to have been interfered with in its construction. The problem of the purpose and date of Stonehenge could possibly be narrowed down from its present vagueness, if not settled, by a few days' excavation near the spot. This, if done at all, should be carried out under the strictest supervision. Personally I confess to a liking for the state of dim conjecture in which we stand with regard to its history."

But Mr. Hardy wants no "dim conjecture" as to the future of Stonehenge.

[This interview is signed by "Our Special Correspondent," but Hardy, who wrote a five-page rough draft in the form of an article (now in the Howard Bliss Collection), must be considered the primary author. Purdy (p. 306) notes that Hardy's draft is "here printed almost verbatim." Bits and pieces of the text are reproduced in James Milne's lively sketches, *A Window in Fleet Street* (London, 1931), pp. 253-264, where Milne ("Our Special Correspondent") again casts Hardy's words into the form of an interview at Max Gate. The haunting, powerful final pages of *Tess of the d'Urbervilles* use as their setting the Stonehenge which is "older than the centuries; older than the d'Urbervilles!"]

A Christmas Ghost-Story

[*Daily Chronicle,* December 28, 1899, p. 8]

[To the Editor of the *Daily Chronicle:*]

Sir,—In your interesting leading article of this morning, on Christmas Day, you appear to demur to the character of the soldier's phantom in my few lines entitled "A Christmas Ghost Story" (printed in the *Westminster Gazette* for Dec. 23), as scarcely exhibiting the primary quality of, say, a Dublin Fusilier, which is assumed to be physical courage; the said phantom being plaintive, embittered, and sad at the prevalence of war during a nominal Æra of peace. But surely there is artistic propriety—and, if I may say so, moral and religious propriety—in making him, or it, feel thus, especially in a poem intended for Christmas Day. One's modern fancy of a disembodied spirit—unless intentionally humorous—is that of an entity which has passed into a tenuous, impartial, sexless, fitful form of existence, to which bodily courage is a contradiction in terms. Having no physical frame to defend or sacrifice, how can he show either courage or fear? His views are no longer local; nations are all one to him; his country is not bounded by seas, but is co-extensive with the globe itself, if it does not even include all the inhabited planets of the sky. He has put off the substance, and has put on, in part at any rate, the essence of the Universe.

If we go back to the ancient fancy on this subject, and look into the works of great imaginative writers, they seem to construct their soldier-shades much on the same principle—often with a stronger infusion of emotion, and less of sturdiness. The Homeric ghost of Patroclus was plaintively anxious about his funeral rites, and Virgil's military ghosts—though some of them certainly were cheerful, and eager for war news—were as a body tremulous and pensive.[33] The prophet Samuel, a man of great will and energy when on earth, was "disquieted" and obviously apprehensive when he was raised by the Witch of Endor at the request of Saul.[34] Moreover, the authors of these Latin, Greek, and Hebrew fantasies were ignorant of the teaching of Christmas Day, that which alone moved the humble Natal shade to speak at all.

In Christian times Dante makes the chief Farinata exhibit a fine scornfulness, but even his Caesar, Hector, Æneas, Saladin, and heroes of that stamp, have, if I am not mistaken, an aspect neither sad nor joyful, and only reach the level of serenity.[35] Hamlet's father, impliedly martial in life, was not particularly brave as a spectre. In short, and speaking generally, these creatures of the imagination are uncertain, fleeting, and quivering, like winds, mists, gossamer-webs, and fallen autumn leaves; they are sad, pensive, and frequently feel more or less sorrow for the acts of their corporeal years.

Thus I venture to think that the phantom of a slain soldier, neither British nor Boer, but a composite, typical phantom, may consistently be made to regret on or about Christmas Eve (when even the beasts of the field kneel, according to a tradition of my childhood[36]) the battles of his life and war in general, although he may have shouted in the admirable ardor and pride of his flesh-time, as he is said to have done: "Let us make a name for ourselves!"

Your obedient servant,

Dec. 25. THOMAS HARDY.

[Hardy's letter to the *Daily Chronicle* is part of a curious minor episode in the poet's lifelong attack on war between nations as a means of settling differences. "A Christmas Ghost-Story," an eight-line poem by Hardy which invoked the reader's sense of pity for "a fellow-mortal" who had fallen "South of the Line, inland from far Durban," appeared in the *Westminster Gazette* on December 23, 1899. Hardy imagined the "puzzled phantom" moaning, and asking the question why Christ's Law of Peace had been "ruled to be inept, and set aside." An editorial in the *Daily Chronicle* on Christmas Day took issue with the sentiment of the poem, although admitting that the poem was "a fine conception." The writer concluded, ". . . we fear that soldier is Mr. Hardy's soldier, and not one of the Dublin Fusiliers who cried amidst the storm of bullets at Tugela, 'Let us make a name for ourselves!' " Hardy's response was swift, and was printed in full by the Editor, who appended a brief note to the effect that he could not argue with a poet. "Mr. Hardy's dead soldier," he concluded, "is rightly admitted to the best company of Christmas ghosts, and we feel the pathetic beauty of the conception, whatever we may think of its metaphysics."]

Memories of Church Restoration

[*The Society for the Protection of Ancient Buildings. The General Meeting of the Society; Twenty-Ninth Annual Report of the Committee; and Paper Read by Thomas Hardy, Esq., June, 1906,* London, 1906, pp. 59-80]

A MELANCHOLY reflection may have occurred to many people whose interests have lain in the study of Gothic Architecture. The passion for "restoration" first became vigorously operative, say, three quarters of a century ago; and if all the mediaeval buildings in England had been left as they stood at that date, to incur whatever dilapidations might have befallen them at the hands of time, weather and general neglect, this country would be richer in specimens to-day than it finds itself to be after the expenditure of millions in a nominal preservation during that period.

Active destruction under saving names has been effected upon so gigantic a scale that the incidental protection of structures, or portions of structures, by their being kept wind- and water-proof through such operations counts as nothing in the balance. Its enormous magnitude is realised by few who have not gone personally from parish to parish through a considerable district, and compared existing churches there with records, traditions, and memories of what they formerly were.

But the unhappy fact is nowadays generally admitted, and it would hardly be worth adverting to on this occasion if what is additionally assumed were also true, or approximately true; that we are wiser now, that architects, incumbents, churchwardens and all concerned, are zealous to act conservatively by such few of these buildings as still remain untinkered, that they desire at last to repair as far as is possible the errors of their predecessors, and to do anything but repeat them.

Such an assumption is not borne out by events. As it was in the days of Scott the First and Scott the Second—Sir Walter and Sir Gilbert—so it is at this day on a smaller scale. True it may be that our more intelligent architects now know the better way, and that damage is largely limited to minor buildings and to obscure places. But continue it does, despite the efforts of this Society; nor does it seem ever likely to stop till all tampering with chronicles in stone be forbidden by law and all operations bearing on their repair be permitted only under the eyes of properly qualified inspectors.

At first sight it seems an easy matter to preserve an old building without hurting its character. Let nobody form an opinion on that point who has never had an old building to preserve.

In respect of church conservation, the difficulty we encounter on the threshold, and one which besets us at every turn, is the fact that the building is beheld in two contradictory lights, and required for two incompatible purposes. To the incumbent the church is a workshop or laboratory; to the antiquary it is a relic. To the parish it is a utility; to the outsider a luxury. How unite these incompatibles? A utilitarian machine has naturally to be kept going, so that it may continue to discharge its original functions; an antiquarian specimen has to be preserved without making good even its worst deficiencies. The quaintly carved seat that a touch will damage has to be sat in, the frameless doors with the queer old locks and hinges have to keep out draughts, the bells whose shaking endangers the graceful steeple have to be rung.

If the ruinous church could be enclosed in a crystal palace, covering it to the weathercock from rain and wind, and a new church be built alongside for services (assuming the parish to retain sufficient earnest-mindedness to desire them), the method would be an ideal one. But even a parish entirely composed of opulent members of this Society would be staggered by such an undertaking. No: all that can be done is of the nature of compromise. It is not within the scope of this paper to inquire how such compromises between users and musers may best be carried out, and how supervision, by those who really know, can best be ensured when wear and tear and the attacks of weather make interference unhappily unavoidable. Those who are better acquainted than I am with the possibilities of such cases can write thereon, and have, indeed, already done so for many years past. All that I am able to do is to look back in a contrite spirit at my own brief experience as a church-restorer, and by recalling instances of the drastic treatment we then dealt out with light hearts to the unlucky fanes that fell into our hands, possibly help to prevent its repetition on the few yet left untouched.

The policy of Thorough in these proceedings was always, of course, that in which the old church was boldly pulled down from no genuine necessity, but from a wanton wish to erect a more stylish one. This I pass over in melancholy silence. Akin to it was the case in which a church exhibiting two or three styles was made uniform by removing the features of all but one style, and imitating that throughout in new work. Such devastations need hardly be dwelt on now. Except in the most barbarous recesses of our counties they are past. Their name alone is their condemnation.

The shifting of old windows, and other details irregularly

spaced, and spacing them at exact distances, was an analogous process. The deportation of the original chancel-arch to an obscure nook, and the insertion of a wider new one to throw open the view of the choir, was also a practice much favoured, and is by no means now extinct. In passing through a village less than five years ago the present writer paused a few minutes to look at the church, and on reaching the door heard quarreling within. The voices were discovered to be those of two men—brothers, I regret to state—who after an absence of many years had just returned to their native place to attend their father's funeral. The dispute was as to where the family pew had stood in their younger days. One swore that it was in the north aisle, adducing as proof his positive recollection of studying Sunday after Sunday the zigzag moulding of the arch before his eyes, which now visibly led from that aisle into the north transept. The other was equally positive that the pew had been in the nave. As the altercation grew sharper an explanation of the puzzle occurred to me, and I suggested that the old Norman arch we were looking at might have been the original chancel-arch, banished into the aisle to make room for the straddling new object in its place. Then one of the pair of natives remembered that a report of such a restoration had reached his ears afar, and the family peace was preserved, though not till the other had said, "Then I'm drowned if I'll ever come into the paltry church again, after having such a trick played upon me."

Many puzzling questions are to be explained by these shiftings, and particularly in the case of monuments, whose transposition sometimes led to quaint results. The chancel of a church not a hundred and fifty miles from London has in one corner a vault containing a fashionable actor and his wife, in another corner a vault inclosing the remains of a former venerable vicar, who abjured women, and died a bachelor. The mural tablets, each over its own vault, were taken down at the refurbishing of the building, and refixed reversely, the stone of the theatrical couple over the solitary divine, and that of the latter over the pair from the stage.

Should disinterment ever take place, which is not unlikely nowadays, the excavators will be surprised to find a lady beside the supposed reverend bachelor, and the supposed actor without his wife. As the latter was a comedian he would probably enjoy the situation if he could know it, though the vicar's feelings might be somewhat different.

Such facetious carelessness is not peculiar to our own country. It may be remembered that when Mrs. Shelley wished to exhume her little boy William, who had been buried in the English cemetery at Rome, with the view of placing his body beside his father's ashes, no coffin was found beneath the boy's headstone, and she could not carry out her affectionate wish.[37]

This game of Monumental Puss-in-the-Corner, even when the outcome of no blundering, and where reasons can be pleaded on artistic or other grounds, is, indeed, an unpleasant subject of contemplation by those who maintain the inviolability of records. Instances of such in London churches will occur to everybody. One would like to know if any note has been kept of the original position of Milton's monument in Cripplegate Church, which has been moved more than once, I believe,[38] and if the position of his rifled grave is now known. When I first saw the monument it stood near the east end of the south aisle.

Sherborne Abbey affords an example on a large scale of the banishment of memorials of the dead, to the doubtful advantage of the living. The human interest in an edifice ranks before its architectural interest, however great the latter may be; and to find that the innumerable monuments erected in that long-suffering building are all huddled away into the vestry is, at least from my point of view, a heavy mental payment for the clear nave and aisles. If the inscriptions could be read the harm would perhaps be less, but to read them is impossible without ladders, so that these plaintive records are lost to human notice. Many, perhaps, deserve to be forgotten; but who shall judge?

And unhappily it was oftenest of all the headstones of the

poorer inhabitants—purchased and erected in many cases out of scanty means—that suffered most in these ravages. It is scarcely necessary to particularise among the innumerable instances in which head-stones have been removed from their positions, the churchyard levelled, and the head-stones used for paving the churchyard walks, with the result that the inscriptions have been trodden out in a few years.

Next in harm to the re-designing of old buildings and parts of them came the devastations caused by letting restorations by contract, with a clause in the specification requesting the builder to give a price for "old materials"—the most important of these being the lead of the roofs, which was to be replaced by tiles or slate, and the oak of the pews, pulpit, altar-rails, etc., to be replaced by deal. This terrible custom is, I should suppose, discontinued in these days. Under it the builder was indirectly incited to destroy as much as possible of the old fabric as had intrinsic value, that he might increase the spoil which was to come to him for a fixed deduction from his contract. Brasses have marvellously disappeared at such times, heavy brass chandeliers, marble tablets, oak carving of all sorts, leadwork above all.

But apart from irregularities it was always a principle that anything later than Henry the Eighth was Anathema, and to be cast out. At Wimborne Minister fine Jacobean canopies were removed from Tudor stalls for the offence only of being Jacobean. At an hotel in Cornwall, a tea-garden was, and possibly is still, ornamented with seats constructed of the carved oak from a neighbouring church—no doubt the restorer's honest perquisite. Church relics turned up in unexpected places. I remember once going into the stone-mason's shed of a builder's yard, where, on looking round, I started to see the Creed, the Lord's Prayer, and the Ten Commandments, in gilt letters, staring emphatically from the sides of the shed—"Oh, yes," said the builder, a highly respectable man, "I took 'em as old materials under my contract when I gutted St. Michael and All Angels', and I put 'em here to keep out the weather: they might keep my blackguard hands serious at the same time; but they don't." A lady once was heard to say that she could not go to morning service at a particular church because the parson read certain of the Commandments with such accusatory emphasis: whether these that had become degraded to the condition of old materials were taken down owing to kindred objections one cannot know.

But many such old materials were, naturally, useless when once unfixed. Another churchwright whom I knew in early days was greatly incommoded by the quantity of rubbish that had accumulated during a restoration he had in hand, there being no place in the churchyard to which it could be wheeled. In the middle of the church was the huge vault of an ancient family supposed to be extinct, which had been broken into at one corner by the pickaxe of the restorers, and this vault was found to be a convenient receptacle for the troublesome refuse from the Ages. When a large number of barrow-loads had been tipped through the hole the labourer lifted his eyes to behold a tall figure standing between him and the light. "What are you doing, my man?" said the figure blandly. "A-getting rid of the rubbage, Sir," replied the labourer. "But why do you put it there?" "Because all the folks have died out, so it don't matter what we do with their old bone cellar." "Don't you be too sure about the folks having died out. I am one of that family, and as I am very much alive, and that vault is my freehold, I'll just ask you to take all the rubbish out again." It was said that the speaker had by chance returned from America, where he had made a fortune, in the nick of time to witness this performance, and that the vault was duly cleared and sealed up as he ordered.

The "munificent contributor" to the expense of restoration was often the most fearful instigator of mischief. I may instance the case of a Transition-Norman pier with a group of shafts, the capitals of which showed signs of crushing under the weight of the arches. By taking great care it was found possible to retain the abacus and projecting parts supporting it, sculptured with the vigorous curled leaves of the period, only the diminishing parts, or the bell of each capital, being renewed. The day after the re-opening of the church the lady who had defrayed much of the expense complained to the contractor of his mean treatment of her in leaving half the old capitals when he should have behaved handsomely, and renewed the whole. To oblige her the carver chipped over the surface of the old carving, not only in that pier, but in *all* the piers, and made it look as good as new.

Four parishes, which could not afford to pay a clerk of works to superintend the alterations, suffered badly in these ecclesiastical convulsions. During the years they were raging at their height I journeyed to a distant place to supervise a case, in the enforced absence of an older eye. The careful repair of an interesting early English window had been specified; but it was gone. The contractor, who had met me on the spot, replied genially to my gaze of concern: "Well now, I said to myself when I looked at the old thing, 'I won't stand upon a pound or two: I'll give 'em a new winder now I am about it, and make a good job of it, howsomever.'" A caricature in new stone of the old window had taken its place.

In the same church was an old oak rood-screen of debased perpendicular workmanship, but valuable, the original colouring and gilding, though much faded, still remaining on the cusps and mouldings. The repairs deemed necessary had been duly specified, and I beheld in its place a new screen of deal,[39] varnished to a mirror-like brilliancy. "Well," replied the builder, more genially than ever, "I said to myself, 'Please God, now I am about it, I'll do the thing well, cost what it will!'" "Where's the old screen?" I said, appalled. "Used up to boil the workmen's kittles; though 'a were not much at that!"

The reason for consternation lay in the fact that the bishop—strictly Protestant—had promulgated a decree concerning rood-screens, *viz.,* that though those in existence might be repaired, no new one would be suffered in his diocese. This the builder knew nothing of. What was to be done at the re-opening, when the bishop was to be present, and would notice the forbidden thing? I had to decide there and then, and resolved to trust to chance and see what happened. On the day of the opening we anxiously watched the bishop's approach, and I fancied a lurid glare in his eye as it fell upon the illicit rood-screen. But he walked quite innocently under it without noticing that it was not the original. If he noticed it during the service he was politic enough to say nothing.

I might dwell upon the mistakes of architects as well as of builders if there were time. That architects the most experienced could be cheated to regard an accident of Churchwardenry as high artistic purpose, was revealed to a body of architectural students, of which the present writer was one, when they were taken over Westminster Abbey in a peripatetic lecture by the late Sir Gilbert Scott. He, at the top of a ladder, was bringing to our notice a feature which had, he said, perplexed him for a long time, why the surface of diapered stone before him should suddenly be discontinued at the spot he pointed out, when there was every reason for carrying it on. Possibly the artist had decided that to break the surface was a mistake; possibly he had died; possibly anything; but there the mystery was. "Perhaps it is only plastered over," cried the reedy voice of the youngest pupil in our group. "Well, that's what I never thought of," replied Sir Gilbert, and taking from his pocket a clasp knife which he carried for such purposes, he prodded the plain surface with it. "Yes, it *is* plastered over, and all my theories are wasted," he continued, descending the ladder not without humility.[40]

My knowledge at first hand of the conditions of church-repair at the present moment is very limited. But one or two prevalent abuses have come by accident under my notice. The first concerns the rehanging of church bells. A barbarous practice is, I believe, very general, that of cutting off the cannon of each bell—namely, the loop on the crown by which it has been strapped to the stock—

and restrapping it by means of holes cut through the crown itself. The mutilation is sanctioned on the ground that, by so fixing it, the centre of the bell's gravity is brought nearer to the axis on which it swings, with advantage and ease to the ringing. I do not question the truth of this; but the resources of mechanics are not so exhausted but that the same result may be obtained by leaving the bell unmutilated and increasing the camber[41] of the stock, which, for that matter, might be so great as nearly to reach a right angle. I was recently passing through a churchyard where I saw standing on the grass a peal of bells just taken down from the adjacent tower and subjected to this treatment. A sight more piteous than that presented by these fine bells, standing disfigured in a row in the sunshine, like cropped criminals in the pillory, as it were ashamed of their degradation, I have never witnessed among inanimate things.

Speaking of bells, I should like to ask cursorily why the old sets of chimes have been removed from nearly all our country churches. The midnight wayfarer, in passing along the sleeping village or town, was cheered by the outburst of a stumbling tune, which possessed the added charm of being probably heeded by no ear but his own. Or, when lying awake in sickness, the denizen would catch the same notes, persuading him that all was right with the world. But one may go half across England and hear no chimes at midnight now.

I may here mention a singular incident which occurred in respect of a new peal of bells at a church whose rebuilding I was privy to, which occurred on the opening day many years ago. It being a popular and fashionable occasion, the church was packed with its congregation long before the bells rang out for service. When the ringers seized the ropes, a noise more deafening than thunder resounded from the tower in the ears of the startled sitters. Terrified at the idea that the tower was falling they rushed out at the door, ringers included, into the arms of the astonished bishop and clergy advancing in procession up the churchyard path, some of the ladies being in a fainting state. When calmness was restored by the sight of the tower standing unmoved as usual, it was discovered that the six bells had been placed "in stay"—that is, in an inverted position ready for the ringing, but in the hurry of preparation the clappers had been laid inside though not fastened on, and at the first swing of the bells they had fallen out upon the belfry floor.

After this digression I return to one other abuse of ecclesiastical fabrics, that arising from the fixing of Christmas decorations. The battalion of young ladies to whom the decking with holly and ivy is usually entrusted, seem to be possessed with a fixed idea that nails may be driven not only into old oak and into the joints of the masonry, but into the freestone itself if you only hit hard enough. Many observers must have noticed the mischief wrought by these nails. I lately found a fifteenth century arch to have suffered more damage during the last twenty years from this cause than during the previous five hundred of its existence. The pock-marked surface of many old oak pulpits is entirely the effect of the numberless tin-tacks driven into them for the same purpose.

Such abuses as these, however, are gross, open, palpable,[42] and easy to be checked. Far more subtle and elusive ones await our concluding consideration, which I will rapidly enter on now. Some who have mused upon the safeguarding of our old achitecture must have indulged in a reflection, which at first sight, seems altogether to give away the argument for its material preservation. It is that, abstractedly, there is everything to be said in favour of church renovation—if that really means the honest reproduction of old shapes in substituted materials. And this too, not merely when the old materials are perishing, but when they are only approaching decay.

It is easy to show that the essence and soul of an architectural monument does not lie in the particular blocks of stone or timber that compose it, but in the mere forms to which those materials have been shaped. We discern in a moment that it is in the boundary of a solid—its insubstantial superfices or mould—and not in the solid itself, that its right lies to exist as art. The whole quality of Gothic or other architecture—let it be a cathedral, a spire, a window, or what not—essentially attaches to this, and not to the substantial erection which it appears exclusively to consist in. Those limestones or sandstones have passed into its form; yet it is an idea independent of them—an aesthetic phantom without solidarity, which might just as suitably have chosen millions of other stones from the quarry whereon to display its beauties. Such perfect results of art as the aspect of Salisbury Cathedral from the north-east corner of the Close, the interior of Henry VII.'s Chapel at Westminster, the East Window of Merton Chapel, Oxford, would be no less perfect if at this moment, by the wand of some magician, other similar materials could be conjured into their shapes, and the old substance be made to vanish for ever.

This is, indeed, the actual process of organic nature herself, which is one continuous substitution. She is always discarding the matter, while retaining the form.

Why this reasoning does not hold good for a dead art, why the existence and efforts of this Society are so amply justifiable, lies in two attributes of by-gone Gothic artistry—a material and a spiritual one. The first is uniqueness; such a duplicate as we have been considering can never be executed. No man can make two pieces of matter exactly alike. But not to shelter the argument behind microscopic niceties, or to imagine what approximations might be effected by processes so costly as to be prohibitive, it is found in practice that even such an easily copied shape as, say, a traceried window, does not get truly reproduced. The old form inherits, or has acquired, an indefinable quality—possibly some deviations from exact geometry (curves were often struck by hand in mediaeval work)—which never reappears in the copy, especially in the vast majority of cases where no nice approximation is attempted.

The second, or spiritual attribute which stultifies the would-be reproducer, is perhaps more important still, and is not artistic at all. It lies in human associations. The influence that a building like Lincoln or Winchester exercises on a person of average impressionableness and culture is a compound influence, and though it would be a fanciful attempt to define how many fractions of that compound are aesthetic, and how many associative, there can be no doubt that the latter is more valuable than the former. Some may be of a different opinion, but I think the damage done to this sentiment of association by replacement, by the rupture of continuity, is mainly what makes the enormous loss this country has sustained from its seventy years of church restoration so tragic and deplorable. The protection of an ancient edifice against renewal in fresh materials is, in fact, even more of a social—I may say a humane—duty than an aesthetic one. It is the preservation of memories, history, fellowship, fraternities. Life, after all, is more than art, and that which appealed to us in the (may be) clumsy outlines of some structure which had been looked at and entered by a dozen generations of ancestors outweighs the more subtle recognition, if any, of architectural qualities. The renewed stones at Hereford, Peterborough, Salisbury, St. Albans, Wells, and so many other places, are not the stones that witnessed the scenes in English Chronicle associated with those piles. They are not the stones over whose face the organ notes of centuries "lingered and wandered on as loth to die,"[43] and the fact that they are not, too often results in spreading abroad the feeling I instanced in the anecdote of the two brothers.

Moreover, by a curious irony, the parts of a church that have suffered the most complete obliteration are those of the closest personal relation—the woodwork, especially that of the oak pews of various Georgian dates, with their skilful panellings, of which not a joint had started, and mouldings become so hard as to turn the edge of a knife. The deal benches with which these cunningly mitred and morticed framings have been largely replaced have already, in many cases, fallen into decay.

But not all pewing was of oak, not all stonework and roof timbers were sound, when the renovators of the late century laid hands on them; and this leads back again to the standing practical question of bewildering difficulty which faces the protectors of Ancient Buildings—what is to be done in instances of rapid decay to prevent the entire disappearance of such as yet exists? Shall we allow it to remain untouched for the brief years of its durability, to have the luxury of the original a little while, or sacrifice the rotting original to instal, at least, a reminder of its design? The first impulse of those who are not architects is to keep, ever so little longer, what they can of the very substance itself at all costs to the future. But let us reflect a little. Those designers of the middle ages who are concerned with that original cared nothing for the individual stone or stick—would not even have cared for it had it acquired the history that it now possesses; their minds were centered on the aforesaid form, with, possibly, its colour and endurance, all which qualities it is now rapidly losing. Why, then, should we prize what they neglected, and neglect what they prized?

This is rather a large question for the end of a paper. Out of it arises a conflict between the purely aesthetic sense and the memorial or associative. The artist instinct and the care-taking instinct part company over the disappearing creation. The true architect, who is first of all an artist and not an antiquary, is naturally most influenced by the aesthetic sense, his desire being, like Nature's, to retain, recover, or recreate the idea which has become damaged, without much concern about the associations of the material that idea may have been displayed in. Few occupations are more pleasant than that of endeavouring to re-capture an old design from the elusive hand of annihilation.

Thus if the architect have also an antiquarian bias he is pulled in two directions—in one by his wish to hand on or modify the abstract form, in the other by his reverence for the antiquity of its embodiment.

Architects have been much blamed for their doings in respect of old churches, and no doubt they have much to answer for. Yet one cannot logically blame an architect for being an architect—a chief craftsman, constructor, creator of forms—not their preserver.

If I were practising in that profession I would not, I think, undertake a church restoration in any circumstances. I should reply, if asked to do so, that a retired tinker or riveter of old china, or some "Old Mortality" from the almshouse, would superintend the business better. In short, the opposing tendencies excited in an architect by the distracting situation can find no satisfactory reconciliation. All that he can do is of the nature of compromise.

Fortunately cases of imminent disappearance are not the most numerous of those on which the Society has to pronounce an opinion. The bulk of the work of preservation lies in organising resistance to the enthusiasm for newness in those parishes, priests and churchwardens who regard a church as a sort of villa to be made convenient and fashionable for the occupiers of the moment; who say, give me a wide chancel arch; they are "in" at present; who pull down the west gallery to show the new west window, and pull out old irregular pews to fix mathematically spaced benches for a congregation that never comes.

Those who are sufficiently in touch with these proceedings may be able to formulate some practical and comprehensive rules for the salvation of such few—very few—old churches, diminishing in number every day, as chance to be left intact owing to the heathen apathy of their parson and parishioners in the last century. The happy accident of indifferentism in those worthies has preserved their churches to be a rarity and a delight to pilgrims of the present day. The policy of "masterly inaction"[44]—often the greatest of all policies—was never practised to higher gain than by these, who simply left their historic buildings alone. To do nothing, where to act on little knowledge is a dangerous thing, is to do most and best.

[Hardy, a member of the Society, was unable to be present to read his paper, and Colonel Eustace Balfour, a Scotsman who believed that his country lagged behind England "in appreciating the value of ancient unrestored buildings," read it for him. The members present expressed their pleasure at the emphasis that Hardy had placed upon "the human associations of ancient buildings, for instance, the pews of churches," and a motion of thanks passed with acclamation. The original *Report* included marginal glosses with the text, and summarized the problem (p. 78) as a "Conflict of the Aesthetic sense with the Antiquarian." When the *Cornhill Magazine* reprinted the speech (August, 1906, pp. 184-196), the glosses were eliminated. The glosses, being merely topical, were in all likelihood not contributed by Hardy, and have been omitted from this reprinting.]

Dorset in London

[Speech published in *The Society of Dorset Men in London* (Yearbook, 1908-1909), London, 1908, pp. 3-7]

THE SOCIETY of Dorset Men that has been formed in this City is now in the fifth year of its existence, and though a very little Society at first, it has grown to an astonishing degree during its moderate span of life. Much as it is indebted to its organisers and conductors for the attainment of its present position, there may be something in the character of the people composing it that has helped it on. A distinguished Scotchman, devoted to psychological study, who knows Dorset very well, has been heard to remark that what I may call the cohesive feeling among Dorset county men away from home largely resembles that among his folk north of the Tweed; and if he is right, this would go far to account for the Society's development by leaps and bounds.

No more curious change has come over London social life of late years than the rise of that almost total disregard of provincialism among its constituents and casual sharers which nowadays pervades the City. Incomers are allowed to preserve personal peculiarities that they formerly were compelled to stifle if they wished to be accepted. This is particularly the case in respect of local accents. A hundred or even fifty years ago the object of every sojourner in the Metropolis from the West—as from East, South and North—was to obliterate his local colour, and merge himself in the type Londoner as quickly as possible. But now Town society has become a huge menagerie, and at what are called the best houses visitors hear with no surprise twangs and burrs and idioms from every point of the compass. It is a state of disregard primarily owing, no doubt, to large conceptions of life, coupled with the influx of Americans every season; though it is now extended to the provincial English, Scotch and Irish. In former times an unfamiliar accent was immediately noted as quaint and odd, even a feature of ridicule in novels, memoirs, and conversations of the date. So that while it was the aim of every provincial, from the squire to the rustic, to get rid of his local articulation at the earliest moment, he now seems rather to pride himself on retaining it, being, in fact, virtually encouraged to do so.

Even dialect-words are respected. Within my own recollection it was, for instance, thought comical to hear in London a West of England man speak of the autumn as "the fall." But now that the American multi-millionaire also speaks of the autumn as the fall, the expression is voted poetical—which indeed it is.

Who knows that country accents and words may not some day be affected by smart society men in Town, like the newest pattern in waistcoats, and members of fashionable clubs go down to the shires with week-end tickets, to get a little private practice? Unless, on the other hand, all local differences become obliterated before that date by the amalgamating effect of perpetual intercourse arising out of endless facilities for travel.

After such a surmise as this, it may not be amiss if we indulge in a brief meditative survey of the many points of contact between our County and the City, and consider what the phrase "Dorset in London" may be felt to mean. We may discover it to contain much more than is apparent at first sight.

For clearness, let us imagine ourselves in the situation of a young man just arrived in London from Dorsetshire, with a half-formed intention of making the capital the scene of his life's endeavours, and a probability of finding there his home and his interests, possibly his grave. We will assume that he is in no hurry to make up his mind, is under no great stress of any sort, and can afford time to look about him.

He pauses, maybe, on Waterloo Bridge, and, Dorset people being impressionable, he experiences as he gazes at the picture before him a vivid sense of his own insignificance in it, his isolation and loneliness. He feels himself among strangers and strange things. Being, however, though impressionable, also a very thorough sort of person, he means to explore the town, and leaning against the parapet of the bridge he looks at his new map to find out his bearings. He perceives that, despite the first strangeness, there are three "Dorset" Streets, a "Dorset" Square, and one or two "Dorset" Roads in the wilderness of brick and stone encampments about him. Also a "Weymouth" Street, a "Blandford" Square and Street, a "Bryanston" Square, Place and Street, a "Melcombe" Place, a "Portland" Place and Street, a "Sherborne" Lane, a "Cranbourne" Street, a "Melbury" Road, a "Bridport" Place, and even a "Bindon" Road. Dorset, either directly, or indirectly through family titles, has certainly set its mark on London nomenclature.

The most conspicuous object before his eyes is St. Paul's Cathedral, rising against the sky from Ludgate Hill. St. Paul's is built of Portland stone. St. Paul's seems, on reflection, to be almost as much Dorset as he is. To be sure, it has been standing here in London for more than two hundred years, but it stood, or rather lay, in Dorset probably two hundred thousand years before it got here. How thoroughly metropolitan it is; its façade thrills to the street noises all day long, and has done so for three or four human lifetimes. But through what a stretch of time did it thrill all day and all night in Portland to the tides of the West Bay, particularly when they slammed against the island during south-west gales, and sent reverberations into the very bottom quarry there. As if to prevent his ever forgetting this geological fact, some of the stones that were quarried for the Cathedral still remain, as is well known, in the lonely cove of the isle, squared and ready, though for some unaccountable reason they were never taken away, like their fellows, to adorn the largest city in the world.

Reflecting on this, he looks towards the Strand end of the bridge, where the lengthy front of Somerset House displays itself, one of the most satisfactory specimens of that order of architecture to be found in London, one which would, indeed, be almost perfect if it could be raised to a somewhat higher level. The substance of this dignified building also hails from Portland, and was buried for ages in the heart of the isle.

Once on this trail our imaginary Dorset young man moves along to follow it up. But, as we have not his leisure, we will not accompany him through all his wanderings to look at more specimens of Dorset stonework—the Whitehall Banqueting House, the Horse Guards, nearly all the churches of Wren, the General Post Office, and many other buildings. London, in brief, teems with edifices of importance in stone from Dorsetshire.

Should he still be in the mood, he may look for Dorset at a lower level—in the paving-blocks of the streets; though these, it is true, have largely given way to wood and asphalt of late. Enormous quantities of these blocks came from another corner of the county—Swanage and the Isle of Purbeck.

(I may observe parenthetically in respect of the "Isle" of Portland and the "Isle" of Purbeck, that our Dorset ancestors must have been as imaginative as Mr. Wemmick in the matter of islands,[45] a brook that you can jump over, or a dribble through an isthmus of pebbles, having been enough, in their view, to entitle a merely peninsular spot to that geographical distinction.)

Not to dwell longer on the extent to which material London is a product of Dorsetshire, let us pass on to what may, perhaps, be still more significant instances of the fact that Dorset has made herself at home in no mean degree in the London of the past.

To begin where we began in our examination of the substantive part of the City—St. Paul's. What probably attracts us most of all among the monuments within the building is that erected to Wellington, a design which has been declared, by better judges than I can pretend to be, to show absolute genius in all its features, to be one of the few instances, in a city where so much of the monumental work is bad, that touch real success in this difficult branch of art. And to whose mind does this fine work—the admiration of connoisseurs from all parts of the world—owe its existence? To the mind of a Dorset man, a man of Blandford, Alfred Stevens—one whose exceptional powers as a creator of beautiful forms were unhappily brought to an early end by the living death of paralysis, to England's great artistic loss.[46]

Our meditative friend may now turn aside to the bookstalls of the neighbourhood, and casually take down from a row of volumes a small one in old-fashioned binding. It contains poems which, as he glances through them, he finds to combine airy vivaciousness and humour in a manner altogether charming. There are whimsical epigrams and songs, graceful and witty sketches in rhyme, poetical qualities that, in the words of Austin Dobson, "lift their possessor above every other writer of familiar verse."[47] The author of all this grace and lightness is Matthew Prior, mostly called Matt, a man who was born at Wimborne. Should curiosity lead our enquirer on, he will discover the tomb of this elegant Dorset genius in Westminster Abbey.

The same investigator may on some succeeding day find himself in Bloomsbury, standing in front of the Foundling Hospital. This institution, which he had always imagined to be eminently metropolitan, he learns to have been established by the indefatigable exertions of a native of Lyme Regis, Thomas Coram, whose name has been given to an adjoining street—one of the few instances in London of a street being called after a person who deserves commemoration. Coram made such great personal sacrifices to further his darling project that he ruined himself by his efforts, and was reduced in his old age to dependence upon charitable subscriptions. His portrait by his friend Hogarth may be seen in the Hospital still, and it should make every Dorset native proud that such a philanthropic being first drew breath on our county's shore.[48]

It would take us all night to dwell upon the history of every Dorset man who has added distinction to London in past times. It is only possible to give a name or two more. That of John Morton, Cardinal and Archbishop of Canterbury, occurs to me. He was Dorset born, hailing from Bere Regis, and was at one time a monk at Cerne Abbas. Bacon describes him as a wise and eloquent man, but in nature harsh and haughty; accepted by the King, envied of the nobility, and hated by the people.[49]

Ashley Cooper, the first Earl of Shaftesbury, is another notable of Dorset origin, having been born at Wimborne St. Giles. Conspicuous rather than good, the most prominent figure in the notorious Cabal Ministry, he is the chief character in "Absalom and Achitophel," the immortal satire of Dryden, whose lines about him testify to his extraordinary ability, even while they mercilessly dissect him:—

> A fiery soul which working out its way,
> Fretted the pigmy body to decay.
>
> . . . .
>
> Great wits are, sure, to madness near allied,
> And thin partitions do their bounds divide;
> Else why should he, with wealth and honour blest
> Refuse his age the needful hours of rest?
> Punish a body which he could not please;
> Bankrupt of life, yet prodigal of ease?

Nor must I forget to mention, as a Dorset man who in his time was a force in London and elsewhere, the Cromwellian Colonel Nathaniel Whetham, whose life and times have lately been made the subject of an interesting volume by two of his descendants.[50]

He was born at Burstock, near Broadwindsor, in 1604, and early became an important man of affairs in the City. When the Civil Wars broke out he served in the Parliamentary Army as a Colonel of Dragoons, and afterwards became a member of Parliament, but on the death of Cromwell he retired to private life in the part of England from which he had sprung.

There are many others from the same little shire who have stepped or ridden up to this City by the old road which comes through High Street, Kensington, and on to Hyde Park Corner. One might almost include Henry Fielding, who was a London magistrate as well as a writer of novels and plays. Though not born in the county, he was closely associated with North-East Dorset, having settled for some time at East Stower. That he knew Dorset like a native is apparent to any Dorset man who makes himself familiar with this keen observer's humorous scenes and dialogues. I may also include, since he has a monument in Westminster Abbey, Sir Richard Bingham, of Bingham's Melcombe, whom Strype calls "a brave soldier,"[51] and Fuller describes as being "*fortis et felix* in all his undertakings."[52] He fought in the battles of Candia and Lepanto, and was engaged in all sorts of adventures by land and sea.

Coming away from his monument the visitor may glance across to Lambeth, and, in addition to that of Cardinal-Archbishop Morton aforesaid, recall the name of Archbishop William Wake, who was born at Blandford in 1657.

Having started on this line of inquiry in the assumed character of a newly-arrived young man, members of the Society can pursue it further in their own. It is an inquiry that may stouten their hearts and set them girding their loins anew. It will enable them to realise that certain men of Dorset have done no small things here in the past. Many of them were excellent things, others less excellent—much less; but all of them things which required energy, determination, and self-reliance. I think—at any rate I hope—that the investigation will tend to lessen that feeling of gloomy isolation to which young men of Dorset stock are peculiarly liable in an atmosphere not altogether exhilarating after their own air—say in days of fog, when the south-west county is known to be flooded with sunshine, or in those days of piercing rawness from the eastern marshes, that seems to eat into the bones, a rawness seldom or never felt in their own shire. They may gradually learn to take these inclemencies philosophically, and to decide, as those noted predecessors of theirs, good and bad, probably decided, that their true locality and anchorage is where what they can do best can best be done.

[The annual banquet of the Society took place in May, 1908, but Hardy, worried by his susceptibility "to influenza and throat-trouble if he read or spoke in London himself," requested the Secretary to read his Presidential Address for him. Nevertheless, the speech was not delivered. Hardy thought later that he might have saved himself the trouble of writing it. *Life*, p. 341.]

Maumbury Ring

[*The Times,* October 9, 1908, p. 11]

THE PRESENT month sees the last shovelful filled in, the last sod replaced, of the excavations in the well-known amphitheatre at Dorchester, which have been undertaken at the instance of the Dorset Field and Antiquarian Club and others, for the purpose of ascertaining the history and date of the ruins. The experts have scraped their spades and gone home to meditate on the results of their exploration, pending the resumption of the work next spring. Mr. St. George Gray, of Taunton, has superintended the labour, assisted by Mr. Charles Prideaux, an enthusiastic antiquary of the town, who, with disinterested devotion to discovery, has preferred to spend his annual holiday from his professional duties at the bottom of chalk trenches groping for *fibulae* or arrow-heads in a drizzling rain, to idling it away on any other spot in Europe.

As usual, revelations have been made of an unexpected kind. There was a moment when the blood of us onlookers ran cold, and we shivered a shiver that was not occasioned by our wet feet and dripping clothes. For centuries the town, the county, and England generally, novelists, poets, historians, guide-book writers, and what not, had been freely indulging their imaginations in picturing scenes that, they assumed, must have been enacted within those oval slopes; the feats, the contests, animal exhibitions, even gladiatorial combats, before throngs of people

> Who loved the games men played with death,
> Where death must win[53]

—briefly, the Colosseum programme on a smaller scale. But up were thrown from one corner prehistoric implements, chipped flints, horns, and other remains, and a voice announced that the earthworks were of the palaeolithic or neolithic age, and not Roman at all![54]

This, however, was but a temporary and, it is believed, unnecessary alarm. At other points in the structure, as has been already stated in *The Times,* the level floor of an arena, trodden smooth, and coated with traces of gravel, was discovered with Roman relics and coins on its surface; and at the entrance and in front of the podium, a row of post-holes, apparently for barriers, as square as when they were dug, together with other significant marks, which made it fairly probable that, whatever the place had been before Julius Caesar's landing, it had been used as an amphitheatre at some time during the Roman occupation. The obvious explanation, to those who are not specialists, seems to be that here, as elsewhere, the colonists, to save labour, shaped and adapted to their own use some earthworks already on the spot. This was antecedently likely from the fact that the amphitheatre stands on an elevated site—or, in the enigmatic words of Hutchins, is "artfully set on the top of a plain,"[55]—and that every similar spot in the neighbourhood has a tumulus or tumuli upon it; or had till some were carted away within living memory.

But this is a matter on which the professional investigators will have their conclusive say when funds are forthcoming to enable them to dig further. For some reason they have hitherto left undisturbed the ground about the southern end of the arena, underneath which the *cavea* or vault for animals is traditionally said to be situated, though it is doubtful if any such vault, supposing it ever to have existed, would have been suffered to remain there, stones being valuable in a chalk district. And if it had been built of chalk blocks the frost and rains of centuries would have pulverized them by this time.

While the antiquaries are musing on the puzzling problems that arise from the confusion of dates in the remains, the mere observer who possesses a smattering of local history, and remembers local traditions that have been recounted by people now dead and gone, may walk round the familiar arena, and consider. And he is not, like the archaists, compelled to restrict his thoughts to the early centuries of our era. The sun has gone down behind the avenue on the Roman Via and modern road that adjoins, and the October moon is rising on the south-east behind the parapet, the two terminations of which by the north entrance jut against the sky like knuckles. The place is now in its normal state of repose and silence, save for the occasional bray of a motorist passing along outside in sublime ignorance of amphitheatrical lore, or the clang of shunting at the nearest railway station. The breeze is not strong enough to stir even the grass-bents with which the slopes are covered, and over which the loiterer's footsteps are quite noiseless.

Like all such taciturn presences, Maumbury is less taciturn by night than by day, which simply means that the episodes and incidents associated therewith come back more readily to the mind in nocturnal hours. First, it recalls to us that, if probably Roman, it is a good deal more. Its history under the rule of the Romans would not extend to a longer period than 200 or 300 years, while it has had a history of 1,600 years since they abandoned this island, through which ages it may have been regarded as a handy place for early English council-gatherings, may have been the scene of many an exciting episode in the life of the Western kingdom. But for century after century it keeps iself closely curtained, except at some moments to be mentioned.

The civil wars of Charles I unscreen it a little, and we vaguely learn that it was used by the artillery when the struggle was in this district, and that certain irregularities in its summit were caused then. The next incident that flashes a light over the contours is Sir Christopher Wren's visit a quarter of a century later. Nobody knows what the inhabitants thought to be the origin of its elliptic banks—differing from others in the vicinity by having no trench around them—until the day came when, according to legend, Wren passed up the adjoining highway on his journey to Portland to select stone for St. Paul's Cathedral, and was struck with the sight of the mounds. Possibly he asked some rustic at plough there for information. That all tradition of their use as an amphitheatre had been lost is to be inferred from their popular name, and one can quite understand how readily, as he entered and stood on the summit, a man whose studies had lain so largely in the direction of Roman architecture should have ascribed a Roman origin to the erection. That the offhand guess of a passing architect should have turned out to be true—and it does not at present seem possible to prove the whole construction to be prehistoric—is a remarkable tribute to his insight.[56]

The curtain drops for another 40 years, and then Maumbury was the scene of as sinister an event as any associated with it, because it was a definite event. It is one which darkens its concave to this day. This was the death suffered there on March 21, 1705-06, of a girl who had not yet reached her nineteenth year. Here, at any rate, we touch real flesh and blood, and no longer uncertain visions of possible Romans at their games or barbarians at their sacrifices. The story is a ghastly one, but nevertheless very distinctly a chapter of Maumbury's experiences. This girl was the wife of a grocer in the town, a handsome young woman "of good natural parts," and educated "to a proficiency suitable enough to one of her sex, to which likewise was added dancing." She was tried and condemned for poisoning her husband, a Mr. Thomas Channing, to whom she had been married against her wish by the compulsion of her parents. The present writer has examined more than once a report of her trial, and can find no distinct evidence that the thoughtless, pleasure-loving creature committed the crime, while it contains much to suggest that she did not.[57] Nor is any motive discoverable for such an act. She was allowed to have her former lover or lovers about her by her indulgent and weak-minded husband, who permitted her to go her own ways, give parties, and supplied her with plenty of money. However, at the assizes at the end of July, she was found guilty, after a trial in which the testimony chiefly went to show her careless character before and after marriage. During the three sultry days of its continuance, she, who was soon to become a mother, stood at the bar—then, as may be known, an actual bar of iron—"by reason of which (runs the account) and her much talking, being quite spent, she moved the Court for the liberty of a glass of water." She conducted her own defence with the greatest ability, and was complimented thereupon by Judge Price, who tried her, but did not extend his compliment to a merciful summing-up. Maybe that he, like Pontius Pilate, was influenced by the desire of the townsfolk to wreak vengeance on somebody, right or wrong. When sentence was about to be passed, she pleaded her condition; and execution was postponed. Whilst awaiting the birth of her child in the old damp gaol by the river at the bottom of the town, near the White Hart inn, which stands there still, she was placed in the common room for women prisoners and no bed provided for her, no special payment having been made to her gaoler, Mr. Knapton, for a separate cell. Someone obtained for her the old tilt of a wagon to screen her from surrounding eyes, and under this she was delivered of a son, in December. After her lying-in, she was attacked with an intermittent fever of a violent and lasting kind, which preyed upon her until she was nearly wasted away. In this state, at the next assizes, on the 8th of March following, the unhappy woman, who now said that she longed for death, but still persisted in her innocence, was again brought to the bar, and her execution fixed for the 21st.

On that day two men were hanged before her turn came, and then, "the under-sheriff having taken some refreshment," he proceeded to his biggest and last job with this girl not yet 19, now reduced to a skeleton by the long fever, and already more dead than alive. She was conveyed from the gaol in a cart "by her father's and husband's house," so that the course of the procession must have been up High-East-street as far as the Bow, thence down South-street and up the straight old Roman road to the Ring beside it. "When fixed to the stake she justified her innocence to the very last, and left the world with a courage seldom found in her sex. She being first strangled, the fire was kindled about five in the afternoon, and in the sight of many thousands she was consumed to ashes." There is nothing to show that she was dead before the burning began, and from the use of the word "strangled" and not "hanged," it would seem that she was merely rendered insensible before the fire was lit. An ancestor of the present writer, who witnessed the scene, has handed down the information that "her heart leapt out" during the burning, and other curious details that cannot be printed here. Was man ever "slaughtered by his fellow man" during the Roman or barbarian use of this place of games or of sacrifice in circumstances of greater atrocity?

A melodramatic, though less gruesome, exhibition within the arena was that which occurred at the time of the "No Popery" riots, and was witnessed by this writer when a small child. Highly realistic effigies of the Pope and Cardinal Wiseman were borne in procession from Fordington Hill round the town, followed by a long train of mock priests, monks, and nuns, and preceded by a young man discharging Roman candles, till the same wicked old place was reached, in the centre of which there stood a huge rick of furze, with a gallows above. The figures were slung up, and the fire blazed till they were blown to pieces by fireworks contained within them.

Like its more famous prototype, the Colosseum, this spot of sombre records has also been the scene of Christian worship, but only on one occasion, so far as the writer of these columns is aware, that being the Thanksgiving service for Peace a few years ago. The surplices of the clergy and choristers, as seen against the green grass, the shining brass musical instruments, the enormous chorus of singing voices, formed not the least impressive of the congregated masses that Maumbury Ring has drawn into its midst during its existence of a probable eighteen hundred years in its present shape, and of some possible thousands of years in an earlier form.

So large was the quantity of material thrown up in the course of the excavations at Maumbury Ring, Dorchester, especially from the prehistoric pit which was unexpectedly struck, that the work of filling in, which has been in progress eight days, is likely to last nearly a week longer. The pit, situated at the base of the bank on the north-west side, between the bank and the arena, was found at the conclusion of the excavations to be 30 ft. deep, and Mr. St. George Gray thinks it is the deepest archaeological excavation on record in Britain.[58] Of irregular shape, and apparently excavated in the solid chalk subsoil, it diminished in size from a diameter of about 6 ft. at the mouth to about 18 in. by 15 in. at the bottom. One of three red-deer antler picks recovered from the deposit in the pit was found resting on the solid chalk floor of the bottom, and worked flint was found within a few feet of the bottom. The picks exactly resemble those which Mr. St. George Gray found in the great fosse at Avebury last May. Roman deposits and specimens were found in the upper part of the pit down to the level of the chalk floor of the arena, but not below it.

[Hardy's antiquarianism was not restricted to such objects as the *fibulae*, bones, and smashed vase-fragments that the shovel of an excavator turned up; and Moberly Bell, manager of *The Times*, who asked Hardy to write this essay on an important archeological enterprise at Maumbury Ring, Dorchester, had ample reason to hope that Hardy might emphasize the men and women who, centuries before, had walked the Dorset downs. There is considerably less fancy than fact in the "tale" called "Ancient Earthworks and What Two Enthusiastic Scientists Found Therein" (1885; subsequently titled "A Tryst at an Ancient Earthwork" in *A Changed Man and Other Tales*, 1913). It recounts, with a deep respect for the achievements of long-vanished "Ancient-British" inhabitants, an amateur archeological expedition comparable to the one conducted by members of the Dorset Field and Antiquarian Club. As the story-teller stares at "the abrupt configuration of the bluffs and mounds," he imagines the spears and shields which were placed there "while their owners loosened their sandals and yawned and stretched their arms in the sun." He adds: "Men must have often gone out by those gates in the morning to battle with the Roman legions under Vespasian; some to return no more, bringing with them the noise of their heroic deeds. But not a page, not a stone, has preserved their fame." The Maumbury excavations afforded Hardy the opportunity to review the entire history of Maumbury, and to tell again the story of the execution of Mrs. Thomas Channing, an event of the early eighteenth century which, like that of an execution he personally witnessed while still a schoolboy, stimulated his imagination.]

Which is the Finest View in Dorset?

[Contribution to a symposium in *The Society of Dorset Men in London* (Year-book, 1915-1916), London, 1915, pp. 31-32]

THERE are views entirely inland, and views partly marine; also there are wide views with no near foreground, and bounded views in which the foreground plays a great part. I can only name a few embracing each kind that have struck me at different times as being good:—

1. From High Stoy, near Minterne.
2. From Bulbarrow, near Ansty.

3. From Castle Hill, Shaftesbury.

4. From the Purbeck Ridge above Creech Grange.

5. From Toller Down to Wynyard's Gap, between Maiden Newton and Crewkerne.

6. From the Highway between Dorchester and Bridport, at a point near Litton Cheney.

7. From Pilsdon.

8. From Golden Cap, near Chideock.

I am sorry to be unable to appraise them in order of merit.

[Hardy's list was printed along with several lists compiled by members of the Society. Perhaps not surprisingly, several of the views cited by Hardy turned up on the other lists.]

The Ancient Cottages of England

[*The Preservation of Ancient Cottages,* London, 1927, pp. 13-16]

I CAN with pleasure support the appeal of the Royal Society of Arts for assistance in its plan towards preserving the ancient cottages of England, having been, first and last, familiar with many of these venerable buildings in the West of England, and having also seen many of them vanish under the hands of their owners, through mistaken views not only on their appearance, but on their substantiality and comfort.

They are often as old as the parish church itself, but in consequence of a lack of distinctive architectural features in most, it is difficult to pronounce upon their exact date. In this district they continued to be built in the old style down to about the middle of the last century, when they were ousted by the now ubiquitous brick-and-slate. By the merest chance I was able, when a child, to see the building of what was probably one of the last of these old-fashioned cottages of "mudwall" and thatch. What was called mudwall was really a composition of chalk, clay, and straw—essentially, unbaked brick. This was mixed up into a sort of dough-pudding, close to where the cottage was to be built. The mixing was performed by treading and shovelling—women sometimes being called in to tread—and the straw was added to bind the mass together, a process that had doubtless gone on since the days of Israel in Egypt and earlier.

It was then thrown up by pitch-forks on to the wall, where it was trodden down, to a thickness of about two feet, till a "rise" of about three feet had been reached all round the building. This was left to settle for a day or two, and then another rise was effected, till the whole height to the wall-plate was reached, and then that of the gables, unless the cottage was hipped, or had a "pinion" end, as it was called. When the wall had dried a little the outer face was cut down to a fairly flat surface with a spade, and the wall then plastered outside and in. The thatch projected sufficiently to prevent much rain running down the outer plaster, and even where it did run down the plaster was so hard as to be unaffected, more lime being used than nowadays. The house I speak of is, I believe, still standing, unless replaced by a colder and damper one of brick-and-slate.

I can recall another cottage of the sort, which had been standing nearly 130 years, where the original external plaster is uninjured by weather, though it has been patched here and there; but the thatch has been renewed half a dozen times in the period. Had the thatch been of straw which had passed through a threshing machine in the modern way it would have required renewal twice as many times during the existence of the walls. But formerly the thatching straw was drawn by hand from the ricks before threshing and, being unbruised, lasted twice as long, especially if not trimmed; though the thatcher usually liked to trim his work to make it look neater.

I have never heard of any damp coming through these mud-walls, plastered and lime-whitened on the outside. Yet as everybody, at any rate every builder, knows, even when brick walls are built hollow it is difficult to keep damp out entirely in exposed situations.

Landowners who have built some of these latter express their wonder that the villagers prefer their old dingy hovels (as they are regarded) with rooms only six feet high, and small dormer windows with little lead squares, to the new residences with nine-feet rooms and wide windows with large panes. The explanation is the simple one that in the stroke of country winds a high room is not required for fresh air, sufficient ventilation entering through the door and window, and that the draught through the hollow brick wall makes the new cottages cold in winter.

I would therefore urge owners to let as many as are left of their old cottages remain where they are, and to repair them instead of replacing them with bricks, since, apart from their warmth and dryness, they have almost always great beauty and charm. Not only so, but I would suggest that their construction might be imitated when rebuilding is absolutely necessary.

[Hardy's contribution was printed together with the longer statement by Stanley Baldwin (1867-1947), at the time Prime Minister, in a pamphlet published by the Royal Society of Arts. The brief note was followed by an address to which contributions should be sent.]

Dedication of the New Dorchester Grammar School

[Address delivered by Thomas Hardy in laying the commemoration stone of the New Dorchester Grammar School, July 21, 1927]

I HAVE been asked to execute the formal part of to-day's function, which has now been done, and it is not really necessary that I should add anything to the few words that are accustomed to be used at the laying of dedication stones. But as the circumstances of the present case are somewhat peculiar, I will just enlarge upon them for a minute or two. What I have to say is mainly concerning the Elizabethan philanthropist, Thomas Hardy, who, with some encouragement from the burgesses, endowed and re-built this ancient school after its first humble shape—him whose namesake I have the honour to be, and whose monument stands in the church of St. Peter, visible from this spot.[59] The well-known epitaph inscribed upon his table, unlike many epitaphs, does not, I am inclined to think, exaggerate his virtues, since it was written, not by his relatives or dependents, but by the free burgesses of Dorchester in gratitude for his good action towards the town. This good deed was accomplished in the latter part of the sixteenth century, and the substantial stone building in which it merged eventually, still stands to dignify South-street, as we all know, and hope it may remain there.

But what we know very little about is the personality of this first recorded Thomas Hardy of the Froom Valley here at our back, though his work abides. He was without doubt of the family of the Hardys who landed in this county from Jersey in the fifteenth century, acquired small estates along the river upwards towards its source, and whose descendants have mostly remained hereabouts ever since, the Christian name of Thomas having been especially affected by them. He died in 1599, and it is curious to think that though he must have had a modern love of learning not common in a remote county in those days, Shakespeare's name could hardly have been known to him, or at the most but vaguely as that of a certain ingenious Mr. Shakespeare who amused the London playgoers; and that he died before Milton was born.

In Carlylean phraseology, what manner of man he was when he walked this earth, we can but guess, or what he looked like, what he said and did in his lighter moments, and at what age he died.[60] But we may shrewdly conceive that he was a far-sighted man, and would not be much surprised, if he were to revisit the daylight, to find that his building had been outgrown, and no longer supplied the needs of the present inhabitants for the due education of their sons. His next feeling might be to rejoice in the development of what was possibly an original design of his own, and to wish the reconstruction every success.

We living ones all do that, and nobody more than I, my retirement from the Governing body having been necessitated by old age only. Certainly everything promises well. The site can hardly be surpassed in England for health, with its open surroundings, elevated and bracing situation, and dry subsoil, while it is near enough to the sea to get very distinct whiffs of marine air. Moreover, it is not so far from the centre of the borough as to be beyond the walking powers of the smallest boy. It has a capable headmaster, holding every modern idea on education within the limits of good judgment, and assistant masters well equipped for their labours, which are not sinecures in these days.

I will conclude by thanking the Governors and other friends for their kind thought in asking me to undertake this formal initiation of the new building, which marks such an interesting stage in the history of the Dorchester Grammar School.

[Early in 1909 Hardy became a Representative Governor of the Dorchester Grammar School. This position, an appointment made by the Dorset Court of Quarter Sessions, Hardy was pleased to accept because his namesake, Thomas Hardy of Melcombe Regis (died 1599), had founded the school. Hardy later became a full Governor, and served in this post until 1925. Less than two years later, in his last public appearance, he delivered this brief address. The cold, crisp windiness of the July day was "by no means a suitable day for a man of Hardy's advanced years" (*Life*, p. 437), but Hardy spoke clearly and resonantly. At the conclusion of the talk, he was "very tired." Purdy gives bibliographical details of an unauthorized edition of the address, printed under the title "The Two Hardys" (p. 249). Hardy's amiable comments on "the walking powers of the smallest boy" refer not only to the site (which he might see from the front gate of his house), but to the fact that he himself had had to walk to school in Dorchester ("Mr. Last's Academy for Young Gentlemen") from his home in Upper Bockhampton, in the parish of Stinsford, a distance of three miles.]

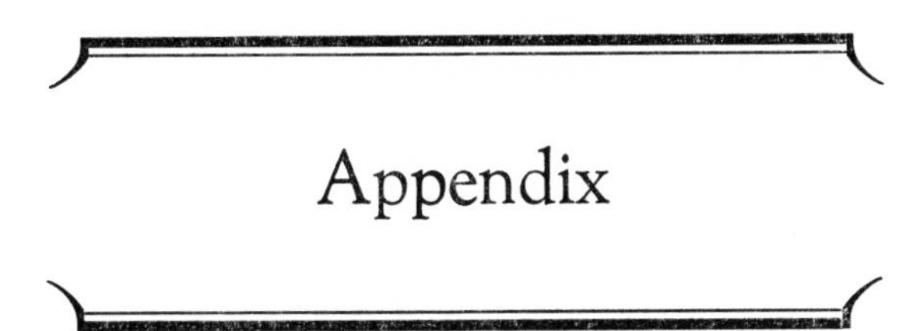

Appendix

Minor Writings

The items for which bibliographical listings and brief comments or quotations are provided here have not been reprinted, because of their brevity and limited inherent interest or because they overlap the selections which have been included. They are described in Part III of Richard Little Purdy's *Thomas Hardy: A Bibliographical Study* (London, 1954), pp. 289-325, with appropriate notations. I have rearranged them in terms of the major categories of this collection, and added a section, "Friends and Family." Uncollected poems and short stories are not included.

On Literary Matters

1. "Thomas Hardy," *Literary World* (Boston) (August 1, 1878), p. 46. Printed anonymously; of doubtful attribution. The author notes that the passion for church "restoration" led to Hardy's specializing in ecclesiastical architecture. ". . . under color of restoring and renovating for a good cause [Hardy] was instrumental in obliterating many valuable records in stone of the history of quiet rural parishes, much to his regret in later years." The sketch takes Hardy's life down to the publication of *The Return of the Native* in the pages of *Harper's Monthly*.

2. *The Squire* at the St. James's Theatre, *Daily News* (January 2, 1882), p. 2. Hardy resented the resemblances between Pinero's play and a dramatization of his novel, *Far from the Madding Crowd*, which he had prepared in collaboration with Comyns Carr, the art critic, before submitting it to the managers of the St. James's Theatre. Assurance that his own play would soon be produced was followed by rejection; then silence; and finally the production of *The Squire*. "My

drama is now rendered useless," Hardy concluded his letter, "for it is obviously not worth while for a manager to risk producing a piece if the whole gist of it is already to be seen by the public at another theatre."

3. "*The Squire* at the St. James's Theatre," *The Times* (January 2, 1882), p. 6. A second strong protest at what Hardy considered the "quite unjustifiable" actions of the management of the St. James's Theatre. The managers replied in both the *Daily News* and *The Times*, on January 3.

4. "English Authors and American Publishers," *Athenaeum* (December 23, 1882), pp. 848-849. Hardy, along with several other authors, rose to the defense of Harper & Brothers, which had been accused of unfair practices. He referred to his own happy experience in supplying a novel for a specified sum of money; when the novel turned out to be one-third longer than expected, he received a "proportionate third above the price agreed on. It is said that other publishers delight in paying an author more than he expects to get, but I believe the excellent practice is not yet universal."

5. "*Two on a Tower*," *St. James's Gazette* (January 19, 1883), p. 14. Hardy denied that the bishop in his novel was "a studied insult to the Church," insisted that "an episcopal position" was essential for the character, added that "one of the most honourable characters in the book, and the hero's friend, is a clergyman," and concluded with the statement that his heroine's "most tender qualities" were woven in with her religious feelings.

6. "A British '*Théatre Libre*,'" *Weekly Comedy* (November 30, 1889), p. 7. Like several others who had been asked how an English "free stage" was to be managed, Hardy chose the occasion to censure the modern theatre as artifice and accessories rather than art. "Nowadays, persons who were devoted to the drama in their youth find as they approach middle age that they cannot by any possibility feel deeply interested in the regulation stage-presentation of life, their impression usually being: First act—it may be so; second act—it surely is not so; third—it cannot be so; fourth—ridiculous to make it so; fifth—it will do for the children." Hardy's dislike of "intolerable masses of scenery and costume" led him to propose something very similar to theatre-in-the-round. Cf. "Why I Don't Write Plays," p. 139.

7. "The Art of Authorship," in *The Art of Authorship*, ed. George Bainton (London, 1890), pp. 320-321. Hardy's contribution to this

symposium denies the value of "studied rules," emphasizes his belief that "a writer's style is according to his temperament," and declares that content (something "to say which is of value") must precede style.

8. "The Merry Wives of Wessex," *Pall Mall Gazette* (July 10, 1891), p. 2. This response to an unfavorable review of *A Group of Noble Dames* concentrated on what Hardy considered undue squeamishness about "the mere tale of a mutilated piece of marble," and conjectured that the reviewer "must be a highly sensitive and beautiful young lady, who herself nourishes an unhappy attachment to a gentleman in some such circumstances as those of the story 'Barbara of the House of Grebe.'" Printed immediately after Hardy's letter came a rejoinder from "Your Sensitive and Beautiful Reviewer," admitting her sex but denying Hardy's "soft impeachment": "I am *not* in love with a mutilated Antinous, either in flesh or in marble; and if my husband, the Earl, were to act like Lord Uplandtowers, I should not bear him eleven idiot children in eight years, but should appeal to Mr. Justice Butt to relieve me from the duty of continuing his noble line." Hardy did not continue the debate.

9. "Mr. Thomas Hardy at Max Gate, Dorchester," *Cassell's Saturday Journal* (June 25, 1892), pp. 944-946. Probably not by Hardy, although Purdy notes that the editor wrote to the author on February 3, 1892, and referred to it as "your article on yourself." One comment by Hardy, quoted directly by "the representative of the *Saturday Journal*," emphasizes the importance of local color: "And I always like to have a real place in my mind for every scene in a novel. Before writing about it I generally go and see each place; no, one can't do with a picture of it."

10. The American Edition of *Tess, Critic* (New York) (September 10, 1892), p. 134. Hardy denied that omission of the Preface in the revised and enlarged American edition of *Tess of the d'Urbervilles* (1892) constituted suppression. ". . . such omission was not intentional on my part, but arose from circumstances of publication over which I had no control at the time."

11. "A Question of Priority," *Westminster Gazette* (May 10, 1893), p. 2. William Archer, in a letter to the *Westminster Gazette*, had raised the possibility that a baptism scene in *Alan's Wife*, a play of some notoriety in 1893, had preceded a comparable scene in *Tess of the d'Urbervilles*. Hardy pointed out that the Swedish magazine in which the story serving as foundation for the play had appeared in January,

1891, and that the chapters of *Tess* being discussed had been at the printers as early as September, 1889.

12. "The Hon. Mrs. Henniker," *Illustrated London News* (August 18, 1894), p. 195. Unsigned. The fullest treatment of Hardy's relationship to this remarkable woman—Florence Ellen Hungerford Henniker, *née* Milnes—may be found in Purdy, Appendix IV, "A Note on the Hon. Mrs. Arthur Henniker," pp. 342-348; references in the *Life* are discreet and relatively uninformative. This sketch accompanied her portrait, and praised "her note of individuality, her own personal and peculiar way of looking at life. . . ."

13. "Hearts Insurgent," *Daily Chronicle* (September 25, 1895), p. 3. Hardy denied that "Hearts Insurgent," later to be reprinted as *Jude the Obscure*, was being bowdlerized during its serialization in *Harper's New Monthly Magazine*. He made a sharp distinction between the "middle-aged readers" for whom he had originally written the novel and "those young ladies for whose innocence we are all solicitous" and who, presumably, formed the primary audience of the magazine. The former audience should wait for publication of the book, "a month hence, under a new title."

14. *The Trumpet-Major, Critic* (New York) (July 4, 1896), p. 8. A charge of plagiarism, raised first in the *Critic*, January 28, 1882, had forced Hardy into several denials, including one in the Preface to the Osgood, McIlvaine reprinting of *The Trumpet-Major*. The matter is treated by Carl Weber in his biography, *Hardy of Wessex: His Life and Literary Career* (Hamden, Connecticut, 1962), pp. 85-86, 92-94, 260. Hardy refers to it here as "a trivial matter," and "a few sentences in a novel written twenty years ago," but the whole controversy was unpleasant.

15. "*Tess* at the Coronet Theatre," *The Times* (February 21, 1900), p. 4. Hardy's denial of authorization for H. A. Kennedy's dramatization of his novel: ". . . I am ignorant of the form it has taken, except in so far as I gather from the newspapers." The play was not favorably reviewed.

16. "Edmund Kean in Dorchester," *Dorset County Chronicle* (Dorchester) (July 10, 1902), p. 11. Two earlier letters (May 29 and June 12, 1902) have been reprinted in Hardy's *Life*, pp. 316-317. Hardy, writing under the pseudonym "History," was certain that Edmund Kean, during his appearance in Dorchester in 1813, did not act in the New Theatre in North-square, for that theatre did not open until 1828.

17. "Serial Rights in Stories," *Athenaeum* (May 16, 1903), p. 626. Another of Hardy's objections to unethical publishing practices, this time the reviving of an old story ("Benighted Travellers") for reprinting as a "new story" in the *Sphere* for May 2nd and 9th, 1903.

18. "*Far from the Madding Crowd*: A Correction," *Spectator* (April 29, 1905), p. 638. Edmund Downey's book, *Twenty Years Ago*, had been reviewed in the *Spectator*, where a statement quoted from the book, to the effect that *Far from the Madding Crowd* had been offered to William Tinsley and then withdrawn because he would not "give a rise" on another publisher's price for it, provoked a letter of denial from Hardy. "The story was produced in response to a request from the late Sir Leslie Stephen, the editor, for a novel for the *Cornhill*, and the opening chapters were sent up to him from the country, and accepted—those to follow being taken on trust—without any negotiation elsewhere. . . ."

19. Henry Mills Alden, *Harper's Weekly* (New York) (December 15, 1906), p. 1814. Alden, editor of *Harper's Magazine*, was the subject of various tributes, including this brief statement by Hardy, on the occasion of his 70th birthday.

20. George Meredith, *Daily News* (February 12, 1908), p. 4. Hardy's friendship with Meredith, which had lasted for some forty years, is briefly attested to on the occasion of the latter's eightieth birthday.

21. The Censorship of Plays, *The Times* (August 13, 1909), p. 4. John Galsworthy had asked Hardy to write a letter which might be used as part of the evidence presented before Lord Plymouth, and a Joint Committee of Lords and Commons, to show that irresponsible censorship deterred men of letters from writing for the stage. Hardy wrote that "something or other—which probably is consciousness of the Censor" operated to prevent men of letters, "who have other channels for communicating with the public, from writing for the stage," and cited an example from his own experience: his abandonment of a scheme for transforming a ballad, "A Sunday Morning Tragedy," into a play because it might never get on the boards.

22. "Mr. Hardy's Poems," *Daily News* (December 15, 1909), p. 6. Hardy objected to a review of *Time's Laughingstocks, and Other Verses* in the *Daily News* (December 13) which not only omitted the second part of the title, but stressed the "disillusion and despair" of the poems. "If this were true it might be no bad antidote to the grinning

optimism nowadays affected in some quarters; but I beg leave to observe that of the ninety odd poems the volume contains, more than half do not answer to the description at all. . . ."

23. "Mr. Hardy's Swinburne Poem," *Daily Mail* (April 5, 1910), p. 5. Unsigned. Hardy explained an allusion to Bonchurch graveyard, on the Isle of Wight, contained in his poem, "The Singer Asleep," written in commemoration of Swinburne and printed in the *English Review*. Cf. Hardy's strong praise for Swinburne in his *Life*, pp. 344-345.

24. A Correction of Misstatements, *Athenaeum* (October 28, 1911), pp. 523-524. Unsigned. Hardy's denial of a story in the *Daily News* of October 23 with its "wholly fictitious" details about his writing and collaborating for the theatre, and its inaccurate remarks about the manner of his disposition of his manuscripts. Hardy added parenthetically that "nearly half" of his manuscripts had been lost.

25. "Charles Dickens: Some Personal Recollections and Opinions," *Bookman* (February, 1912), p. 247. For this Dickens Centenary Number, Hardy, like the other contributors, was asked several questions about the influence which Dickens had exerted over his imagination, his opinion as to which was the greatest of Dickens's books, etc. Hardy answered that, although he had attended readings by Dickens at the Hanover Square Rooms, he did not know Dickens personally, and his literary efforts did not owe much to his influence. "No doubt they owed something unconsciously, since everybody's did in those days."

26. William Dean Howells, *Harper's Weekly* (New York) (March 9, 1912), Part II, p. 33. Howells, now seventy-five, must have been pleased to receive this tribute (among many others printed in a special supplement): "I do not remember that a single word except of praise—always well deserved—has ever been uttered on your many labors in the field of American literature. You have, too, always beheld the truth that poetry is the heart of literature, and done much to counteract the suicidal opinion held, I am told, by young contemporary journalists, that the times have so advanced as to render poetry nowadays a negligible tract of letters."

27. Sudermann's *The Song of Songs*, in Hermann Sudermann, *The Song of Songs*, trans. Beatrice Marshall (London, 1913), pp. ix-x. John Lane, requesting advice on whether to withdraw Sudermann's novel from circulation (he was being threatened by government prosecution), was particularly concerned with the opinions of established

novelists such as Hardy. Hardy advised withdrawal "as a practical question," and concluded: "A translation of good literary taste might possibly have made such an unflinching study of a woman's character acceptable in this country, even though the character is one of a somewhat ignoble type, but unfortunately, rendered into the rawest American, the claims that the original (which I have not seen) no doubt had to be considered as literature, are largely reduced, so that I question if there is value enough left in this particular translation to make a stand for." Lane reissued the novel in 1913, but the translation was a new one. Hardy permitted the reproduction of his letter in Lane's Introduction, which summarized the controversy.

28. "The War and Literature," *Book Monthly* (April, 1915), p. 434. The editor asked a number of writers and critics, "What effects, so far as they can be estimated ahead, is the Great War likely to exercise on English literature?" Hardy's answer: "Ultimately for good; by 'removing (from literature) those things that are shaken, as things that are made, that those things that cannot be shaken may remain.'—Heb. xii.27."

29. *Far from the Madding Crowd*: Programme (Turner Films, Ltd., November 16, 1915), pp. 2-11. A straightforward synopsis of the novel, written for a special showing of the film at the West End Cinema.

30. The Harper Centennial, in *The Harper Centennial 1817-1917* (New York, 1917), p. 12. Privately distributed, this volume contains a third-person statement by Hardy, with the charming sentence, "Although aware that they had handed on the torch for a good many decades it had not struck him that the period could be so long as it proves to be."

31. American Editors, *The Times* (November 13, 1918), p. 5. At this dinner, given for American editors by Cecil Harmsworth at Dr. Johnson's house, Hardy sent as his message Edward's lines, in *King Henry VI*,

> "Now breathe we, Lord; good fortune bids us pause,
> And smooth the frowns of war."

32. "Tolstoy's Works," *The Times* (April 29, 1922), p. 17. George Bernard Shaw had written a letter to *The Times* appealing for support of a complete edition of the works of Leo Tolstoy, specifically the Oxford University Press translation by Aylmer Maude which was pro-

jected for the Tolstoy Centenary of 1928. Hardy's note, appended to Shaw's letter, agreed with the opinion that a good translation of Tolstoy's works "should be made practicable by the concentration of effort on one production."

33. Horace Moule, *London Mercury* (October, 1922), p. 631. Hardy's note accompanied the poem "Ave Caesar," by Horace Moule, which had originally appeared in *Once a Week* in the summer of 1862. Its subject was the interior of the Coliseum, as painted by Gérôme; Moule had seen the painting at the International Exhibition in 1862. The *London Mercury* was printing in the early 1920's a series of poems that deserved re-examination, and Hardy was paying tribute to the memory of his friend.

34. *Tess of the d'Urbervilles, John o' London's Weekly* (October 24, 1925), p. 125. Hardy's note, addressed to the "Gentle Reader," prefaced a reprinting of *Tess*, the first serial publication of the definitive text (i.e., that of the Wessex Edition), with "a fragment of one chapter here embodied having been discovered but a short while ago." Hardy added that in his view the experiences of the heroine could have led to the same issue "last week" just as much as "fifty years back."

35. *Saturday Review* (November 7, 1925), Supplement, p. xiv. The magazine having reached "the Psalmodic age of three-score and ten," Hardy sent a congratulatory message, and added that he had been a faithful reader for more than sixty-eight years.

36. "The dram of eale," *The Times* (June 17, 1926), p. 15. Hardy, stimulated by a leading article with its comment on a famous passage in *Hamlet*, I, iv, wrote a letter about his own effort, in the 1860's, to elucidate its meaning. "I give it here, since it may pass in the crowd of conjecture on what Shakespeare really did write as being not much worse than the rest.

> "The dram of ill
> Doth all the noble substance leaven down
> To his own scandal."

Reminiscences and Personal Views

37. "The Waterloo Ball," *The Times* (December 17, 1888), p. 4. The question of where the Duchess of Richmond held her ball the night before Waterloo has puzzled a great many historians; Hardy sought to locate the site when he visited Brussels on two separate occa-

sions (1876 and 1896), and there is a striking footnote on the matter in *The Dynasts*, III, VI, ii. Hardy attempted to reconcile conflicting statements by assuming that "the Duchess of Richmond, during her stay in Brussels, gave more than one ball," or that a child may have remembered "a small dance" and magnified it in her memory as she grew older.

38. "How Authors Write," *Phonographic World* (New York) (July, 1889), p. 252. Hardy was responding to an inquiry about his "method of transferring thoughts to paper," as indeed several other authors were; he wrote in longhand, and when he dictated, he did so to another longhand writer. He found the systems of Taylor and Pitman the best of several inadequate choices, and concluded that "the system which successfully grapples with the vowel difficulty has yet to be invented." He concluded by saying that he had never used a typewriter.

39. "The Tree of Knowledge," *New Review* (June, 1894), p. 681. Hardy joined Hall Caine, Mrs. Edmund Gosse, Israel Zangwill, and Walter Besant, among others, in answering questions about the need for candor between the sexes and the best method for informing a young girl about the physiological basis of marriage. The problems were of some concern to Hardy because of his work on *Jude the Obscure*. He insisted that "a girl should certainly not be allowed to enter into matrimony without a full knowledge of her probable future in that holy estate, and of the possibilities which may lie in the past of the elect man"; recommended "a plain handbook on natural processes, specially prepared," for both the daughter and for "innocent youths"; and concluded with the melancholy observation that civilization had never succeeded in creating "a satisfactory scheme for the conjunction of the sexes."

40. "The Duchy of Cornwall and Mr. Thomas Hardy," *Dorset County Chronicle* (Dorchester) (January 17, 1895), p. 4. Hardy insisted that his negotiations for the site of Max Gate had been entirely pleasant, despite a report to the contrary published in an American newspaper and reprinted in the *Dorset County Chronicle*.

41. "The Disappearance of an Englishman at Zermatt," *The Times* (July 8, 1897), p. 10. Hardy, informed by some English ladies that an Englishman had disappeared from the very mountain trail he was walking along, "slowly searched all the way down the track for some clue to the missing man" (*Life*, p. 294), and then wrote to *The Times*

to say that his inspection had convinced him "no human body could fall over at any point and lie invisible." He was discounting any "sinister rumour" that implied foul play. The exertion of the search exhausted him on his arrival in Geneva, and he had to lie in bed awhile to rest.

42. "The Curse of Militarism," *Young Man* (June, 1901), p. 191. Hardy was contributing to a symposium on the article "The Curse of Militarism," by William Clarke, which had appeared in the May issue of the *Young Man*. "Aggressiveness being one of the laws of nature, by condemning war we condemn the scheme of the universe; while by exalting war we exalt sentiments which all worthy religions agree in calling evil, and whose triumphs the world would do well to escape by self-annihilation."

43. The Royal Buckhounds, *Humanity* [Journal of the Humanitarian League] (August, 1901), pp. 155-156. Hardy was delighted that the Royal Buckhounds had fallen, and to a meeting celebrating the event he wrote that his views on sport in general were extreme. ". . . that is, I hold it to be, in any case, immoral and unmanly to cultivate a pleasure in compassing the death of our weaker and simpler fellow-creatures by cunning, instead of learning to regard their destruction, if a necessity, as an odious task, akin to that, say, of the common hangman. In this view the hunting of tame stags is but a detail."

44. The Beauty of Wessex, *Sphere* (September 7, 1901), p. 288. Hardy denied that the "rather impressive and lonely" heath district of Wessex could be seen to advantage by a party of visitors who had "adhered for the most part to the London highway and the branch highway passing through the heath district," and who subsequently had been quoted in the *New York Times Saturday Review of Books and Art* to the effect that only "illusions produced by the novelist" could make such country beautiful. Hardy specified a number of picturesque inland and marine views, most of them lying "miles out of the regular way," and few of them reachable except on foot.

45. "The Wessex of Thomas Hardy," *Guardian* (April 16, 1902), p. 551. A review in the *Guardian* of April 9, in the course of remarks about B. C. A. Windle's *The Wessex of Thomas Hardy*, had accused Hardy of committing "an historical wrong which it will be very difficult to undo" by applying the name of Wessex to Dorsetshire (instead of Hampshire). Hardy's letter pointed out that he included six counties in his Wessex, and that "above all" he had "exhibited its area in a

map whose outline coincides with that given to the old kingdom by historians of early England." Hardy's correction of other misstatements of fact in the review led to an unrepentant answer by "The Reviewer," printed in the same issue.

46. A *Daily Chronicle* interview, *Daily Chronicle* (February 9, 1905), p. 3. Hardy's reticence led to the writing of several deplorable interviews, with much faked matter about his family background. This one, by W. Smithard, was printed on February 8, and Hardy immediately wrote that it had been obtained through a misapprehension on his part; that it did not accurately reflect his opinions; and that Mr. Smithard had not identified himself as a journalist.

47. Walter Tyndale's Water-Colours, *Catalogue of an Exhibition of Water-Colours of Wessex (Thomas Hardy's Country)*, by Walter Tyndale, The Leicester Galleries (London, June-July, 1905), pp. 5-6. Hardy suggested several of the subjects to Tyndale, who endured "many a scorching sun and dripping cloud . . . in our uncertain climate" to paint them. They are reproduced in *Wessex*, by Walter Tyndale and Clive Holland (London, 1906).

48. A Commission on Spelling Reform, *Daily Chronicle* (August 29, 1906), p. 4. Hardy approved of the formation of a Commission on Spelling Reform, recommended that its members represent every nationality save the English, and added that he was "struck with the advantage of having this reform of English spelling taken in hand by an eminent American of Dutch extraction."

49. "Louis Napoleon and the Poet Barnes," in F. H. Cheetham, *Louis Napoleon and the Genesis of the Second Empire* (London, 1909), unpaged leaf inserted between p. 378 and p. 379. This anecdote, which reached the publisher too late for insertion in its proper place, is more briefly recounted in the *Life* (pp. 175-176). Hardy wrote it down on October 17, 1885, after a visit to William Barnes, and there noted that Mr. Hann's people seemed to have been of his mother's stock. It recounts a near-fight which took place when Louis Napoleon visited the Damers, "who then lived at Carne House" near Dorchester, and played an unpleasant practical joke on Barnes's usher.

50. "Some Old-Fashioned Psalm-tunes Associated with the County of Dorset," *The Society of Dorset Men in London: Year-book, 1910-1911* (London, 1910), pp. 103-106. Ten tunes, reproduced in facsimile, with an introductory note: "We are indebted to Mr. Thomas Hardy, O. M. (Past President), for the following collection of old-time Psalm-

tunes, which he has culled from various sources and transcribed, and we are sure they will prove of interest to our Members."

51. "How Shall We Solve the Divorce Problem?", *Nash's Magazine* (March, 1912), p. 683. Laws affecting divorce in England and Wales were being censured as unrealistic, and Florence Fenwick Miller, contributing to this same symposium, called them "monstrous"; reform was in the air. Hardy, under a brief contribution entitled "Laws the Cause of Misery," wrote, "As the present marriage laws are, to the eyes of anybody who looks around, the gratuitous cause of at least half the misery of the community, that they are allowed to remain in force for a day is, to quote the famous last word of the ceremony itself, an 'amazement,' and can only be accounted for by the assumption that we live in a barbaric age, and are the slaves of gross superstition." He recommended liberalization of the marriage laws, but thought it unlikely that "bigots" would permit it.

52. "Performing Animals," *The Times* (December 19, 1913), p. 9. *The Times*, on December 17, printed an article, "Performing Animals: The Psychology of Pain in Man and Beast," which minimized the sensibility of animals to pain: "Pain to an animal represents an unpleasant experience begun and ended sharply. It is unrelated. It has no social or moral significance. It is not terrible in the wide sense." Hardy's response to this was a pointed, vigorous denunciation of the failure of imagination on the part of the "Correspondent." "It seems marvellous that the 20th century, with all its rhetoric on morality, should tolerate such useless inflictions as making animals do what is unnatural to them or drag out an unnatural life in a wired cell. I would also include the keeping of tame rabbits in hutches among the prohibited cruelties in this kind."

53. "Rheims Cathedral," *Manchester Guardian* (October 7, 1914), p. 7. Purdy (p. 159) identifies this letter as having been "commenced at least as a personal letter to Sydney Cockerell, though never sent." It begins with regret at the "mutilation of a noble building, which was almost the finest specimen of mediaeval architecture in France"; declares that the restoration, particularly of the "magnificent stained glass," will be partial and unsatisfactory; calls for determination of whether the bombardment was "accidental, or partly accidental, or contrary to the orders of a superior officer"; and continues with a fierce attack upon the "disastrous blight" wrought upon "the glory and nobility" of Germany by the writings of Nietzsche, with his followers,

Treitschke, Bernhardi, etc. The letter provoked a number of correspondents to defend Nietzsche; Bernard Gilbert, for example, noted Nietzsche's remark, in *Ecce Homo*, that "the German is incapable of conceiving anything sublime"; and other anti-German utterances of Nietzsche were cited as evidence that Hardy's characterization of "this writer's bombastic poetry" was unjust.

54. "A Reply to Critics," *Manchester Guardian* (October 13, 1914), p. 6. Hardy's rebuttal emphasized the inflammatory remarks of Nietzsche, e.g., "Ye shall love peace as a means to new wars, and the short peace better than the long. . . . I do not counsel you to conclude peace but to conquer. . . . Beware of pity." Hardy went on: "He used to seem to me (I have not looked into his works for years) to be an incoherent rhapsodist who jumps from Machiavelli to Isaiah as the mood seizes him, and whom it is impossible to take seriously as a mentor." Clement Shorter reprinted Items 53 and 54 in a pamphlet entitled *Letters on the War*.

55. "Trade Unionism," *Shop Assistant* (June 21, 1919), p. 405. Hardy, asked to define his concept of progress, wrote the single sentence, "I favour social re-adjustments rather than social subversions—remembering that the opposite of error is error still."

56. "A League of Thinkers," *New World* (July, 1921), p. 109. In the May issue, Leo Tolstoy, son of the novelist, proposed "an internal, intellectual, spiritual and moral organisation" to be called a "League of Thinkers." It would precede the formation of "any true 'Society of Nations.'" Hardy, asked to comment (along with George Bernard Shaw and others), expressed approval: "Though I have not as yet had time to consider closely the ways and means of promoting it, or how the Thinkers are to get themselves listened to by the Doers, think they never so wisely, I believe there are ways, and that it is only in those ways salvation lies, if there can be any salvation at all for a world that has got itself into such a deplorable welter, which seems to threaten a new Dark Age, to last may be for centuries before 'the golden years return.'"[1]

57. "World Peace," *The Times* (December 24, 1921), p. 11. Hardy, asked for a statement appropriate to the season, wrote, "Though my faith in the bettering of nations was shattered by the brutal unreason of the Continental instigators of the war, the omens now seem favourable."

58. Weymouth, *The Times* (July 6, 1926), p. 13. A civic delegation

from Weymouth, England, was attending the Independence Day celebrations of Weymouth, Massachusetts, and Hardy's message was read to the assemblage. ". . . we remember its venerable record as being the town second in antiquity in the State of Massachusetts, and its striking history of romantic and tragic vicissitude. . . ." Hardy concluded with the hope that its future success might not be "entirely of a material kind."

59. Country-dances and "The College Hornpipe" (as formerly danced in Wessex), *E. F. D. S.* [English Folk Dance Society] *News* (September, 1926), pp. 384-385. Hardy had been asked the identity of the dance he was thinking of in *Under the Greenwood Tree*, and he replied that it must have been "The College Hornpipe," as it was the only one he remembered that began with six-hands-round. In the course of his letter he distinguished "country dances" from the "folk dances," but added that the history of the former puzzled him. Country dances, supposedly more genteel, "superseded and extinguished the latter from a hundred to a hundred and fifty years ago. . . ."

60. English Country-dances, *Journal of the English Folk Dance Society*, Second Series (1927), pp. 53-54. Hardy's hypothesis that the country-dance might have been a successor to the true folk-dance (Item 59) aroused some controversy. The novelist insisted in a second letter that he held "no strong views," but cited a number of "rather formidable facts" to buttress his position, and ended by saying that his historical sketch of the development of these dances applied only to the west and southwest of England; also, to "the Wessex village of seventy to eighty years ago, before railways."

61. Cruel Sports, *The Times* (March 5, 1927), p. 7. The League for the Prohibition of Cruel Sports held a meeting in Taunton to protest "blood sports," i.e., hunting and coursing, and to recommend substitution of the drag and the mechanical hare. Hardy's message, one of several read in support of the movement, consisted of two sentences: "The human race being still practically barbarian it does not seem likely that men's delight in cruel sports can be lessened except by slow degrees. To attempt even this is, however, a worthy object which I commend."

62. South African Farmers, *Dorset County Chronicle* (Dorchester) (July 14, 1927), p. 8. A group of South African farmers, touring southwestern England and about to come to Dorchester as guests of the Mayor of Dorchester and the Dorset Farmers' Union, were greeted by

Hardy with the hope that "the weather here, so uncertain by comparison with their own, will not unduly depress."

Friends and Family

63. "The Late Mr. T. W. H. Tolbort, B. C. S., *Dorset County Chronicle* (Dorchester) (August 16, 1883), p. 10. Hardy's friendship with Hooper Tolbort flourished during his "years of architectural pupillage" (*Life*, p. 32), and remained warm during many years of separation. He admired Tolbort's "extraordinary facility in the acquisition of languages," and believed that his transliterations of Persian texts into Roman characters were remarkable for the age. Tolbort received his general education at Barnes's school in South-street, but much of his knowledge of nine tongues was self-taught. ". . . his genius, as far as it showed itself, was receptive rather than productive, though there is reason to suppose that had his life been longer spared he would have given to the world in his maturer years much valuable original work." Tolbort died Deputy Commissioner of Umballa, India, and was buried in the Dorchester Cemetery there. Hardy was unable to publish the MS. of Tolbort's last work, *The Portuguese in India*, despite a poignant appeal in the form of a letter from the dying Tolbort.

64. "Recollections of 'Leader Scott,'" *Dorset County Chronicle* (Dorchester) (November 27, 1902), p. 5. Lucy Baxter (1837-1902) was daughter to the Reverend William Barnes, and wrote a biography of him, *The Life of William Barnes, Poet and Philologist* (1887). Her own fame derived from a series of works on Italian art and literature, published under the pseudonym of "Leader Scott." Hardy, who knew her from childhood, lost sight of her for twenty years after she turned twenty-two; but met her once more at her father's rectory, and then again when he and his wife were staying at Florence in 1887. The anecdote about the Piazza dell' Annunziata, scene of the incidents recounted in Browning's "The Statue and the Bust," is retold in the *Life*, p. 199. Her death at Florence on November 10, 1902, stimulated the writing of this informal obituary which was also printed in *The Times* on the same day.

65. Obituary: Jemima Hardy, *Dorset County Chronicle* (Dorchester) (April 7, 1904), p. 4. Unsigned: attributed by Purdy to Hardy on the basis of a statement by Mrs. Hardy, "If anything was written, he must have done it" (p. 309). It seems less likely that Hardy was responsible for the wording of the one-sentence obituary for Thomas

Hardy, Sen., which appeared in the *Dorset County Chronicle* (Dorchester) (July 28, 1892), p. 16, although Purdy (p. 300) attributes it to him. "Mrs. Hardy was a woman of strong character and marked originality, with the keenest love for literature; and much of her son's work in prose and verse was based upon her memories and opinions."

66. Note: Jemima Hardy, *Daily Chronicle* (April 9, 1904), p. 4. This note corrects misstatements about Hardy's mother, speaks briefly about the education which she provided her son, and adds that she preferred to remain in "the original inconvenient" house after it had passed out of her hands, and "was enabled to do [so], as long as she chose, by the courtesy of the present possessor."

67. Obituary: "Laurence Hope," *Athenaeum* (October 29, 1904), p. 591. Adela Florence Nicolson (1865-1904), a poetess who specialized in "tropical luxuriance and Sapphic fervour," attracted considerable notice with *The Garden of Kama* (1901), a volume of "translations" that went through several editions. Intensely grief-stricken after the death of her husband, Lieut.-General Malcolm Nicolson, C.B., she committed suicide in Madras on October 4, 1904. "The author was still in the early noon of her life, vigour, and beauty, and the tragic circumstances of her death seem but the impassioned closing notes of her impassioned effusions."

68. Obituary: Mary Hardy, *Dorset County Chronicle* (Dorchester) (December 2, 1915), pp. 8-9. Unsigned; but Hardy sent a copy of this obituary to Sydney Cockerell as his work. "Under an often undemonstrative exterior she hid a warm and most affectionate nature." Cf. Hardy's emotion-laden note on her interment in the *Life*, p. 371. Much of the obituary is devoted to her twin interests, art and music.

69. Hopkins's "Thomas Hardy and His Folk," *Westminster Gazette* (June 4, 1926), p. 6. Hardy objected strenuously to an article by R. Thurston Hopkins that had been printed in the *Westminster Gazette* on June 2, and that not only invented details about himself but created a "half-brother" who gardened and wrote poetry. "I suppose Mr. Hopkins thinks it humorous to hoax an editor, and perhaps it is; but I must ask you to withdraw these misleading statements nevertheless." The editor did; and so did the offending author, in two letters printed on June 8 and June 11.

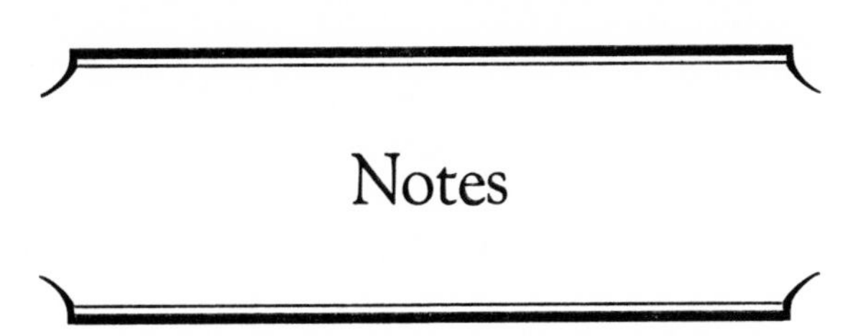

Notes

I. PREFACES TO HARDY'S WRITINGS

1. Hardy's general reference to the seven kingdoms of the Anglo-Saxon Heptarchy (Northumbria, East Anglia, Mercia, Essex, Sussex, Wessex, and Kent) is consonant with his saying elsewhere that the geographical limits of these vanished kingdoms were impossible to fix with certainty. Cf. his remarks about "Wessex" in the *Life,* pp. 122-123. The number of kingdoms in the Heptarchy varied at different times. The *O.E.D.* lists the first use of the term as in 1576, and the very concept may be a convenience of later historiographers. The period of time denoted is a broad one, from the arrival of the Anglo-Saxons (449) to the supremacy of Egbert of Wessex (ninth century).

2. Weatherbury is usually identified as Puddletown, named after the Puddle (also called "the Piddle" or the Trent).

3. For a detailed explanation of such divination (Chapter XIII of *Far from the Madding Crowd*), see Ruth A. Firor's *Folkways in Thomas Hardy* (New York, 1962), pp. 43-45; for St. Valentine folklore, p. 142; the shearing-supper, pp. 144-145. The "Harvest Home" denotes a festival, or "Feasting Day," to celebrate the bringing home of the last of the harvest. "Fuddling" refers to drinking bouts. (Hardy was particularly pleased by Helen Paterson's illustration for the Bible-and-key episode, which first appeared in *Cornhill Magazine* when the novel was being serialized there. Long after she had married William Allingham, the poet, Hardy referred to her as "the best illustrator" he ever had.)

4. For a discussion of the sources used by Hardy in authenticating the historical details, see Evelyn Hardy's *Thomas Hardy: A Critical Biography* (London, 1954), pp. 171-173. William R. Rutland's *Thomas Hardy: A Study of his Writings and their Background* (Oxford, 1938) names *Dumouriez and the Defence of England against Napoleon,* by J. Holland Rose and A. M. Broadley, as a book that contains contemporary documents comparable to those Hardy mentions in his Preface (p. 189), and points out that Broadley inscribed the copy of this volume that Hardy owned. Yet, as

Rutland notes, "the greater part of *The Trumpet-Major* is indebted, not to the printed, but to the spoken word," and Hardy says as much in his Preface. The oblique reference to Hardy's "mistaken" belief in thinking that the drilling scene of the local militia, as given in Gifford's *History,* referred to rural England is treated sympathetically by Carl J. Weber in his article, "A Connecticut Yankee in King Alfred's Country," *Colophon,* n.s., I (June, 1936), 525-535. Hardy's plagiarism of a passage in A. B. Longstreet's *Georgia Scenes* (1835) is explainable by the fact that the passage had been reprinted in Gifford. Hardy was much offended by the charges of unethical behavior made by several American magazines and by the *Academy* (February 18, 1882).

5. Cf. *The Tempest,* IV. i. 148-158.

6. The first spot is the tower standing in Charborough Park, a few miles south of Wimborne Minster; it is 120 feet high, and Hardy describes it (accurately) as having been built "in the Tuscan order of classic architecture." The second spot is a hill near Milborne St. Andrew, between Blandford and Dorchester, on which a shaft or obelisk (known locally as "Milborne Speer" or "Ring's-Hill Speer," since it rises from an entrenched earthwork), is located. This is the site of the observatory. See Hermann Lea's *Thomas Hardy's Wessex* (London, 1913), pp. 194-200.

7. Rutland (p. 206) identifies the "professor of the tongue in question" as Sir George Douglas, who, at Hardy's request, wrote several letters discussing the expressions that Farfrae used, and even went so far as to compile a list of phrases (drawn from the *Graphic*'s serial version) unsuitable for a Scotsman. Hardy eliminated or corrected these phrases in the second edition.

8. "The duty of an historian does not call upon him to interpose his private judgment in this nice and important controversy; but he ought not to dissemble the difficulty of adopting such a theory as may reconcile the interest of religion with that of reason, of making a proper application of that theory, and of defining with precision the limits of that happy period, exempt from error and from deceit, to which we might be disposed to extend the gift of supernatural powers. From the first of the fathers to the last of the popes, a succession of bishops, of saints, of martyrs, and of miracles, is continued without interruption; and the progress of superstition was so gradual and almost imperceptible, that we know not in what particular link we should break the chain of tradition."—Edward Gibbon, *The Decline and Fall of the Roman Empire,* Chapter XV.

9. In Hardy's short story "The Withered Arm," Gertrude Lodge bared her "poor curst arm; and Davies, uncovering the face of the corpse, took Gertrude's hand, and held it so that her arm lay across the dead man's neck, upon a line the colour of an unripe blackberry, which surrounded it." Her shriek was a sign that "the turn o' the blood," as predicted by the conjuror,

had taken place. But the double shock—both physical and mental—proved too much for her. "Her blood had been 'turned' indeed—too far. Her death took place in the town three days after." Some residents of Dorset still believed in this mode of curing otherwise incurable illnesses when Hardy was a child in Dorchester; it was called "turning the blood."

10. The reception accorded *Tess* was, of course, one of the literary scandals of the late Victorian Age. Hardy's shock at such stern reproofs as those published in the *Quarterly Review* ("It seems only that Mr. Hardy has told an extremely disagreeable story in an extremely disagreeable manner . . ."), the *Saturday Review* ("Few people will deny the terrible dreariness of this tale, which, except during a few hours spent with cows, has not a gleam of sunshine anywhere . . ."), and the *National Review* (where Tess was called "A Prig in the Elysian Fields"), was not significantly offset by the praise of H. W. Massingham, Richard Le Gallienne, William Watson, and (in 1893) Lionel Johnson. Hardy's concessions to Grundyism at the time of serial publication should have warned him that worse trouble lay ahead with book publication in November, 1891. Matters were not helped by the addition of a subtitle, *A Pure Woman,* which intensified the storm. Many years later he wrote that "the book, notwithstanding its exceptional popularity, was the beginning of the end of his career as a novelist" (*Life,* p. 240).

11. Schiller's letter was written at Jena on March 1, 1795, and refers to the criticism of Jacobi. *Correspondence Between Schiller and Goethe from 1794 to 1805,* trans. L. Dora Schmitz (London, 1877), I, 58.

12. The "disrespectful phrase," in the first sentence of the last paragraph of *Tess,* reads as follows: " 'Justice' was done, and the President of the Immortals, in Aeschylean phrase, had ended his sport with Tess." Hardy borrowed the phrase from a book he had purchased (in 1862) with the prize-money earned for an architectural design: Theodore A. Buckley's English translation of Aeschylus's *Prometheus Bound* (1849), a volume in Bohn's Classical Series. Carl J. Weber writes, in *Hardy of Wessex* (p. 129), "Hardy expected the reader to understand, by his quotation marks around 'justice' and his allusion to Aeschylus, that his, Hardy's, own explanation was neither of these. His was an indictment of an intolerant society that could condemn a woman of Tess's integrity and courage and humility." See Rutland's slightly different interpretation in *Thomas Hardy* (pp. 232-233). The phrase, incidentally, did not appear in the serialized version, but was added, much in the nature of an afterthought, to the manuscript Hardy submitted to James R. Osgood, McIlvaine & Co. for book-publication. For a brief review of the comments made by contemporary critics, see Edmund Blunden's *Thomas Hardy* (London, 1958), pp. 71-76.

13. Hardy's gibe at "this great critic" who had patronized him was an answer to Andrew Lang's notorious attack, in the *New Review* of February, 1892 (pp. 247-249), which said, in part: "The conclusion of *Tess* is rather

improbable in this age of halfpenny newspapers and appeals to the British public. The black flag would never have been hoisted, as in the final page. But one is afraid of revealing the story to people who have not yet read it. The persistent melancholy they perhaps like, or perhaps can make up their minds to endure. . . . Here are all the ingredients of the blackest misery, and the misery darkens till 'The President of the Immortals has finished his sport with Tess.' I cannot say how much this phrase jars on one. If there be a God, who can seriously think of Him as a malicious fiend? And if there be none, the expression is meaningless. . . . However, tastes differ so much that the blemishes, as they appear to one reader, of Mr. Hardy's works may seem beauty-spots in the eyes of another reader. He does but give us of his best. . . ."

14. Cf. note 1.

15. *King Lear*, IV. i. 38-39.

16. Michael Ott, in his article on Torquemada for *The Catholic Encyclopedia* (New York, 1912), XIV, 7836, quotes the contemporary Spanish chronicler, Sebastian de Olmedo (*Chronicon magistrorum generalium Ordinis Praedicatorum,* fol. 80-81), who called Torquemada "the hammer of heretics, the light of Spain, the saviour of his country, the honour of his order." The phrase "hammer of heretics" has also been applied to Pierre d'Ailly (1350-1425), president of the council that condemned John Huss; to St. Augustine; and to John Faber (1478-1541), writer of German polemics, among them *Malleus Hereticorum*.

17. Hamlet is speaking (in the gravediggers' scene): "How absolute the knave is! We must speak by the card, or equivocation will undo us. By the Lord, Horatio, these three years I have taken note of it; the age is grown so picked that the toe of the peasant comes so near the heels of our courtier, he galls his kibe" (*Hamlet,* V. i. 148-153).

18. Cf. Psalms 115:17.

19. "It would have been better not to write it" (source unidentified).

20. William Walsham How (1823-1897), the first Bishop of Wakefield, and a figure of some distinction because of, among other things, his charitable works for the poor people of the East End of London, wrote an irate letter to the *Yorkshire Post* (June 8, 1896) calling it "garbage"; claimed that he had thrown the novel into the fire (Hardy, "knowing the difficulty of burning a thick book even in a good fire, and the infrequency of fires of any sort in summer," was "mildly sceptical"); and then sent a letter of complaint to W. F. D. Smith, Esq., M.P., which resulted in "the quiet withdrawal of the book from the library, and an assurance that any other books by the same author would be carefully examined before they were allowed to be circulated." Hardy's note in the *Life* (p. 277) seethes with barely controlled passion: "Of this precious conspiracy Hardy knew nothing, or it might have moved a mind which the burning could not stir to say a word

on literary garrotting." The reviews were mixed, and, in general, unsettling to a sensitive writer; insinuations about the autobiographical elements in the novel, a charge that he was attempting to establish a sinful "anti-marriage league" (made by Margaret Oliphant), and the fear of actual threats against his person led to Hardy's renunciation of the novel as an art-form and to some sour thoughts about humanity in general. It is not surprising, perhaps, that Hardy read *King Lear* with renewed interest later that year. Nevertheless, there were friendly reviews by Edmund Gosse and Havelock Ellis, among others, and a letter of encouragement from a long-time hero, Swinburne.

21. Diderot wrote to this effect in his article on Natural Law in the *Encyclopédie* (1755). Rousseau's furious and eloquent article on Political Economy, published in the same issue of the *Encyclopédie,* was a criticism of Diderot's position.

22. "The conflagratory bishop" is still another reference to the Bishop of Wakefield. Hardy's dry comment, that the Bishop had doubtless burnt his novel in despair at being unable to burn its author, was widely quoted in England. See note 20.

23. *Athenaeum,* November 23, 1895, p. 710. The reviewer called *Jude the Obscure* "a titanically bad book," and its author a man who had run "mad in right royal fashion."

24. In *Blackwood's* (January, 1896) Mrs. M. O. W. Oliphant, in an article entitled "The Anti-Marriage League," referred to *Jude the Obscure* as "the strongest illustration of what Art can come to when given over to the exposition of the unclean." Hardy derived some meager comfort from Macaulay's remark, in his essay on Byron, "We know of no spectacle so ridiculous as the British public in one of its periodical fits of morality," but was understandably upset by Mrs. Oliphant's hyperbolic language ("Nothing so coarsely indecent as the whole history of Jude . . . has ever been put in English print;—that is to say, from the hands of a master . . ."). See note 20. Another woman, Miss Jeannette Gilder, wrote a scathing review in the *New York World* (December 8, 1895), protesting that she had to open the window "and let in the fresh air" after finishing the story. (See the *Life,* pp. 279-281, for the amusing sequel.) Hardy's scattered dicta on the status of reviewing in the declining years of the century were the product of a rich experience.

25. Portland, "the peninsula carved by Time out of a single stone," served as the scene of *The Well-Beloved.* Hardy often refers to Portland as "The Isle of Slingers" and "The Isle by the Race" in his fictions about Wessex; but it is indeed a peninsula, and in his time was connected by a narrow bank of pebbles to the mainland. For Hardy's word "obsolescent" (p. 36), read "obsolete." Civilization had extorted its payment from the residents of Portland long before Hardy's death. "It is with regret that we notice the

extermination of these idiosyncrasies," one traveller wrote in 1913, "for Portland has altered out of all recognition during the last few generations" (Hermann Lea, *Thomas Hardy's Wessex,* p. 202).

26. The novel, under the title *The Pursuit of the Well-Beloved,* appeared as a serial in the *Illustrated London News* (October 1–December 17, 1892). Hardy did not approve of its form when it came time to prepare it for publication as a book; he revised extensively, particularly at the beginning and end, and altered the outcome in a way that surprised readers familiar with the serial version. The story took four years to get into hard covers, during which time Hardy wrote and published *Jude the Obscure;* depending on one's preference, one may nominate either *The Well-Beloved* or *Jude* as Hardy's last novel. For bibliographical details, see Purdy, pp. 92-96.

27. Hardy's debt to Wordsworth, although less than that to Browning and Shakespeare, is more substantial than critics generally realize. Hardy quotes "Lines Written in Early Spring" and the Ode on Immortality in *Tess of the d'Urbervilles,* and "Resolution and Independence" in *The Woodlanders;* these annotations indicate that Hardy, who earned a substantial part of his early fame from the portrayal of Dorset rustics, approved of Wordsworth's concept of poetry, choice of subject-matter, and employment of a "language really used by men." Here he quotes, for his own purpose, from "Lines Composed a Few Miles above Tintern Abbey on Revisiting the Banks of the Wye During a Tour. July 13, 1798," 23-48.

28. Hardy's use of the famous phrase from *Biographia Literaria* (Chapter XIV) reminds us how troublesome the first reviewers found Hardy's "supernatural spectators of the terrestrial action, certain impersonated abstractions, or Intelligences, called Spirits." (See, on pp. 141-146, the letters that Hardy wrote to *The Times Literary Supplement* on February 5 and 19, 1904.) The most thorough study of how Hardy used his Spirits, written with the prerequisite sympathy for Hardy's intentions that many critics have lacked, is James Osler Bailey's *Thomas Hardy and the Cosmic Mind: A New Reading of* The Dynasts (Chapel Hill, N.C., 1956).

29. "The inheritors of unfulfilled renown
Rose from their thrones, built beyond mortal thought,
Far in the Unapparent."

—Percy Bysshe Shelley, *Adonais,* 397-399.

30. "Oh, write no more the tale of Troy,
If earth Death's scroll must be!
Nor mix with Laian rage the joy
Which dawns upon the free:
Although a subtler Sphinx renew
Riddles of death Thebes never knew."

—Percy Bysshe Shelley, *Hellas,* 1078-1083.

31. "But thought's the slave of life, and life time's fool;
And time, that takes survey of all the world,
Must have a stop."

—*I King Henry IV,* V. iv. 81-83.

32. The incomprehensibility of the universe as a staggering thought is developed at some length in Part I, "The Unknowable," of Herbert Spencer's *First Principles* (1862), the first volume in what was to become a ten-volume work, *Synthetic Philosophy.*

33. Hardy is remembering Francis Bacon's famous passage in the *Novum Organum* (Lib. I, xxxix): "Quatuor sunt genera idolorum quae mentes humanas obsident. Iis (docendi gratia) nomina imposuimus: ut primum genus, *idola tribus;* secundum, *idola specus;* tertium, *idola fori;* quartum, *idola theatri* vocentur." *Bacon's Novum Organum,* ed. Thomas Fowler (Oxford, 1889).

34. "Look at the end of work, contrast
The petty done, the undone vast,
This present of theirs with the hopeful past!
I hoped she would love me; here we ride."

—Robert Browning, "The Last Ride Together," 52-55.

Hardy met Browning at social gatherings, and greatly admired his poetry. For a listing of other specific borrowings from Browning, see Carl J. Weber's *Hardy of Wessex,* pp. 269-276. Hardy's reference to the approaching night (in the line immediately following the quotation) may be either a direct reminiscence of John 9:4, or of the famous concluding line of Chapter IX ("The Everlasting Yea") of Carlyle's *Sartor Resartus:* "Work while it is called Today; for the Night cometh, wherein no man can work."

35. The "dozen minor novels" were " A Changed Man," "The Waiting Supper," "Alicia's Diary," "The Grave by the Handpost," "Enter a Dragoon," "A Tryst at an Ancient Earthwork," "What the Shepherd Saw," "A Committee-Man of 'The Terror,' " "Master John Horseleigh, Knight," "The Duke's Reappearance," "A Mere Interlude," and "The Romantic Adventures of a Milkmaid."

36. "Not for these I raise
The song of thanks and praise;
But for those obstinate questionings
Of sense and outward things,
Fallings from us, vanishings;
Blank misgivings of a Creature
Moving about in worlds not realised,
High instincts before which our mortal Nature
Did tremble like a guilty Thing surprised. . . ."

—William Wordsworth, "Ode: Intimations of Immortality from Recollections of Early Childhood," 143-151.

37. Heine's views on the rights of the human soul, and on the manner in which the State and the forces of organized religion move to interfere with such rights, are scattered throughout his writings. See, for example, his chapters on the history of German philosophy in *Works* (London, 1906), V; and such remarks as the following: "It is injurious to the interests of religion herself and her sacred character that she be invested with special privileges, that her servants should be endowed by the state, above all others, and in return should pledge themselves to uphold the state in order to retain that endowment . . ." (*The Poetry and Prose of Heinrich Heine,* ed. Frederic Ewen, New York, 1948, p. 607).

38. The parable of the good Samaritan, Luke 10:29-37.

39. Though these were not quite the words Frederic Harrison used in an essay published in the *Fortnightly Review* (1920) and subsequently reprinted in *Novissima Verba: Last Words* (London, 1921), pp. 27-34, the sense was accurately reported: "My philosophy of life is more cheerful and hopeful than that of these Lyrics—but they do not at all diminish my entire admiration for *The Dynasts* and for the *Romances*." Hardy, who liked Harrison personally, may have been partially mollified by the journalist's praise of him as "a warm friend, a gracious host, rich with every kind of public and private virtue"; but Harrison's categorical judgment, "This monotony of gloom, with all its poetry, is not human, not social, not true," was bound to irk him. (Harrison was reviewing *Collected Poems,* published by Macmillan and Co., Ltd., in 1919.)

40. Hardy's reference is to Joseph Maunsell Hone's "The Poetry of Mr. Hardy," *London Mercury,* V (February, 1922), 396-405. "The suggestion of an untruth" to which Hardy objected was contained in remarks such as the following: "Schopenhauer's myths have for [Hardy] only a figurative value—and not always even that. He feels in them no consoling power. Schopenhauer himself, on the other hand, could find ecstasy in his pessimism. . . . Mr. Hardy refuses the consolation which the Frankfort sage offered to the faithful. He is a bad Schopenhauerian—as one would say, a 'bad Catholic.'" Or, again: "Mr. George Moore, in the course of one of his passionate arguments about the incompatibility of Catholic philosophy and literature, asserts that 'The length of the sleep out of which we came and the still greater length of the sleep which will very soon fall upon us' are the springs from which all poetry flows: a surprisingly exclusive definition, surely, but Mr. Hardy's case reminds one of it—for his best poetry has no other sources than these." Hone (1882-1959) was later to write biographies of Bishop Berkeley, George Moore, and William Butler Yeats.

41. "O that 't were possible
After long grief and pain
To find the arms of my true love
Round me once again!"

—Alfred, Lord Tennyson, *Maud,* Part II, 141-144.

42. Matthew Arnold, after quoting several passages from Burns's poetry, concedes that the application of ideas to life "is a powerful one; made by a man of vigorous understanding, and (need I say?) a master of language. But for supreme poetical success more is required than the powerful application of ideas to life; it must be an application under the conditions fixed by the laws of poetic truth and poetic beauty. Those laws fix as an essential condition, in the poet's treatment of such matters as are here in question, high seriousness;—the high seriousness which comes from absolute sincerity." ("The Study of Poetry," *Essays in Criticism, Second Series,* London, 1941, pp. 33-34.) Cf. his remark that Wordsworth's "superiority arises from his powerful use, in his best pieces, his powerful application to his subject, of ideas 'on man, on nature, and on human life,'" in his essay on Wordsworth (1879), as well as similar remarks in *On Translating Homer: Last Words* (1862), and in "Joubert" (1864).

43. Mars Hill, where Saint Paul delivered his address to the Athenians (probably gathered on the edge of the Agora). Acts 17:22.

44. Hardy, like Voltaire in *Candide,* regards Pangloss as the symbol of the incorrigible optimist, the man who refuses to allow his convictions to be corrupted by facts.

45. Gil Blas, who writes out the homilies composed by an archbishop, promises to tell the churchman when their quality shows signs of failing. The archbishop suffers a stroke, and mental problems interfere with the writing of effective homilies; but when Gil, in a rash moment of truthfulness, tells the archbishop as much, he is dismissed summarily for his opinion. (Book VII, Chapters 2-4.)

46. Wordsworth was deploring the submergence of the works of Shakespeare and Milton by "frantic novels, sickly and stupid German Tragedies, and deluges of idle and extravagant stories in verse," and announced that he thought of his own poems as a "feeble endeavour" to counteract "this degrading thirst after outrageous stimulation." *Preface to the Second Edition of Several of the Foregoing Poems, Published, with an Additional Volume, under the Title of "Lyrical Ballads"* (1802). The allusion to "high thinking" is a reminiscence of the lines,

> "Plain living and high thinking are no more:
> The homely beauty of the good old cause
> Is gone; our peace, our fearful innocence,
> And pure religion breathing household laws."
> —*Poems Dedicated to National Independence and Liberty,*
> Pt. I, No. XIII, "Written in London, September, 1802."

47. This concept of the relationship between religion and poetry is Arnoldian, and echoes passages in *Culture and Anarchy* (1869), where the finest Greek art and poetry are identified as uniting "the idea of beauty and of a human nature perfect on all sides" with "a religious and devout en-

ergy"; and in "The Study of Poetry" (*Essays in Criticism, Second Series,* 1888), where Arnold predicts that "most of what now passes with us for religion and philosophy will be replaced by poetry," and even goes so far as to say, "The strongest part of our religion today is its unconscious poetry."

48. John 8:32: "And ye shall know the truth, and the truth shall make you free."

49. Heb. 12:27: "And this word, Yet once more, signifieth the removing of those things that are shaken, as of things that are made, that those things which cannot be shaken may remain." Cf. p. 247, item 28.

50. "The Man of science seeks truth as a remote and unknown benefactor: he cherishes and loves it in his solitude: the Poet, singing a song in which all human beings join with him, rejoices in the presence of truth as our visible friend and hourly companion. Poetry is the breath and finer spirit of all knowledge; it is the impassioned expression which is in the countenance of all Science."—William Wordsworth, *Preface, Second Edition of Lyrical Ballads.*

51. *In Memoriam,* LXXXVII, 21-22, written after Tennyson's nostalgic visit to Trinity College, Cambridge, which stirred memories of The Apostles and "the master bowman" (Hallam).

II. Prefaces to the Works of Other Writers

1. Hardy sometimes uses the older name, Well-bridge, and the house is the old manor of a branch of the Turbervilles; here Tess and Angel Clare came to spend their honeymoon; here also Tess confessed and Angel became an apostate. The history of the house probably goes back to Sir John Turberville, knight and sheriff of Dorset in 1652. Bertram C. A. Windle, *The Wessex of Thomas Hardy* (London, 1916), pp. 101-105.

2. Norris Mill Farm, because of its situation in the Valley of Great Dairies, is often regarded as the original of Talbothays, where Tess worked in the dairy and where Angel Clare fell in love with her.

3. Hardy's insertion.

4. Hardy's insertion.

5. The belief that a witch frequently assumes the shape of a hare, "and haunts the downs and hills at night time, being only visible at the dead of night," is expressed in an old Dorset song, "The Haunted Hare." Supposedly only a silver bullet can kill the hare. See J. S. Udal, "Witchcraft in Dorset," *Proceedings of the Dorset Natural History and Antiquarian Field Club,* XIII (1892), 42. The folk attitude toward a hare is ambivalent, however, and many widely disseminated superstitions suggest that the hare is a positive sign (for example, the rabbit's foot brings good luck). Here Hardy is talking about the killing of an animal which may fall under the category of a taboo; belief in fire as punishment for breaking an established taboo is quite common.

6. Old South is terrified by a tall elm that becomes his personal enemy as it grows older, larger, and stronger: "Little did I think, when I let that sapling stay, that a time would come when it would torment me, and dash me into my grave." And indeed it does. Even when cut down, the tree frightens the old man to the extent that he dies by sundown of the next day. *The Woodlanders,* Chapters II and XIII.

7. The gates of Came Wood led to the church where William Barnes served as rector (1862–1886), in Winterborne Came. For the importance of barrows to Hardy's concept of Wessex, see Ruth Firor, pp. 265 ff. Conquer Barrow is 40 paces in diameter, 9 feet high, and hollow in the center; it is located on the West Stafford boundary. Leslie Valentine Grinsell, in the definitive work on this subject, *Dorset Barrows* (Dorchester, England, 1959), writes that it is "placed on the denuded rampart of a probable henge monument with entrance at S.E." (p. 105).

8. Roughly equivalent to "no trace at all."

9. Apparently a reference to the use of *a-* (from *on*) followed by the gerund form, as in Barnes's "Winter A-Comèn":

"Noo rwose is a-bloomèn red to-day,
Noo pink vor your breast or head to-day,
A-deckèn the geärden bed to-day,
Do linger a-noddèn low."

10. "Yes, you, like a ghostly cricket, creaking where a house was burned:
'Dust and ashes, dead and done with, Venice spent what Venice earned.
The soul, doubtless, is immortal—where a soul can be discerned.' "
—Robert Browning, "A Toccata of Galuppi's," XII.

11. "Or sweetest *Shakespear* fancies childe,
Warble his native Wood-notes wilde. . . ."
—John Milton, *L'Allegro,* 133-134.

12. "Behold, ye speak an idle thing;
Ye never knew the sacred dust.
I do but sing because I must,
And pipe but as the linnets sing. . . ."
—Alfred, Lord Tennyson, *In Memoriam,* XXI, 21-24.

13. A commonplace; used, for instance, in William Johnson Cory's "On Livermead Sands":

"For waste of scheme and toil we grieve,
For snowflakes on the wave we sigh,
For writings on the sand that leave
Naught for to-morrow's passer-by."

Cf. Walter Savage Landor's "Well I Remember How You Smiled," and Matt. 7:26.

14. Hardy's guess is not supported by the biographical evidence. See

George Sherburn's *The Early Career of Alexander Pope* (Oxford, 1934), pp. 27-44, where facts are carefully sorted from family tradition and posthumous myth. Cf. William John Courthope's earlier biography, *The Life of Alexander Pope* (London, 1889), pp. 1-12.

15. *King Henry V,* II. iv. 17, 19-20.

16. The *Dictionary of National Biography* was first edited by Sir Leslie Stephen (1832-1904) between 1882 and 1891; after his retirement as editor, Sir Leslie contributed articles on various figures.

17. Thomas Carlyle, "Project of a National Exhibition of Scottish Portraits," *Critical and Miscellaneous Essays* (London, 1899), IV, 404.

III. On Literary Matters

1. William Wordsworth, "Elegiac Stanzas Suggested by a Picture of Peele Castle, in a Storm, Painted by Sir George Beaumont," 15.

2. Ruth Firor (p. 117) traces "Wide-O," the conjuror in *The Mayor of Casterbridge* (Chapter XXVI), back to the itinerant leeches of the Middle Ages who came to country fairs complete with monsters and performing animals. Hardy's understanding of the importance of homeopathic magic in Dorset folkways is well illustrated in the "barbarous remedy" proposed for the dying Mrs. Yeobright: the fat of adders, caught alive if possible. (*The Return of the Native,* Book IV, Chapter VII.)

3. The point is a troubled one. Giles Dugdale, in *William Barnes of Dorset* (London, 1963), pp. 5-7, discusses Hardy's reasons for believing that 1800 was the year of Barnes's birth: "Hardy never gave his reasons for supposing the Barnes family tradition to be incorrect, and although he saw a good deal of Lucy Baxter in Florence, while she was writing her father's biography, he clearly did not persuade her to share his preference. In his own copy of the Life, Hardy inserted a letter dated July 18, 1925, from Captain Acland, Curator of the Dorchester Museum, giving reasons for believing him to have been wrong.

"Before the centralized registration of births at Somerset House such doubts, even in urban areas, were frequently raised. . . . Although no official record of William Barnes's birth has yet been discovered, his own family's traditional belief that he was born on February 22, 1801, should surely now also be generally accepted. Certain it is that his baptism was entered in the register at Sturminster Newton Church on March 22, 1801, and it seems unlikely that in such a devout home a delicate child would have remained unbaptized for thirteen months." Dugdale's view seems wholly convincing. The *D.N.B.* gives 1801 as the year of birth.

4. Printed "some time" in the original.

5. William Mulready (1786-1863), a genre painter whose emphasis on textured surfaces, narrative values, and sentimental poses is perhaps best shown in his illustrations for *The Vicar of Wakefield* (e.g., "Choosing the

Wedding Gown"). The Pre-Raphaelites detested Mulready and Sir David Wilkie (1785-1841), and considered them lacking in high seriousness. One of Mulready's claims to fame: his design of the first penny postage envelope for Rowland Hill (1840).

6. William Barnes became a "ten years' man" on March 2, 1838, when he put his name on the books of St. John's College, Cambridge; during this decade many of his most intensive investigations of archaeological and etymological problems took place. On February 28, 1847, the Bishop of Salisbury ordained him, and he became the pastor of Whitcombe. In 1850 Barnes was graduated B.D. at Cambridge, and two years later resigned his curacy.

7. See note 1.

8. "There is one glory of the sun, and another glory of the moon, and another glory of the stars: for one star differeth from another star in glory" (I Cor. 15:41).

9. *Othello,* I. iii. 134-135.

10. Matthew Arnold, "The Study of Poetry," *Essays in Criticism, Second Series* (1888): "In poetry, as a criticism of life under the conditions fixed for such a criticism by the laws of poetic truth and poetic beauty, the spirit of our race will find, we have said, as time goes on and as other helps fail, its consolation and stay."

11. A viewpoint often expressed by Symonds, as in his essay "The Provinces of the Several Arts": "If we are right in defining art as the manifestation of the human spirit to man by man in beautiful form, poetry, more incontestably than any other art, fulfils this definition and enables us to gauge its accuracy. For words are the spirit, manifested to itself in symbols with no sensual alloy. Poetry is therefore the presentation, through words, of life and all that life implies. . . . The best poetry is that which reproduces the most of life, or its intensest moments." *Essays Speculative and Suggestive* (London, 1893), p. 100.

12. Gen. 40:23.

13. The reasoning here is Aristotelian, and derives ultimately from the *Poetics:* "The distinction between historian and poet is not in the one writing prose and the other verse—you might put the work of Herodotus into verse, and it would still be a species of history; it consists really in this, that the one describes the thing that has been, and the other a kind of thing that might be. Hence poetry is something more philosophic and of graver import than history, since its statements are the nature rather of universals, whereas those of history are singulars." (Translated by Ingram Bywater.)

14. "For verily I say unto you, Till heaven and earth pass, one jot or one tittle shall in no wise pass from the law, till all be fulfilled" (Matt. 5:18).

15. "Have I commandment of the pulse of life?" (*King John*, IV. ii. 92). The phrase is, to be sure, a commonplace.

16. Censure of the obsession with detail which characterized the realistic fiction of post-Flaubertian novelists was as common in France as in England: see George J. Becker's *Documents of Modern Literary Realism* (Princeton, N.J., 1963) for representative arguments, particularly in the second section, "The Battle over Naturalism," pp. 159-425. The passage here quoted appears in H. A. Taine's *History of English Literature,* trans. H. Van Laun (New York, 1874), II, 258.

17. "To Dianeme," 5-10, in *Hesperides.*

18. Matt. 7:16: "Do men gather grapes of thorns, or figs of thistles?"

19. Joseph Addison, *The Spectator,* No. 267, Saturday, January 5, 1712; ed. G. Gregory Smith (London, 1950), II, 296.

20. "He who makes every effort to select his theme aright will be at no loss for choice words or lucid arrangement." *Horace on the Art of Poetry,* ed. Edward Henry Blakeney (London, 1928), p. 42.

21. *"Écorché":* an anatomical figure.

22. Probably the proverb, "You may take a horse to the water, but you can't make him drink," extant in many forms. G. L. Apperson, in *English Proverbs and Proverbial Phrases* (London, 1929), p. 314, dates his first citation *c.* 1175.

23. Thomas Carlyle, *The French Revolution,* Part One, Book I, Chapter II, "Realised Ideals"; also in *Past and Present,* Book IV, Chapter I, "Aristocracies." Cf. William Blake's remark, "Every Eye Sees differently. As the Eye, Such the Object," in "Annotations to Sir Joshua Reynolds's Discourses," *c.* 1808, in *The Complete Writings of William Blake,* ed. Geoffrey Keynes (London, 1957), p. 456.

24. The sense (but not the exact wording) of Comte's discussion of social dynamics, or "theory of the natural progress of human society." See *The Positive Philosophy of Auguste Comte,* translated and condensed by Harriet Martineau, with an introduction by Frederic Harrison (London, 1896), pp. 299-302.

25. "I grant you, friends, if that you should fright the ladies out of their wits, they would have no more discretion but to hang us: but I will aggravate my voice so that I will roar you as gently as any sucking dove; I will roar you as 'twere any nightingale."

—*A Midsummer-Night's Dream,* I. ii. 81-86.

26. For the benefit of the reader who may wish to recall the number of a particular one, the five commandments alluded to are quoted here. The first commandment (Exod. 20:3): "Thou shalt have no other gods before me." The third (20:7): "Thou shalt not take the name of the Lord thy God in vain; for the Lord will not hold him guiltless that taketh his name in vain." The seventh (20:14): "Thou shalt not commit adultery." The ninth (20:16): "Thou shalt not bear false witness against thy neighbour." The sixth (20:13): "Thou shalt not kill."

27. The refrain to the entrance chant of the choristers, repeated at l. 121, l. 139, and l. 159, in *Agamemnon,* as numbered in H. W. Smyth's edition of the text for the Loeb Classical Library (London, 1926).

28. "L'homme est visiblement fait pour penser. C'est toute sa dignité et tout son mérite; et tout son devoir est de penser comme il faut." *Pensée* 146.

29. William Wordsworth, "Lines Composed a Few Miles above Tintern Abbey, on Revisiting the Banks of the Wye during a Tour," 91.

30. *The Tempest,* IV. i. 156-158.

31. See *I. Prefaces,* note 5.

32. "Have you heard the argument? Is there no offence in't?" *Hamlet,* III. ii. 242.

33. Eph. 1:5.

34. William Morris often repeated his appeal for an "Art made by the people as a joy to the maker and the user." Hardy may have had in mind a passage in Morris's speech to the members of the Birmingham Society of Arts and School of Design (February 19, 1879) which speaks of the "grin of pleasure" that "common fellows" brought "to the carrying through of those mazes of mysterious beauty, to the invention of those strange beasts and birds and flowers that we ourselves have chuckled over at South Kensington." *The Collected Works of William Morris,* ed. May Morris (London, 1914), XXII, 40.

35. "Dan Chaucer, well of English undefyled,
On Fames eternall beadroll worthie to be fyled."

—Edmund Spenser, *The Faerie Queen,* Book IV, canto II, stanza 32.

The quotation attributed to Hardy is probably garbled.

36. "On dit que la poésie se meurt: la poésie ne peut pas mourir. N'eût-elle pour asile que le cerveau d'un seul homme, elle aurait encore des siècles de vie, car elle en sortirait comme la lave du Vésuve, et se fraierait un chemin parmi les plus prosaïques réalités. En depit de ses temples renversés et des faux dieux adorés sur leurs ruines, elle est immortelle comme le parfum des fleurs et la splendeur des cieux" (George Sand, *André,* Chapter III).

37. Henry James's disapproval of Hardy's fictions led to an exchange of letters with Robert Louis Stevenson in 1892. James thought *Tess* "chock-full of faults and falsity," yet admitted that it had "a singular beauty and charm." Stevenson, answering from "Polynesia," said that the novel was "one of the worst, weakest, least sane, most *voulu* books" he had yet read. "I should tell you in fairness I could never finish it; there may be the treasures of the Indies further on; but so far as I read, James, it was (in one word) damnable. *Not alive, not true,* was my continual comment as I read; and at last—*not even honest!* was the verdict with which I spewed it from my mouth. I write in anger? I almost think I do; I was betrayed in a

friend's house—and I was pained to hear that other friends delighted in that barmicide feast. I cannot read a page of Hardy for many a long day, my confidence [in him] is gone. So that you and Barrie and Kipling are now my Muses Three." This extraordinary outburst from a writer who had often expressed his admiration of Hardy was almost completely suppressed by Sidney Colvin when he edited *The Letters of Robert Louis Stevenson to his Family and Friends* (New York, 1899), II, 330-331; but Hardy learned of it nevertheless. See Dan H. Laurence's "Henry James and Stevenson Discuss 'Vile' Tess," *Colby Library Quarterly* (May, 1953), pp. 164-168. The letter from Stevenson to James is now in the Houghton Library at Harvard.

38. Swinburne's letter to the *Spectator* was printed June 7, 1862, pp. 632-633, as a protest against a review (printed in the issue of May 24, 1862) of George Meredith's *Modern Love, and Poems of the English Roadside, with Poems and Ballads.* It was the only thing he ever wrote about Meredith's works. *The Swinburne Letters,* ed. Cecil Y. Lang (New Haven, 1959), I, 51-53, and V, 283.

39. *Saturday Review,* October 24, 1863, pp. 562-563.

40. The reference is to Letter 82 (October, 1877) of *Fors Clavigera,* in Ruskin's *Works,* edited by E. T. Cook and Alexander Wedderburn (London, 1907), VII, 233-235.

IV. Reminiscences and Personal Views

1. Exod. 20:17: "Thou shalt not covet thy neighbour's house, thou shalt not covet thy neighbour's wife, nor his manservant, nor his ox, nor his ass, nor any thing that is thy neighbour's."

2. London.

3. "Dante, pacer of the shore
Where glutted hell disgorgeth filthiest gloom,
Unbitten by its whirring sulphur-spume—
Or whence the grieved and obscure waters slope
Into a darkness quieted by hope. . . ."
—Robert Browning, *Sordello,* Book the First.

4. Christian's flight from the City of Destruction takes him first through the Slough of Despond (Bunyan's *Pilgrim's Progress*).

5. Mark 5:11-14.

6. "Some mute, inglorious Milton here may rest,
Some Cromwell, guiltless of his country's blood."
—Thomas Gray, *Elegy Written in a Country Churchyard,* 59-60.

7. "To-morrow, and to-morrow, and to-morrow,
Creeps in this petty pace from day to day
To the last syllable of recorded time,

And all our yesterdays have lighted fools
The way to dusty death."

—*Macbeth,* V.v. 19-23.

8. Matt. 6:34.

9. Persons who hold land tenure "at the will of the lord according to the custom of the manor," by copy of the manorial court-roll *(O.E.D.).*

10. *Pilgrim's Progress.* In Part I, Giant Despair beats his prisoners, Christian and Hopeful, in Doubting Castle, from which they later escape; in Part II, Great-heart slays Giant Despair, and Doubting Castle is demolished.

11. F. P. Verney, "Peasant Properties in Auvergne: Jottings in Auvergne," *Contemporary Review,* XLII (December, 1882), 954-972.

12. Robert Burns, "To a Mouse, on Turning Her up in Her Nest with the Plough, November, 1785."

13. An allusion to the story told by Cicero in *Tusculanarum Quaestionum libri quinque* (5.61), and often repeated, in which Damocles, the courtier of Dionysius I, overpraised the happiness of the tyrant, and was punished by being ordered to feast and enjoy himself with a sword, hanging by a hair, above his head.

14. At the hiring-fairs one would advertise his vocation by an appropriate garb and symbol. These twice-yearly events are referred to in *Tess of the d'Urbervilles* (Chapter XXIII) and in *Far from the Madding Crowd* (Chapter VI). The Candlemas fair (February 2) was apparently a more colorful and interesting occasion than the Martinmas fair (November 11); workers would agree to begin work on April 6, Lady Day, Old Style, and then migrate to their new homes (as described in Chapters LI and LII of *Tess*). See Ruth Firor, pp. 174, 229, 255-257.

15. "An Englishman entering on life, finds to all great questions an answer ready made. A Frenchman entering on life finds to all great questions simply suggested doubts. In this conflict of opinions he must create a faith for himself, and, being mostly unable to do it, he remains open to every uncertainty, and therefore to every curiosity and to every pain. . . ." This, and much more in similar vein, may be found in Taine's *History of English Literature,* translated by H. Van Laun (New York, 1874), pp. 535-541, where the great French critic expresses a preference for Musset over Tennyson. Cf. his chapter, "The Past and the Present," pp. 313-336.

16. Lady Day, commemorating the Annunciation of the Blessed Virgin, has been March 25 ever since the setting of the date of Christ's Nativity as December 25. After the Gregorian calendar replaced the Julian calendar in England (1752), differences between the Old and the New Style resulted in the celebration of "Old Lady Day" in parts of England several days after March 25.

17. *1 Henry IV.* I. 3-4. "Charles's Wain" is an old name for the Dipper.

18. "The hexagon to the bee": an oft-noted comparison during the eighteenth century. Oliver Goldsmith wrote, in *An History of the Earth, and Animated Nature* (1774), "Each cell is like that of the bee, hexagonal."

19. II Sam. 6:3-8.

20. Jaques is speaking:

"O worthy fool! One that hath been a courtier,
And says, if ladies be but young and fair,
They have the gift to know it; and in his brain,
Which is as dry as the remainder biscuit
After a voyage, he hath strange places cramm'd
With observation, the which he vents
In mangled forms. O that I were a fool!"

—*As You Like It,* II. vii. 36-42.

21. In law, a reference to "the moral rule which requires probity, justice, and honest dealing between man and man, as when to say that a bargain is 'against conscience' or 'unconscionable,' or that the price paid for property at a forced sale was so inadequate as to 'shock the conscience.' " Henry Campbell Black, *Black's Law Dictionary* (St. Paul, Minnesota, 1951), p. 376.

22. "Scholars," of course, denotes students.

23. A phrase that came into currency after the publication of *Ivanhoe* (1819), by Sir Walter Scott. Cedric, in the novel, seeks to restore the Saxon line to the throne of England; his most famous thrall is Wamba, who risks his life to save him.

24. Joseph Arch (1826-1919) played an important role in forming the Warwickshire Agricultural Labourers' Union (1872); an agricultural trade-union movement, that same year, known as the National Agricultural Labourers' Union; and other organizations dedicated to the improvement of the lot of farm-workers. See "The Disaster to Farming," in R. C. K. Ensor's *England 1870-1914,* in *The Oxford History of England,* XIV (Oxford, 1960), 115-121.

25. A remark by Ulysses, in the famous speech on the transiency of love and life, "One touch of nature makes the whole world kin . . ." (*Troilus and Cressida,* III. iii. 175).

26. A rustic in Shakespeare's *As You Like It,* who confesses to Touchstone that he has never been at court, and who emerges with considerable dignity from a name-calling session with the clown: "Sir, I am a true labourer. I earn that I eat, get that I wear, owe no man hate, envy no man's happiness, glad of other men's good, content with my harm, and the greatest of my pride is to see my ewes graze and my lambs suck" (III. ii. 77-81).

27. *Ibid.,* 25-26.

28. The "Possibilists" were French Socialists who, in the early 1880's, advocated the undertaking of reforms in areas where such reforms were immediately possible. M. Émile Louis Victor de Laveleye (1822-1892), who

earned his reputation for works on Socialism, political economy, and the language and literature of Provence and for translations, claimed that the habitual motive of man's actions is the pursuit of what is useful to him; i.e., he tried to show what it is possible for man to acquire. Gladstone congratulated him for his "known powers and wide sympathies."

29. Without offspring or descendants.

30. *1 Henry IV,* I. iii. 10-13. The speaker is Thomas Percy, Earl of Worcester.

31. A graveyard or charnelhouse, i.e., a gathering-place of skulls.

32. "Durnovaria" is one form of the name for Dorchester, Dorsetshire, and is connected by some historians with the old British name *Dwrinwyn,* a settlement by the *Dwr,* or the dark water of the Frome. Eilert Ekwall, in *The Concise Oxford Dictionary of English Place-Names* (Oxford, 1960), p. 148, notes that the Welsh *dwrn* means, literally, "fist," and *gwarae* "play"; hence, the British name, alluding to a place where fist-play is conducted, would refer to the Roman amphitheatre. "The real Dorset form was no doubt *Dorn-gweir,* with Co[rnish] *dorn* corresponding to Welsh *dwrn.* By substitution the Brit[ish] name was adopted as OE *Dornwaru,* or the name was abbreviated to *Dorn,* from which was formed OE *Dornwaru* 'the Dorchester people.' This was combined with OE *ceaster* 'Roman station.' "

33. *The Iliad,* XXIII. 59-110. The shade of Patroclus appears and begs for a speedy burial. In Virgil's *Aeneid,* VI. 477-532, appear the military ghosts to whom Hardy refers.

34. I Sam. 28:3-25.

35. Farinata appears in Canto X of *La Commedia;* the others are mentioned briefly in Canto IV.

36. One of Hardy's best-known poems, "The Oxen," begins with the lines,

"Christmas Eve, and twelve of the clock.
'Now they are all on their knees,'
An elder said as we sat in a flock
By the embers in hearthside ease,"

and ends with Hardy's hope that "it might be so."

37. Shelley had expressed a desire to be buried with William (d. 1818), but those who were attempting to carry out his wish discovered that the stone which supposedly marked the grave of William rested over the body of an adult; the remains of William could not be found. Hence, Shelley had to be buried by himself. See Hugh Elliot's letter to *The Times Literary Supplement,* November 4, 1920; Walter Edwin Peck, *Shelley: His Life and Work* (London, 1927), II, 299-300; and Newman Ivey White, *Shelley* (New York, 1940), II, 383.

38. "Milton's gravestone outside St Giles's, Cripplegate, inscribed 'J.M. 1671', was taken away and lost, [George] Vertue tells us, before 1721—

during the 1704 restoration of the church presumably—and there was no memorial there till Samuel Whitbread put up the present bust by Bacon, the detestable Gothic setting of which is an outrage of the 1860's. . . ." Katharine A. Esdaile, *English Church Monuments 1510 to 1840* (New York, 1947), p. 115.

39. The wood of fir or pine, cut into boards.

40. It was from the hands of Sir Gilbert Scott (1811-1878) that Hardy received the prize medal for his essay in 1863 (*Life,* p. 404). The career of Sir Gilbert was one of the most energetic and productive of the Victorian Age; his studies of Augustus Welby Northmore Pugin's architectural achievements (both the buildings and the writings) led to the development of a Gothic style of considerable distinction. Among the more than seven hundred structures to whose design he contributed were the Martyrs' Memorial at Oxford, the Albert Memorial, St. Pancras Station, and several buildings of Glasgow University. His work on the Home and Colonial Offices in London was carried out in classic or renaissance style. Hardy was particularly impressed by his lifelong efforts to restore or renovate important architectural works of the past, such as Ely Cathedral and the cathedrals at Hereford, Lichfield, Salisbury, and Ripon. At the very end of his life Sir Gilbert founded the Society for the Protection of Ancient Buildings, before which Hardy was to read this paper some two decades later. It is ironic, in the anecdote recounted here by Hardy, that Sir Gilbert was calling to the attention of his students an anomaly in an architectural detail of Westminster Abbey; Pugin, Sir Gilbert's hero, had been frustrated in carrying through many of his most important plans for authentic Gothic details in the designs for the new Houses of Parliament at Westminster, and by exactly such devices as plaster groining.

41. "Camber": the condition of being slightly arched or convex above, i.e., a flattened arch *(O.E.D.).*

42. An echo of Prince Hal's comment to Falstaff, "These lies are like their father that begets them; gross as a mountain, open, palpable" (*I Henry IV,* II. iv. 249-251).

43. "Where light and shade repose, where music dwells
Lingering—and wandering on as loth to die;
Like thoughts whose very sweetness yieldeth proof
That they were born for immortality."

—William Wordsworth, "Inside of King's College Chapel, Cambridge," 11-14.

44. "The Commons, faithful to their system, remained in a wise and masterly inactivity."—Sir James Mackintosh, *Vindiciae Gallicae* (1791), Chapter I.

45. Mr. Wemmick, in *Great Expectations,* lives a circumspect life as clerk to Mr. Jaggers, the lawyer; but has pronounced views on the value of

living his own life when away from the office: "No, the office is one thing and private life is another. When I go into the office, I leave the Castle behind me, and when I come into the Castle, I leave the office behind me" (Chapter XXV). After Pip and Mr. Wemmick cross a plank that leads across "a chasm about four feet wide and two deep" into the Castle, Mr. Wemmick hoists up the bridge, makes it fast, and thereby cuts off communication with the outside world. The Castle thus becomes a protected island. Cf. Pip's feeling of security in Chapter XXXVII: "The flag had been struck, and the gun had been fired, at the right moment of time, and I felt as snugly cut off from the rest of Walworth as if the moat were thirty feet wide by as many deep. Nothing disturbed the tranquillity of the Castle. . . ."

46. Alfred George Stevens (1818-1875) studied in Rome (1841-1842) under Bertel Thorwaldsen, the famous sculptor, before returning to England to become a teacher at the new School of Design, Somerset House, London. His designs of cast-metal furniture and stoves attracted favorable comments at the Great Exhibition (1851). He is perhaps best remembered for his design of the Wellington monument at St. Paul's Cathedral, although his work on the decorations of Dorchester House, London (1858-1862), indicate the quality of his mature skills in possibly even fuller measure. Many of his works are on display at the Tate Gallery.

47. ". . . in the art of Hudibrastic or octosyllabic verse he himself is second to none." Austin Dobson, "Matthew Prior," *Eighteenth Century Vignettes, Third Series* (London, 1923), III, 260.

48. Thomas Coram (1668?-1751) established the famous hospital for foundling infants (1739) which today is known as the Thomas Coram Foundation for Children. (See the article on Foundling Hospitals in the *Encyclopaedia Britannica,* IX, 14th ed., for an interesting account of the history of this institution.) Coram was also an important agent in early settlement schemes for Georgia and Nova Scotia.

49. "This year also died IOHN MORTON, *Archbishop of Canterburie, Chancellor of England,* and *Cardinall.* Hee was a Wiseman, and an Eloquent, but in his nature harsh, and haughtie; much accepted by the King, but envied by the *Nobilitie,* and hated of the *People.*" Francis Bacon, *The Historie of the Raigne of King Henry the Seventh* (London, 1622), pp. 198-199.

50. Catherine Durning Whetham and William Cecil Dampier Whetham, *A History of the Life of Colonel Nathaniel Whetham* (London, 1907).

51. John Strype, *A Complete History of England* (London, 1719), II, 613.

52. "In his youth [Sir Richard Bingham] traced most parts of the world to search for service and find fit objects for his valour. He was at the siege of Saint Quentin in France, the sacking of Leith in Scotland, served in Candia under the Venetian against the Turk; then returned into the Netherlands,

being observed to be *fortis et felix* in all his undertakings." Thomas Fuller, *The Worthies of England,* ed. John Freeman (London, 1952), p. 150.

53. Algernon Charles Swinburne, "Faustine," 65-66.

54. H. St. George Gray conducted excavations in Maumbury Ring in 1908, 1909, 1910, 1912, and 1913, and reported in full detail on his findings to the members of the Dorset Natural History and Antiquarian Field Club. Describing his work in 1908, he wrote, "This is undoubtedly one of the deepest archaeological excavations on record in Great Britain" (*Proceedings,* XXIX, 272), but he may well have used the superlative in private conversation with Hardy, a fellow-member of the Club. It was Gray's work that convinced Englishmen of the prehistoric origins of the site, and led to the view that the Romans merely adapted for their own uses an embankment that was already there. A member of the Taunton Castle Museum staff, Gray acquired much of his experience in the service of General Pitt-Rivers.

55. John Hutchins, *The History and Antiquities of the County of Dorset* (London, 1861-1870), 3rd edition, II, 796: "This is artfully set on the top of a plain, declining to the north-east, whereby the rays of the sun falling upon the ground hereabouts are thrown off to a distance by reflection, and the upper end of the amphitheatre, for the major part of the day, has the sun behind the spectators."

56. The trip of Sir Christopher Wren to which Hardy alludes probably took place in the spring of 1697. The twelve days spent on the journey came at a crucial point in his planning for St. Paul's choir, but Sir Christopher's personal intervention had become necessary: for various reasons Portland stone had not been delivered to Ludgate Hill for a full two-year period. For the fullest account of how Portland stone was used in the construction of this great cathedral, see Jane Lang's *Rebuilding St. Paul's after the Great Fire* (London, 1956), *passim.*

57. See "The History of the Dorchester Gallows," by the Rev. S. E. V. Filleul, in *Proceedings of the Dorset Natural History and Antiquarian Field Club,* XXXII (1911), 61-69. Other writers on the unfortunate fate of Mrs. Channing are less convinced than Hardy of her innocence. F. J. Harvey Darton, who also consulted the contemporary record of the trial proceedings, had no doubt that she was guilty; see *The Marches of Wessex* (London, 1922), p. 200. Both Hardy and Darton read *Serious Admonitions to Youth, in a Short Account of the Life, Trial, Condemnation, and Execution of Mrs. Mary Channing, Who for Poisoning Her Husband Was Burnt at Dorchester on Thursday, March the 21st, 1705-6, with Practical Reflections.* London: printed for Benjamin Bragge, at the Black Raven, in Paternoster Row, 1706.

58. See note 54.

59. In St. Peter's Church, Dorchester, a tablet commemorates Hardy's ancestor: "To the memorye of Thomas Hardy, of Melcombe Regis, in the County of Dorsett, esquier, whoe endowed this Burroughe wth a yearely

revenew of 50 £; and appoynted out of it, to be employed for y[e] better mayntenance of a preacher 20 £; a schoolmaster twenty Powndes; an husher twenty nobles; the alms women five markes. The Baylives and Burgisses of Dorchester, in testimony of their gratitude, and to commend to posterity an example soe worthy of imitation, have erected this monument. He dyed the 15th of October, Anno: Do: (1599). The just shall be had in everlasting remembrance." Frank R. Heath, in *Dorset* (London, 1905), identifies him further as a member of a Jersey family called Le Hardie, "the ancestor of the naval hero whose monument is on Blackdown, and of the novelist and poet, who needs none" (p. 144).

60. Hardy seems to have recalled Carlyle's remarks on the family background of Teufelsdröckh: "To us it appeared, after repeated trial, that in Weissnichtwo, from the archives or memories of the best-informed classes, no Biography of Teufelsdröckh was to be gathered; not so much as a false one. He was a stranger there, wafted thither by what is called the course of circumstances; concerning whose parentage, birthplace, prospects, or pursuits, curiosity had indeed made inquiries, but satisfied herself with the most indistinct replies" (*Sartor Resartus,* Chapter III). "His Life, Fortunes, and Bodily Presence, are as yet hidden from us, or matter only of faint conjecture" *(ibid.)*.

Appendix

1. "The world's great age begins anew,
    The golden years return,
   The earth doth like a snake renew
    Her winter weeds outworn:
   Heaven smiles, and faiths and empires gleam,
   Like wrecks of a dissolving dream."

—Percy Bysshe Shelley, *Hellas,* 1060-1065.

Index

INDEX

INDEX